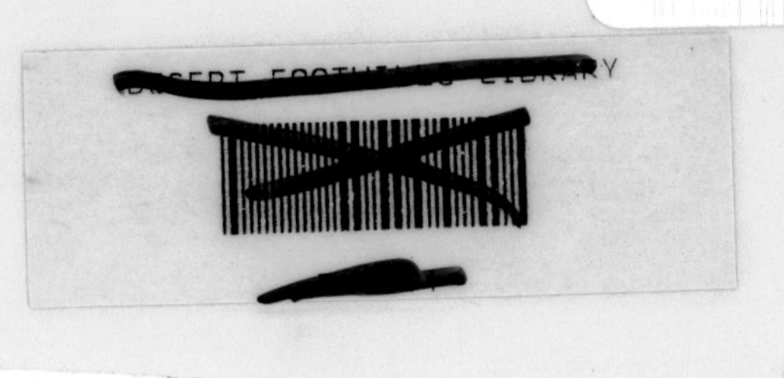

Wagenvoord, James.
The swim book.

THE SWIM BOOK

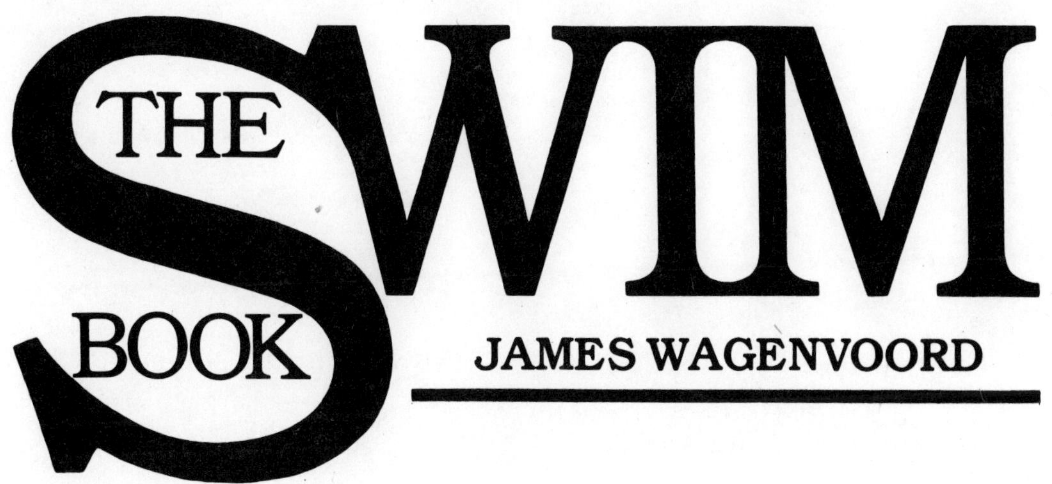

THE BOBBS-MERRILL COMPANY, INC. / *Indianapolis* / *New York*

Published by The Bobbs-Merrill Company, Inc.
Indianapolis/New York

Manufactured in the United States of America
First Printing

Library of Congress Cataloging in Publication Data
Wagenvoord, James.
The swim book.
1. Swimming. I. Title.
GV837.W23 797.2'1 79-5381
ISBN 0-672-52622-0

ACKNOWLEDGEMENTS

This book would not have been possible without the help and time given by many friends and organizations.

Princeton University Swimming Coach, Rob Orr and members of the Princeton Swim team, Pam Phillips, Charlotte Teidemann, Beth Mauer, Nancy Conroy, John Christensen, Bill Specht, Dan Sikes and Mark Wingerter gave of their skill and patience in demonstrating individual strokes. Much of the photographic recording of their efforts was done by Dr. Emmett Wilson, an excellent photographer and a great friend of competitive swimming. Alice Wagenvoord was of immense help in developing the basic attitude for this book, and with Mike Fisher, a fellow student at the University of Hawaii, demonstrated outstanding swimming skill for our cameras.

A special thanks to James Hunt, Jr., Stephanie Hunt, and Fiona St. Aubyn and to Dr. Hemming Atterbom, Director of the Human Performance Laboratory of the University of New Mexico; C. Carson Conrad, Director of the President's Committee on Physical Fitness; Sam Cynamon of the American Red Cross; and Ted Haartz, Chairman of AAU Master Swimming for the Amateur Athletic Union of the U.S..

Sincere thanks must also go to Ron Morganstein and Ralph DiMeglio of Photo Lettering Inc.; Vincent Apicella of CGS Complete Graphic Service, Inc.; Michael Kogan of Action Photo, Inc.; John Dornan and Richard Traub of Berkey K&L, New York, and Alan Galowitz and Donald Demcsik of Galowitz Photographics, New York, for their care and superb effort in meeting difficult schedules.

An Oak Alley Book Created and Produced by James Wagenvoord Studio, Inc.

EDITOR—James Wagenvoord

DESIGN—Marta Norman

SENIOR EDITOR—JoAnne Blackwelder

WRITERS—James Wagenvoord, Douglas Colligan, Christopher Hallowell, Joel Homer, Jean Baur

ILLUSTRATIONS—Stephen Laughlin

COPY EDITOR—Ted Johnson

EDITORIAL RESEARCH—Barbara Binswanger Alice Wagenvoord, Dewey Thompson

RESEARCH PHOTOGRAPHY—James Wagenvoord, Dr. Emmett Wilson

INDEX—Maro Riofrancos

ART ASSISTANTS—Lorna Bieber, Kathy Woloch

PROOFREADERS—Eva Galan, Kristine Kalazs, Meredith Helleberg

Contents

Think Better, Feel Better

You can't go anywhere these days without running into someone who has a personal formula for fitness. Getting or staying "in shape" is on just about everyone's mind. The only problem is, many people have trouble sticking to a self-designed fitness regimen. For every jogger or bicyclist you meet, you will probably meet two or three ex-joggers and ex-bicyclists. "I'm just tired of being chased by dogs and getting sideswiped by cars" is how one friend put it the day he retired his 10-speed. Joggers too are finding that there are not only runners' "highs," there are runners' "lows" as well. It can be hard to get out there on a cold, damp winter morning or a steamy summer afternoon. This is not to say jogging hasn't done a lot to promote good health habits in those people who can get past this discomfort block. Of course it has. (But it's also meant a booming practice for podiatrists who are called on to treat runners' injuries).

What many people forget is that long before there were sky-blue nylon running shoes and titanium 10-speed bikes, there was an exercise healthier than running or bicycling. That exercise was and is swimming. Ben Franklin saw how "delightful and wholesome an exercise" it is, and a lot of ex-joggers and ex-cyclists have rediscovered it as well.

Many of the advantages of swimming are quite obvious. Unlike running, it is truly an all-weather exercise. While the jogger has to worry about the weather, the traffic, and the man-eating dogs that haunt his route, all the swimmer has to concern himself with is access to a

pool. And with the minimum of equipment required—a pool, a bathing suit, a body—the swimmer can concentrate on the exercise itself.

Simplicity and convenience aren't the only reasons for the upsurge in swimming's popularity. The sport also improves both the inner and outer you in a way that no other can. It can do as much for your psyche as for your body. It does this in ways that psychologists are only now beginning to understand.

PSYCHIC CHEMISTRY

To start, swimming is an aerobic, or oxygen-using, exercise. As you will see in later chapters, aerobic exercise works wonders for your heart, circulatory system, and general fitness. And it gives you a special kind of mental fitness as well. According to Dr. Kenneth Cooper, one of the special effects of aerobic excerise is that it increases the amount of oxygen that gets absorbed into your body and circulated in your blood. More oxygen circulating means more of that gas is getting to your brain, where some interesting results can occur.

For one thing, says Cooper, a brain well supplied with oxygen and other nutrients is more alert and awake. Rather than wear you out, swimming can work like a real tonic to your mind. Some of this effect, doctors say, is the direct result of higher doses of oxygen. In the past few years doctors have been experimenting with oxygen the way some clinicians experiment with drugs, and they have found it has some surprising effects on the brain.

For example, doctors at the U.S. Naval Hospital in Long Beach, California, got some amazing results using carefully controlled doses of oxygen on their patients. They had been using a technique called hyperbaric oxygenation, sealing patients in airtight tanks filled with oxygen under pressure. The tanks originally had been used to treat deep-sea divers who suffered from the bends, but in time the doctors discovered that the same

This matter of breathing is most important. One cannot swim, or do anything else, unless one breathes comfortably.

—EDWIN TENNEY BREWSTER, *Swimming*, 1910

containers and high levels of oxygen could be used to speed up healing in patients suffering from serious burns, carbon-monoxide poisoning, and inflamed bone tissue. At the same time doctors also noticed other effects.

People previously thought to be senile or suffering some kind of memory lapse because of poor circulation to their brains recovered dramatically. Memories improved after a spell in the oxygen-rich chamber. There were even cases in which eyesight improved. Doctors are certain the increased oxygen is responsible for such changes, though they aren't sure how it works. One guess is that certain improvements in circulation come about as a result of this oxygen dose, and weak but living brain cells perk up.

Taking a dose of oxygen—that is, breathing it from a pressurized tank—can do tremendous things for the body and mind when you're in the middle of an exercise workout, when your body is low in oxygen because you are using it up at a faster rate than average. Doctors who have given athletes whiffs of oxygen, usually at 66 percent concentration, have found it causes a real energy boost. Fatigue diminishes, endurance increases, breathing is more calm, and the athletes are more relaxed.

Appropriately enough, it was a swimming team that introduced the idea of using oxygen as a special sports aid. The 1932 Japanese Olympic swimming team had a good year at the International Games, in part because each swimmer took a whiff of oxygen before stepping up on the starting blocks. This got coaches interested in using it for other sports. Today it's common to see an oxygen tank close to a team's bench.

All the evidence points to the fact that oxygen is an energizer for both the mind and body. Short of carrying around your own private supply in a couple of pressure tanks, the best way to get it, the healthiest way, is by having your body work for it as you swim.

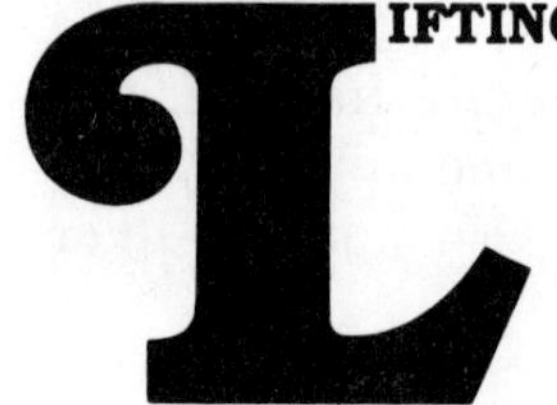

IFTING EMOTIONAL WEIGHTS

Doctors also think that swimming gains you a dose of another helpful natural chemical, called norepinephrine. This is a brain chemical which, among other things, carries messages between brain cells and also seems to be a natural antidepressant. Researchers now know there is a chemical as well as a psychological element in depression. One clue they have is that depressed people tend to have low levels of norepinephrine, while people who are in good moods have high levels. One thing that seems to change the level of norepinephrine in your system is exercise.

In the past couple of years, psychiatrists at both the University of Wisconsin and the University of Virginia have been prescribing exercise sessions instead of analysis sessions for their depressed patients. The results have been impressive. After about two months of steady, three-times-a-week exercise sessions, depression was usually significantly reduced. Whether or not it was the norepinephrine theory in action, the psychiatrists couldn't say, but clearly the exercise was good for their patients.

You're already aware of the toll that stress can take on your health. Problems like ulcers, asthma attacks, even headaches can be triggered by an overload of stress. Your mind has a great deal to do with the health of your body. Fortunately, doctors now know what people have long suspected: You can improve your state of mind by the way you use your body.

A University of California researcher named Herbert de Vries found that a surprisingly modest amount of exercise can give you good stress protection. De Vries determined a system for measuring a person's tension by taking special readings of electrical activity in muscle tissue. The higher the reading, the greater the tension. After just 15 minutes of mild exercise, de Vries found the

tension in his patients dropped by 20 percent. Once this daily 15-minute workout became a habit, the muscle electrical activity lowered to 75 percent of what it had been. In this instance, the mild exercise acted as a kind of natural tranquilizer.

RESTORING THE BODY'S BALANCE

A carefully paced swim a few times a week can do a lot more for breaking you free of the hold of everyday stress than any drug or chemical you can buy. And it can do it without dangerous side effects. Probably no one knows this better than Dr. Hans Selye of the University of Montreal, who pioneered modern medicine's studies of what stress can do to you and for you. Stress, says Selye, is not necessarily bad for you. Feeling happy is a kind of stress, but no one willingly avoids it. Problems come, he says, when your body or mind gets overloaded with too much of a single kind of stress.

As he states in his book *Stress Without Distress*, "In stress research we have found that, when completion of one particular task becomes impossible, diversion, a voluntary change of activity, is frequently as good as—if not better than—a rest. For example, when either fatigue or enforced interruption prevents us from finishing a mathematical problem, it is better to go for a swim than just to sit around."

And he follows his own advice. Although he routinely works a 12-hour day, he also takes the time both in the morning and in the evening to do some light exercises and go for a swim.

Another theory about why exercise seems to banish depression, according to Dr. Gabe Mirkin in *The Sports Medicine Book*, is the way it changes the salt levels in the brain of the depressed person. It's already known that strenuous exercise lessens painful menstrual cramps in women. According to Mirkin, it has also been used, in combination with a diuretic treatment program, to lessen some of the depression that comes with the onset of the menstrual period. Some of this tension and depression, researchers suggest, is brought on by raised hormonal levels, which in turn can cause the woman's body and brain to retain a higher-than-average amount of salt.

From studying athletes who have taken too many salt tablets, doctors know that high concentrations of salt can bring on personality changes and feelings of lethargy. Exercise helps the body shed this excess salt, as you probably already know if you've ever tasted your own salt-rich perspiration. In addition, diuretic drugs help the body drain off the salt in the urine.

Don't think that because you're in water you don't sweat. Swimming coaches have found that their athletes can lose up to three pounds of their body weight in the course of a rough training day. They estimate practically all of that is fluid loss.

The exercise of swimming is one of the most healthy and agreeable in the world. After having swam for an hour or two in the evening, one sleeps coolly the whole night, even during the most ardent heat of summer.

—BENJAMIN FRANKLIN, *The Art of Swimming*

ENDING INSOMNIA

Daily exercise seems to help another problem that is largely psychological: insomnia. Sleep expert and psychologist Dr. Peter Hauri of Dartmouth University points out that exercise is one of the best natural sleep medicines. Sleep doctors believe that at least half of all insomnia is caused by psychological problems, usually depression. If that's true, then maybe an exercise like swimming induces sleep indirectly, by getting rid of depression. It is also possible, other experts believe, that by exercising you increase your body's natural hunger for the deep, satisfying sleep the body needs to recover after physical work.

However, if you plan to use your swimming as a sleeping pill, you must make it a habit. Swimming once or twice will not work. A burst of unaccustomed exercise will probably keep you wide awake instead of helping you sleep, since you'll more than likely be tossing and turning all night with sore muscles. In order to get the sleep-inducing benefits of exercise, the experts say, you have to exercise consistently.

It is a well-authenticated fact that the American people in the last twenty years have degenerated physically more than any other nation, unless possibly the French.

–Life and Adventures of Professor Robert Emmet Odlum, 1885

Another point to remember, according to Dr. Hauri, is to exercise fairly early in the day—in the morning, or not too late in the afternoon. Done too close to bedtime, exercise can be a stimulant—getting your system stirred up—instead of a relaxant. Only trial and error will tell you if your exercise is getting in the way of your sleep. If it seems to, simply schedule your swimming sessions earlier in the day.

APPETITE CONTROL

Exercise can also help control what for some of us is a stress-reaction habit and what for others is just a plain bad habit: overeating. We sometimes put into our bodies more calories than we can use, and the result is we end up with more pounds to carry around.

It's not that we're not interested in health and sports. There are probably few nations more sports-crazy than ours. The only problem is that we're interested in sports more as spectators than as players. To make matters worse, we gobble snacks as we lounge in front of the TV set or sit in the stands watching a game. It's a kind of nervous-spectator syndrome that has probably put many a sedentary sports fan in an early grave. It's almost as though we're substituting the sensation of playing a game for the less healthy sensation of overeating as we watch one.

People eat, or overeat, for a lot of reasons—to alleviate boredom, to compensate for the lack of something (affection, success), or to comfort themselves in a stressful situation. Nutritionist Dr. Jean Mayer has even claimed that overeating can come with doing less and less, leading a sedentary life. As some individuals get less active they feel hungrier, or at least they eat more. In spite of the fact that they are exercising less, their appetite control breaks down.

As you'll see in the following chapter, developing an exercise routine is one way of bringing your appetite back in line with your body's needs. Exercise burns

I am in that temper that if I were under water, I would scarcely kick to come to the surface.

-JOHN KEATS,
Letter to Benjamin Bailey
21 May 1818

calories, but beyond that you may find that it eliminates or at least weakens some of the deeper psychological urges that keep you chewing long after you know that you've eaten your share. For that reason many people report that some of their nastier habits—smoking, drinking a little too much, and eating a little too much—are easier to control once they've inserted a steady diet of exercise into their days and weeks.

SELF-IMAGE

You may not feel you need any special exercise to counter stress, relieve depression, or overcome insomnia, and maybe you don't. But the benefits are very broad, and though you may be more or less satisfied with your life now, perhaps you just don't know how much better it can be.

In one test carried out at Purdue University, a group of 60 middle-aged men, most of whom were out of condition, were put on an exercise regimen of four and a half hours of workouts per week. Activities included calisthenics, swimming, and running. As fitness programs go, it was pretty grueling, and done under strict medical supervision. It paid off in many ways.

Gradually the men began to get in better shape. Other changes were noticeable. They felt better in general. At the beginning of the exercise program they took tests measuring certain facets of their personalities—emotional stability, imagination, self-confidence, and self-sufficiency. After a few weeks they were given another personality test. A curious pattern started to surface. The men who had made the biggest improvement in physical condition also showed the biggest positive changes in their personality characteristics. They had greater emotional stability, more self-confidence, and a greater sense of self-sufficiency. Other, similar studies done at the Mayo Clinic and the

California Human Performance Laboratory had similar results. The better shape your body is in, the better your psychological health.

It's not hard to see why this should be. If you feel physically fit and prove it to yourself during your workout sessions in the pool, that fit feeling can translate into a real boost in self-confidence. You probably recall how you felt when you were out of shape. You didn't feel sick exactly, but somehow you just didn't feel right. Your body may have seemed sluggish. Both physical and mental work tired you more easily. Your concentration flagged. You may also have gained a few extra pounds so your clothes didn't feel comfortable. This vague feeling of malaise translates directly into the kind of image you project to others. If you don't feel that your body is in tune, your attitude about yourself suffers.

THE DUCK OR THE EGG

According to Dr. Roy Shephard, a physiologist at the University of Toronto, being out of shape draws us into a vicious circle of gradually lowering physical and mental fitness. Physical exertions that didn't seem difficult—climbing a flight of stairs, hauling a suitcase through a crowded airport—become tremendously hard work. Soon it starts to feel as though every mildly demanding feat is too much of an effort. We feel worn out and tired all the time, and we start to get depressed because we feel that way. We would like to be in better shape but feel much too dragged out to start exercising. It seems like a no-win situation. We aren't in shape and we think we're too out of shape to start trying.

It's at these times, Shephard theorizes, that our self-image takes a turn for the worse. We start to have a distorted view of how we really are. Our bodies all of a sudden seem awkward, clumsy. Almost anything physical or even mental seems to be beyond us. It seems to take too much of an effort just to get through the day.

SELF-CURING

Naturally, the best cure is to shake loose this lethargy with exercise. If you're faithful to your swimming program and can make it through the initial aches and pains of getting your body to move again, you'll find your mind's fitness will improve right along with your body's. Suddenly those physical chores seem much easier. You feel more graceful, more sure of yourself. The more you work at it, the better you'll feel. Shephard says that in one test done with a group of elderly exercisers, before-and-after psychological screening showed that some people had tremendous surges of improvement in their self-images while others had none at all. What made the difference was how intensely the person exercised. The really intense exercisers had the biggest improvement in self-image, while those who worked out less benefited less psychologically.

Shephard cites another interesting case—a group of Toronto radio-telegraph operators who decided to take exercise breaks instead of coffee breaks during their day. After adopting a weekly schedule of four hours of exercise, one group showed tremendous improvement in how they performed their jobs. Ratings of both attention and concentration went up. They came away from their exercise periods refreshed and ready to start work with new enthusiasm. In some Eastern European countries, the exercise break is already part of workers' daily routines for these reasons. People end up having more alert minds than any amount of coffee drinking could give them.

One of the big advantages of involvement in swimming is that it frees one of many of the limiting images that come to mind when people talk about "sports." "I used to play sports as a kid, but I don't anymore" is something you probably hear a lot from people now out of shape. It's most likely that sport was baseball, basketball, or football, some kind of team sport you don't play and enjoy most of your life. Those games are fine

Swimming stands apart from ordinary games, for it gives employment to nearly every muscle and more particularly the respiratory muscles of the chest, a development of the highest importance to every human being.

–ARCHIBALD SINCLAIR,
Swimming and Lifesaving, 1906

when you're young and fit, but for your adult years you need something you can do either by yourself or with others. Something relatively simple with no elaborate equipment. And something that puts you back in touch with your body. That's what swimming does. It helps you rediscover fitness on your own terms and following your own personal tempo of development. It is sport in its purest, most enjoyable form.

EMOTIONAL PAMPERING

Sheer enjoyment is an important factor. In one physical-fitness survey that asked Americans why they exercised, the President's Council on Physical Fitness and Sports found that people offered four main reasons. The largest number of people said they did it for the sake of good health. The second largest number said they exercised because they felt better in general as a result. The third reason given was to keep in shape and stay slim, and the fourth was solely for the pure enjoyment of doing it.

That brings up perhaps the most important psychological reason for exercise: fun. Many people, even those who used to play sports as kids, may never really have enjoyed them. Team sports were often too loaded with the tension of competition: the struggle to make the team, another struggle for first string. Then constant drill and practice so that when the big day came you could go out and beat the hell out of the other team. Getting ahead and winning were what pulled a lot of people into sports. Pure enjoyment of the sport or game frequently never even enters one's head.

Yet you know yourself that passing from childhood to adulthood doesn't immunize you against that basic urge to go out and have fun, to turn your body loose without worrying about keeping score. For many this release of playfulness comes when they're out dancing. For others it might be when they're playing a favorite piece on a musical instrument. For many others it comes when the body is operating smoothly and effortlessly in a favorite sport. (You'll find hints at the end of this chapter on how to capture those special moments.)

Taking time out of your day for your swim gives you a chance to be a little selfish in a positive way. It lets you pamper yourself, get off by yourself to be alone with your own thoughts, and give yourself time to let off a little steam in a healthy way. People may criticize you for hanging out at your favorite local bar, but no one is going to make any comments about your swim time. It's cheaper than buying drinks, and, as swimming expert Dr. Paul Hutinger of Western Illinois University sums up simply, "You will feel better."

WATER EUPHORIA

Besides bringing you all the aerobic benefits, swimming has a few emotional features uniquely its own. Just floating or drifting in water has remarkable effects on your psyche. One of the first to discover this was neurophysiologist Dr. John Lilly.

He was curious about a theory that the brain needs outside stimulation from the five senses to stay alert and awake. Without those senses reporting anything, the theory went, the brain simply goes to sleep.

To find out if this was true, Lilly devised an ingenious test. He had a lightproof, soundproof tank built and filled with water warmed to slightly below body temperature. He also added a heavy solution of Epsom salts to make the water more buoyant. That way he could easily float near the surface, letting his arms and legs dangle freely. The tank cut off all outside sound and light from his ears and eyes, and the water helped to blur any feedback from his sense of touch.

One of the first things he noticed when he slipped into his tank was just how totally soothing it was. The muscles in his body uncoiled completely, and he could feel the body tension slip away. Being in a controlled water environment, Lilly says, made him aware of something he had never before noticed—how hard the body has to work against the force of gravity. Stop and think about it. Much of your routine muscular efforts are made just to hold your body upright in the earth's gravitational field. This is not only a complex muscular effort your body has to worry about, but one that occupies your brain as well. Millions of nerve cells are constantly kept working to coordinate all your muscle activity, helping you keep your balance on land. Your brain has to juggle the complex feedback from sight, sound, and your other senses to keep that balance. Once you're in the water, however, you don't have to worry about gravity, and as a result your brain is free from the constant blur of calculations and corrections it makes.

The water had a soft roll, completely without any sharp waves. The confident half of my mind said it was beautiful and the other half said nothing yet. With a new awareness of them, I could feel my bone joints and muscles working as though I were roaming my body inspecting each one of them and finding them all right. I knew beyond any kidding that this swim was dangerous, and the knowledge sharpened me.

–R. V. CASSILL,
The Swimmers at Pallikula

So in this sense there is a kind of sensory deprivation when you're in water, although Lilly prefers the term "sensory isolation" as being more accurate. Your mind is cut off from complex stimulation, and so is your body's largest sense organ, your skin. Once you're in the water, you're in a world without gravity, and in many ways without as many limits on what you can do. In this world of zero-G you can give a quick lunge with your hands and feet and glide in any direction you choose. The water enveloping you has a hypnotic, soothing effect. You are most likely only vaguely aware of the borders of your pool. As far as your mind and body are concerned, you are not in a pool but in a whole different world. Given all this, it's not surprising that NASA astronauts learned how to move and work in space by practicing in underwater tanks built specifically for them.

FLOATING FREE

As to the brain theory, Lilly did find there was less stimulation coming into his brain from the outside, but it did not have the stupefying effect it was expected to have. He was amazed to find that with less outside

I have often noticed that even a few minutes of this self-forgetfulness is tremendously invigorating. I wonder if we don't waste most of our energy just by spending most every waking minute saying hello to ourselves.

—ANNIE DILLARD, *Pilgrim at Tinker Creek*

stimulation, the brain paradoxically became more active. He found his mind settling into waking dreams and trances; he even had experiences he could only describe as mystical. He was mentally isolated from the outside world and felt tremendously comfortable about it.

The total effect of his floating experience was a special kind of serenity, the kind you get, for example, from a particularly satisfying session of meditation. In certain ways he found it even more satisfying. In time Lilly began finding many uses for his session in the water: ". . . for a rest, to get away from the business of one's life . . . to be able to think free of the physical fatigue of the body."

This does not necessarily mean slipping into the pool is going to take you to your own personal nirvana or that every swim will be full of mystical experiences; nevertheless, you probably will feel some effects similar to those Lilly described: the sense that you've left your day-to-day world and its problems behind; a feeling of "specialness," of being in an environment meant just for your fun and relaxation. As much as they might run or pedal, no jogger or bicyclist can ever duplicate this experience out on a cinder track or on a road. The swimmer's world is like no other.

Sports psychologist Dr. Richard Suinn found this out in talking to Olympic-quality athletes. Suinn, who specialized in counseling and devising mental training techniques for U. S. competitors in the Olympics, helped skiers and other athletes increase their competitive drive by having them run an entire race in their minds as vividly as possible. Essentially it was a complete mental re-creation of racing in the form of a deliberately concocted, tightly controlled dream. One of the more vivid descriptions of a mental race came from a swimmer. She had meticulously set up the scene in her mind's eye—walking toward the edge of the pool, standing up on her starting block, and dropping into her takeoff crouch—all in a crisp black-and-white picture. As soon as she hit the water after the imaginary starting gun was fired, the scene would come alive in Technicolor when the cool water enveloped her body.

INTERIOR RHYTHMS

Probably the best way to get insights into the world of the competition-class swimmer is to listen to someone who has made a career of spending hours and even days in the water. Marathon swimmer Diana Nyad told one reporter, "I can't tell you what it's like when I'm swimming strongly and in unison with the water. I get to this point inside myself where I feel, I mean *I just know,* I was made to live in the water."

Some of the lure of swimming, some of its special qualities, she has found, seem related to the discoveries that Dr. John Lilly made in his sensory-isolation tank. That feeling of being apart from the everyday world and its concerns is an automatic benefit of the sport. In her autobiography, *Other Shores,* Ms. Nyad said she once worried about what she at first thought were bizarre experiences during her hours-long swims.

For one thing, she noticed that after a while her vision became practically useless. The constant hypnotic rhythm of moving her head back and forth as she swam seemed to blur her ability to focus, and eventually that whole sense began to phase out. In fact, her vision would get so distorted that her trainer, following in the support boat, had to act as her eyes, guiding her by a prearranged system of blasts on a police whistle to tell her when to change direction.

Even that was of limited use, because weird things would happen to her hearing as well during a long swim. At one point her trainer tried to alleviate some of the boredom of her record-breaking trek across Lake Ontario by rigging up giant loudspeakers on the escort boat and blasting loud music in her direction as she plowed through the water. Although the racket practically deafened everyone aboard the boat, Nyad says she can't remember having heard a note the whole time she was in the water.

INNER WORLDS

These bizarre experiences worried Nyad until she came upon a report of John Lilly's work with his isolation tank. Then she saw the connection. "No outside stimulation can penetrate to the swimmer," she writes. "Besides sight and hearing, other senses fail. The tactile sense is distorted because of the immersion time. Taste and smell are obliterated in the water." And the result? Her mind produced its own stimulation and entered an entirely different level of consciousness. Swimming became for her a form of deep meditation.

This is why you hear the founders of Esalen, the Mecca of sensitivity training and body awareness, say, "Sport is a Western yoga. The Dance of Shiva. Pure play, the delight in the moment, the Now." And why you hear professional swimmers making remarks like, "The rhythm of a hand entering the water . . . is so balanced, so monotonous, that at times you feel as though the sound of your hand slapping the surface is the only sound on earth."

For this reason you shouldn't be surprised to hear many psychologists describe sports on the highest level as an experience that goes beyond mere exercise. "There is a philosophical aspect to swimming," says Dr. Hemming Atterbom, Director of the Human Performance Laboratory at the University of New Mexico. He has worked with and studied thousands of athletes, including Olympic swimmers, as part of his investigations of what happens to the body during an athletic event. "It's almost like a meditation, because there's a turning in on oneself. When a jogger is out running he's passing all that different scenery which he can use to distract

himself. But with a swimmer, that's not possible. You have to turn into yourself. It's the only way to go."

He continues, "You're alone with yourself completely and it's like being isolated out in the desert. Swimmers have told me that after they've been swimming awhile they feel a certain kind of euphoria. They feel calm, relaxed." The special nature of the sport actually forces the swimmer, Atterbom concludes, to turn in on himself. "If you don't do it, you'll go bananas."

PACING

Something as basic as focusing on the sensation of the water sweeping past your body as you swim can heighten enjoyment of your time in the pool. Since you've already taken the step of choosing swimming as your fitness sport, you may as well take the time to appreciate some of the unique physical sensations that come with it.

As you swim you'll find that your body settles into a steady, even pace. It's also not a bad idea to mentally swim the pool—that is, mark it off by the number of strokes—if you want to switch over, say, from the crawl to the backstroke. If you can tell by the number of strokes just when the edge of the pool is coming up, you don't have to be looking nervously over your shoulder trying to avoid a head-to-poolside collision. That way you can enjoy some of the benefits of the backstroke without worrying about succumbing to the nervousness that swimming "blind" like this can induce. After all, swimming is supposed to be relaxing, not a test of nerve. You'll find that after a while you can even swim the pool with your eyes closed—you will be able to tell when you're finishing a lap by counting your strokes. Also getting in the habit of counting strokes helps you analyze the efficiency of your swimming. As you get better, you'll notice it takes you fewer strokes to do a lap. It's a crude measure of progress, but it works.

Finally, you can use the time spent swimming by

yourself to do a little self-coaching. Maybe you feel you're rolling your hips too much as you kick, or that the timing of your breathing is a little off in the crawl stroke. Spend a few laps just concentrating on that. You'll find the time and the distances will slip by amazingly quickly when you focus your attention on your working body.

PAUSING

Finally, to avoid the boredom or the monotony of swimming along at your own personal pace, Dr. Atterbom has some simple advice. "Take a break now and then. Talk to some people at poolside or just pause and relax a bit in the water," he says. If you do anything for too long a time, it's bound to wear you down psychologically. That's why many Olympic swimmers don't continue to swim in later life. Those years of grueling training, five to six hours a day, have drained all the pleasure out of the sport for them. Since you're not going to be swimming for Olympic gold, learn to pace yourself psychologically as well as physically. Work for the maximum enjoyment of your workouts. Take the time to appreciate the special qualities of swimming: the graceful sensation of gliding through the soothing, low-gravity world of the pool; the way the water envelops you, shutting you up in your own personal world; and finally that special sense of aliveness that comes when your whole body is working as one smoothly operating, synchronized whole. Suddenly everything will click. You will have settled on a whole new plateau of relaxation. You will become what writer George Leonard describes in his book *The Ultimate Athlete*: "an Olympian figure as soft and strong as flowing water, as pervasive and inevitable as gravity."

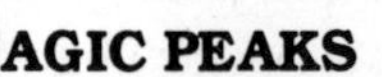

MAGIC PEAKS

When it all comes together in the right way—the movement, the exertions, your breathing, your thinking, your whole awareness—a sport can have an almost

Swimming is the most necessary accomplishment of almost all outdoor sports and pastimes: and every man or boy in the kingdom ought to learn to overcome his dread of the water, and even to delight in it.

-JOHN LEAHY,
The Art of Swimming in the Eton Style, 1875

mystical feel to it. It's not purely physical. If it were, you could duplicate it anytime you chose. It's not intellectual either, or you could figure out how to do it. It's an intuitive experience that just seems to happen. As you'll soon see, there are tricks you can use in trying to reach it.

The constant motion and rhythmic use of your body as you move through the water have a soothing, hypnotic effect on your mind. Being literally immersed in your exercise world has an added isolating and liberating effect on your concentration that you may notice. Instead of going stale with boredom, you may find your brain getting hyperactive with random thoughts. It can be a little unnerving at first. You may even find simple mental jobs like keeping track of how many laps you've swum tricky because of all these distractions. In many ways it's a level of awareness above and beyond the "highs" of other sports. Although many sports psychologists have been able to confirm the existence of these magic times, no one can agree on what to call the experience. One athlete described that special feeling that comes with it this way: "You are totally involved in what you're doing. Your body feels good. Your body is awake all over. Your energy is flowing very smoothly. You feel relaxed, comfortable, energetic." Many people call it a "high." University of Chicago psychologist Dr. Mihaly Csikszentmihalyi calls it the "flow" of sports, and another psychologist, Dr. Gayle Privette of the University of West Florida, calls it "peak performance."

PREPARATIONS

Whatever you want to call this "peak" state, you can enjoy your workouts more if you're ready for it. The way to reach this special swimmer's yoga, this special state of mind, once mystified psychologists. After studying both professional and experienced amateur athletes (as well as dancers, musicians, writers, and artists) who have experienced this special feeling, they have finally been able to break it down into some of its basic elements. By incorporating some of these into your workout, you can do your mind as well as your body a world of good.

You can't realistically expect this flow or peak emotional feeling to come every time you dive into the pool. The experience would get pretty boring if that did happen. But you can increase the odds of its happening with the right kind of mental preparation. The preparation is not very complicated.

Focus your attention. For many reasons, psychological as well as physical, your exercise sessions are extremely important to your health. Take them as seriously as you do the rest of your day. This doesn't mean you should face every time in the pool with the grim determination of a swimmer getting ready to make his or her first Channel crossing. But just think about what you're doing. Letting your mind get distracted by worries about your work or other preoccupations will get in the way of your enjoyment. Try to relax a little. Let your body settle into a natural swimming rhythm and enjoy its hypnotic regularity. Psychologist Dr. Gayle Privette says this kind of full focus of your attention can ease you into the feel of a peak performance.

Have a pre-swim ritual. One thing Dr. Mihaly Czikszentmihalyi noticed about athletes experiencing what he calls the "flow" of exercise, was that each had a kind of pre-event ritual. Some of it is practical—slipping off your street clothes and putting on a bathing suit. Some of it may be habit—dipping your hand or foot into the water to test the temperature. In either case, the effect is to help your mind gradually shift its focus from whatever it was on before. This helps you block out distractions and focus your mental energies on what is to come.

Don't force your body. Part of the reason for keeping a sharp mental focus on how you swim is to know exactly what the strong points *and* the limitations of your body are. According to sports psychologists, one thing that separates the professional from the amateur athlete is that the professional, during any given workout, can

> Learn fairly to swim; as I wish all men were taught to do in their youth. They would, on many occurrences, be the safer for having that skill, and on many more the happier, as freer from painful apprehensions of danger, to say nothing of the enjoyment in so delightful and wholesome an exercise.
>
> —BENJAMIN FRANKLIN, *The Art of Swimming*

gauge more exactly just how far and how safely he can push himself. It's a more calculated but ultimately more beneficial attitude. The professional keeps careful track of his fitness level and knows, by carefully monitoring how his body is functioning during a given workout, if it's time to step up the intensity of the exercise. Your body has certain rhythms that will tell you these things. Learn to read them, and don't abruptly make impulsive moves, say, to double your lap time "just to see if I can do it." Even if you can, what's likely to happen, if you're not prepared, is that you'll be a stiff and sore wreck, and you may start to hate your time in the pool.

Make your exercise a habit. Once you get over the hump of adjusting to minor aches and pains of a new exercise regime, you will probably find this advice really isn't hard to follow. In time, your exercise should become an addiction, a "positive addiction," to use one psychologist's phrase. Even if you haven't been particularly active in the past, you will find that your pool time will become as necessary and as permanent a part of your daily schedule as mealtimes. Even better, once your body has reached a certain level of training, it also will begin to develop its own smooth, spontaneous style of moving. Certain of your practiced motions will become automatic, effortless. The more effortless and spontaneous your style is, the more likely you are to enjoy your workouts and occasionally get the "flow," the "peak performance," or the "swimmer's high" that makes sport so special.

The main thing to remember is that you are exercising for your mind as well as your body. Everything that happens to your outside is going to have a rejuvenating effect on the inner you. This won't be evident at first, but the more you work at it, the more you'll notice not only how smoothly and effortlessly your body performs in the water but what a difference it makes in your land-based life. After a while you will discover what many other people are beginning to find once they slip into the water: swimming is a very special state of mind.

Discover Your Body

There is no exercise that can form, stretch, and tone up your body better than swimming. There is literally no other as free from the problems of injuries that plague other fitness regimens. It's probably the most physically demanding and rewarding way to help your body come alive. And that is the single most important total benefit: that sense of being alive.

One of the most complete studies in support of a vigorous regimen's ability to sustain life was a study of 17,000 Harvard Alumni done by Dr. Ralph Paffenbarger, Jr. at Stanford University's School of Medicine. For ten years he kept track of all these men: their state of health and their exercise habits, even including how many steps they climbed in an average day. What he found was that if you have a healthy, normal heart, moderate exercise is better for it than very little, and strenuous exercise is best of all. There was a definite pattern in his findings. Men ranging in age from 35 to 72 who had strenuous exercise habits (even those who hadn't been particularly athletic in college) lowered their risk of heart attack. What's Dr. Paffenbarger's advice? At least two and a half to three hours per week of some kind of strenuous activity. Those he recommended were swimming, tennis, and running.

Doctors point out that tennis is an excellent conditioner *if* you are quite good at it. Long rallies require constant running back and forth, which is a great workout—but you can't have long rallies unless you can hit the ball consistently; for a great majority of weekend

tennis players, the average point is won or lost in two or three strokes. Some doctors have become more outspoken about the other sport Paffenbarger mentions, jogging. One doctor, on hearing of this recommendation, agreed with it in principle but added, "When people start on vigorous exercise, *especially* jogging, they may strain their knees and have a good deal of pain, they may develop foot problems, or they may be doing more than is good for their hearts." And that leaves swimming.

STRENGTHENING YOUR HEART

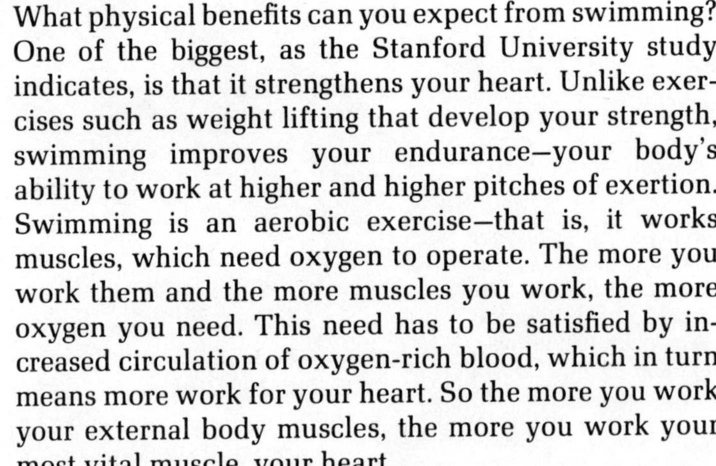

What physical benefits can you expect from swimming? One of the biggest, as the Stanford University study indicates, is that it strengthens your heart. Unlike exercises such as weight lifting that develop your strength, swimming improves your endurance—your body's ability to work at higher and higher pitches of exertion. Swimming is an aerobic exercise—that is, it works muscles, which need oxygen to operate. The more you work them and the more muscles you work, the more oxygen you need. This need has to be satisfied by increased circulation of oxygen-rich blood, which in turn means more work for your heart. So the more you work your external body muscles, the more you work your most vital muscle, your heart.

Like any muscle that gets exercised, the heart eventually gets stronger and can do the same amount of work with less strain than before. The harder you work your heart—within your limits, of course—the more efficient it will get. After your heart has become accustomed to workouts, you will find that its resting beat, its pulse rate when you are sitting quietly, is slower than it was before you started exercising. Suppose you had the "average" pulse rate of about 72 beats per minute. You may find that after you've been exercising a while, your resting rate may drop to 60, even 50, beats per minute. In other words, the heart is doing the same job of supplying your body with the blood it needs but is doing it in fewer beats.

It's easy enough to find your own heart resting rate. Simply sit still for a few minutes and take your pulse by touching the artery near the base of your jaw or at the base of the hand inside of one of the your wrists. Count the beats for a full minute. If your pulse is around 75 beats a minute, you're about average. Below that, you are probably already in good shape. A pulse rate of over 80 beats, however, is a sign that maybe it's time for more serious working out.

BIGGER ARTERIES, BETTER BLOOD

Another reason why your heart will have to work less is the effect exercise has on blood circulation to your heart and the rest of your body. Doctors have found that after a steady schedule of exercise, the coronary arteries that supply blood to your heart get larger, keeping your heart muscle more efficiently fueled and making a heart attack less likely. This improved circulation means that backup arteries that supply the heart also enlarge, so that if one gets blocked up, others keep the heart going with no incidence of any heart problem.

Everyone should strive for basic fitness for its own sake, an idea fatally ignored by most of the American spectating public.

–DIANA NYAD, *Other Shores*

Improved circulation may mean that your blood pressure drops below what it is now. Your network of blood vessels increases with exercise, making it less difficult for blood to circulate to different areas of your body. You will in effect have the blood flowing through more vessels, easing the amount of push your heart will have to give to move blood around. Some doctors think this is why athletes may suddenly surge up from a plateau of exercise fitness. Your body signals you that it's ready to do more work when this broader feeder network to muscles is ready.

Just as important, the quality of the blood itself also changes. For one thing, the level of certain kinds of fats, called triglycerides, goes down in your blood. These fats clog blood vessels and have been implicated in heart attacks. Fewer fats again mean a lower risk of heart trouble.

A second important effect on the blood is that its oxygen-carrying ability improves. As you exercise, your body taps into both a natural body sugar, called glycogen, which is stored in your muscle tissue, and your body fat for its energy. But your body can't burn these body fuels efficiently without oxygen, which it gets from your blood, specifically from your oxygen-carrying red blood cells. These have a special red pigment, hemoglobin, which absorbs oxygen from your lungs and carries it off to where it is needed in your body.

MOVING IS VITAL

Amazingly enough, doctors have found that the more you exercise, the more you can increase the total volume of your blood supply in general, and the number of hemoglobin-carrying red blood cells in particular. The result is that by working out you develop a body that can carry around and use more oxygen than ever before. After a year of steady exercise an average man may increase the total volume of his blood supply by as much as a whole quart. And the more blood you have circulating, the more oxygen there is readily available to fuel your body's working.

EFFICIENT ENZYMES

With more oxygen circulating in your body, something else happens as you keep on swimming, working the muscles of your body: Your muscles get better at using the oxygen brought to them. In order to extract oxygen from your blood, your muscles have certain enzymes. What seems to happen with exercise is that the more these enzymes have to work at getting that oxygen, the better they get at collecting it. The result is your muscles are able to absorb oxygen at a faster rate and work more smoothly, with less effort. In a word, they "flow."

Another part of the body's oxygen-supply system also improves—your lungs. The lungs themselves have a fixed capacity for how much air they can take in, but how

much of that capacity is actually used will depend on your level of fitness. Your lungs take in air when they expand and let out carbon dioxide when they contract. Just how much air comes in depends on how much your lungs can contract. And how much your lungs can contract depends on the muscles around your rib cage and your diaphragm, your main breathing muscle. Those muscles take air into your lungs by creating a vacuum–expanding the belly and chest–and they force air out by compressing the lungs. If you don't do much exercise as a rule, these breathing muscles get out of shape and are less able to expand and contract as fully as they once did. When this happens, you aren't able to take in as much air as before or do it in as short an amount of time. That is where swimming helps tremendously. It creates large oxygen demands in your muscles, which in turn send the message to your brain, which finally steps up your breathing rate to keep the oxygen supplied to your blood-rich lungs.

MUSCLE SORENESS

You may notice after you've begun exercising that your chest and your stomach muscles feel sore. Part of the reason for this soreness is that you've been working them harder than usual in doing the mechanics of breathing. Also, biochemically these muscles are sore because they themselves didn't get enough of the oxygen they are trying to provide for the whole body.

As already mentioned, muscles need oxygen to burn the fuel that they have stored inside. In well-conditioned muscles or muscles operating within their normal limits, the body sugar, glycogen, provides energy and gives off waste chemicals which are picked up by your bloodstream and shuttled back to your lungs, where you expel them as carbon dioxide and water vapor. If your muscles are working beyond this comfortable limit and can't get enough oxygen, a different chemical reaction takes place and that glycogen becomes something called lactic acid.

This gradually slows muscle contractions and will give you stiff, aching muscles, even cramps, if you push too hard.

You will probably feel this soreness as you start up a new exercise using new muscles until the oxygen supply gradually increases in that area and the muscles accumulate more glycogen. Even if you are fit, you may notice this aching sensation as you increase your swimming distance. If you handle it right, this process can benefit your endurance, because swimming until your muscles ache slightly will drain off your muscles' glycogen supply but will also condition your muscles to store more of that body's energy source the next time. So the next time you swim it may take longer to tire yourself out. The payoff is a stronger, more resilient body. And it shows.

FEELING GOOD

People talk about the "glow" of good health. That glow has a sound scientific basis. One reason is the effect we have mentioned of increasing vascularization—that is, improving the network of blood vessels in your body. As your body begins to exercise more, it makes its demands for more and more oxygen. In response to this, blood vessels grow and spread to feed oxygen-hungry muscles. These vessels are the pipeline for nutrients that all body cells need, and since your body tissue—everything from bone to muscle and skin—is made up of these cells, how well they are nourished will show in your complexion, in your resistance to disease, and in your general physical appearance.

Beyond that there is the improvement in muscle tone you get from a steady habit of swimming. If you don't use your muscles, as you probably already know, they slacken and can eventually get overwhelmed with fat. You not only don't feel as fit when you lose your muscle tone, you don't look as well either. A well-used muscle

THE SWIMMING OF A FROG AND A MAN COMPARED
The definition of swimming is, I believe, to keep yourself afloat and make progress. It matters little how this is done—in what mode or form—as long as it is done.

-JOHN LEAHY,
The Art of Swimming in the Eton Style, 1875

never totally relaxes. It settles into a state of mild contraction even when it's not in use. Doctors routinely use this tone—this state of being partly contracted, this tautness—as an indicator of health. Lack of tone is simply a sign that your body has gotten weaker, something you feel soon enough when you do anything strenuous. But this feeling of weakness will soon disappear when you get into your swimming program.

Although doctors haven't figured out why, steady exercise also affects your digestive system. People with the beginnings of an ulcer sometimes find that with exercise their condition lessens or even disappears. One reason is probably the relaxing, stress-relieving effects of exercise. Another seems to be that when you're in condition, less gastric acid is produced. Exercise also works on the lower part of your digestive system as a natural laxative; it seems to speed up the contractions of the intestines, moving food and digested waste along quickly.

CLEARING THE SMOKE

If you smoke, you may already feel a little guilty about your habit. From the Surgeon General's warning and dozens of articles, you probably know what the evils of smoking are—risk of emphysema, lung cancer, and other respiratory problems, as well as heart disease—and you may be wondering whether your smoking habit will fit in with your exercise program. It would be nice to say that swimming will cure you of smoking, but life isn't that simple. Smoking is a tough habit to break, and no one solution works for everyone. But swimming *may* help you quit, or at the very least diminish some of the damage you're doing to your body.

For many, smoking is a stress release. They feel better when they light up. Just as a matter of psychological habit, if you can obtain relief from stress by kicking and splashing away your tensions, you might lessen your compulsion to smoke.

Although he's seen many people quit smoking after starting a swimming fitness program, Dr. Hemming Atterbom, Director of the Human Performance Laboratory at the University of New Mexico, is not sure why or how it happens. It seems to be a "chicken-or-egg" situation, he says. As you become more conscious about fitness, you may become more concerned about what your smoking is doing to you. That may give you the psychological motivation you need to quit.

Certainly when you exercise you're more aware of what smoking does to you. After a strenuous workout you'll be gasping for breath and spitting up mucus collected in your lungs. You are now placing new oxygen demands on your heart and lungs and making them work harder to overcome the smothering effect of smoking. Smokers' lungs are less resilient, and the carbon monoxide you inhale with the smoke reduces your red blood cells' ability to carry oxygen. Also, nicotine is a vasoconstrictor—that is, it causes your blood vessels to shrink in diameter, making it harder for your heart to circulate blood.

As you swim you balance out some of these negative effects. Exercise speeds up circulation, which helps clean out wastes and poisons, such as carbon monoxide, from your system more quickly. Swimming increases the amount of oxygen-carrying hemoglobin in your red blood cells, which helps to compensate for the cells' reduced ability to carry oxygen. And finally, even though nicotine impairs circulation because of its constricting effect on blood vessels, swimming helps counter that by stimulating the spread of more capillaries in muscle tissue to satisfy the increased demand for oxygen. So, even if your circulation isn't what it should be because of smoking, it is still better than it would be if you didn't do any swimming.

Of course, the best thing you can hope for is that the "positive addiction" to swimming, as some psychologists call a good exercise habit, will overtake your negative addiction to smoking. In fact, if you hope to quit smoking, you should also know that even with exercise to turn to, it can be difficult. On the average, says Dr. Atterbom, it takes anywhere from nine months to a year to break free of the physical and psychological addiction. Beyond that, it takes roughly seven years for your body to recover fully from the negative effects of smoking.

BURNING THE FAT

No catalog of the physical benefits of exercise would be complete without talking about the biggest visible change that happens: losing fat. Diets will help you take off weight, but, as you probably know if you've ever relied totally on diets, they don't work forever. Sooner or later, if you don't exercise, those pounds start creeping back on your frame and you have a new battle to fight all over again.

Exercise burns up calories, and since calories are stored on your body in fat, the fat content of your body gets used up. Depending on the speed at which you swim, you can burn from 350 to 420 calories an hour. As you exercise you are building up muscle tissue and dissolving the excess fat on your body. It takes a while to get your body melted down, so don't expect instant results. It may be as long as a month before your body begins to show the effect. But if you maintain the same caloric intake after you exercise as you did before, the fat will start to go. Experts calculate that to lose one pound of fat you have to burn up 3,500 calories over and above your normal caloric requirement. So in about a week and a half of heavy swimming, you could actually trim as much as one pound off your body even if you only maintain your food intake habits.

Another way exercise helps you lose weight is that it acts as a kind of natural diet pill. Your "appestat" —food control center—doesn't fluctuate as wildly as it may have in the past. For some reason exercising seems to act as an appetite suppressant for some people. One theory is that exercise draws blood away from your stomach to your hard-working muscles, so you may not even feel like eating immediately after a workout. Over a longer stretch of time, exercise seems to stabilize the level of blood sugar in your body. And since sharp drops in blood-sugar levels trigger hunger attacks, you become more immune to problems like binge eating. Your appetite levels off and becomes easier to control.

One precaution, however. Don't confuse getting slim with losing weight. You may even find that you weigh a little more as you exercise more. The reason is simply that your body is replacing fat with muscle. Since muscle tissue is denser, heavier, you may weigh more than you expect. But since muscle is also more compact, you will be slimmer-looking. So as you get further along on your swimming regimen, don't look at the dial on your bathroom scale, look in the mirror. That's where the results will show. And, best news of all, the slimming effect will first happen where your body stores most of its fat: on your hips, your thighs, your buttocks, and your midsection.

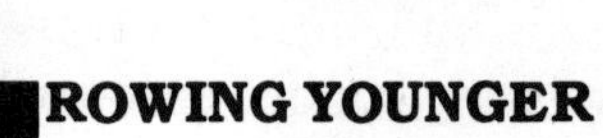

GROWING YOUNGER

All of swimming's effects can add up to one invisible benefit that adds a special zing to your life: an extension of your healthy life span. According to Dr. Paul Hutlinger of Western Illinois University, one of the signs of the aging process is that your body is less able to do physical work. As you get older the physical strength you have naturally diminishes. Studies of men show that between the ages of 45 and 55, an individual can lose up to 13 percent of his work capacity. In general, the aging process starts at about 25, and the ability of your body to do physical work diminishes at the rate of about 1 percent a year.

I can swim like a duck.

-WILLIAM SHAKESPEARE, *The Tempest*

Along with this discovery has come another revelation: that exercise can slow down or even stop part of this aging process. For example, in the Purdue University study mentioned in the last chapter, researchers found that after six weeks of strenuous workouts three hours a week, some of the people in their seventies had the physical age of people 20 or even 30 years younger.

SLOWING NATURE'S CLOCK

In another study noted by Dr. Hutlinger, a group of exercisers were studied over a 10-year period. Careful records were kept of all the body's variables affected by age—weight, blood pressure, oxygen uptake in the body, heart rate at rest, and maximum heart rate. After years of either running a total of 14 miles per week or swimming a total of 5 miles per week, the men in the study seemed to have stopped much of the body's aging. Their weight stayed the same all those years, as did their blood pressure and pulse when at rest. And their maximum heart rate, the rate at which their hearts had to beat when exercising at their peaks, actually declined. Lastly, the capacity of their lungs increased by almost 20 percent over what it had been. As far as most physical measurements are concerned, their bodies had stopped aging ten years before.

According to Dr. Hutlinger, the key to this peak condition was the way the men exercised. During each workout they pushed themselves to 80 percent or more of their maximum heart rate. (As a rule of thumb, your maximum heart rate is 220 minus whatever your age is. So, according to this formula, if you are 31 your maximum heart rate is 189.) Your actual maximum heart rate may vary depending on what kind of condition you're in now; but whatever it is, to get the most anti-aging benefits from your workout, you should do it at roughly 80 percent of capacity. (One regimen Dr. Hutlinger recommends highly is swimming the distance of 2,000 yards a day, five days a week.) Hutlinger is giving this theory of sustained youth the acid test in what is known as the Masters Swimming Program, a national group of swimming enthusiasts, many of them former swimming stars, who like to compete for the exercise and for the fun of it. It was set up in 1970 to give swimmers of all ages a chance to compete on an equal basis of age. Masters races are held for swimmers in their twenties, swimmers in their thirties, and all the way up to those in their eighties. No world records are set at these competitions, at least no records that get very much recognition. But no one really cares. It is as much a social event as a sporting event. After studying master swimmers such as himself, Hutlinger has concluded that pitched at the right intensity, a steady schedule of this kind of swimming can be one of the best rejuvenators around.

E SWIMMER'S BODY

What does it take to be a swimmer? Just the ability to swim and lack of fear of the water. But if you want to get really particular, there *is* something called the competitive swimmer's body. It's a general build that swimming coaches look for in young swimmers. Man or woman, the ultimate swimmer's shape for both speed and efficiency is, first of all, tall—six feet or over for a man, five and one-half to six feet for a woman. For minimum water resistance, the swimmer should be thin as well as long. Thin ankles, strong wrists, and long arms and legs are definite assets for the swimmer. So is a powerful upper torso: strong back, broad and powerful chest, and strong abdominal muscles.

RIBBON WINNING SHAPES

Good body symmetry—an even distribution of muscles—is another plus. That means that while the world class swimmer is stroking through the water he or she doesn't have to compensate for a lopsided surge of power coming from one part of the body. Muscle groups that are important in swimming include the "lats," the *Latissimus dorsi* muscles that begin under the arm and fan out to the lower back; the triceps, that long muscle on the back of each upper arm; the deltoids, which surround the shoulder; the biceps, the classic muscleman bulge on the upper arm; and pectorals, or chest muscles. Thin but strong hips, on which the body pivots as it swims, are an added advantage.

This is why Mark Spitz could perform so superbly in the water. The combination of years of intense training and a body already well designed for efficiency in the water paid off in Spitz's record breaking sweep of gold medals in the Olympics. He was a combination of long, lean lines and power. His arms, for example, were well muscled and very long for his body size. Also he had, and further developed in training, a concentration of powerful muscles in his shoulders, neck, and back. Biomechanically, he was an efficient swimming machine with a high strength-to-body-mass ratio.

The evolutionists tell us that we have lost many of our natural powers, as a penalty for our having neglected to use them, and that these various losses are proved by the disappearance of such more or less useful portions of our anatomy as tails, hair on our bodies, the muscles for cocking our ears, twitching our skin, etc., etc. Unfortunately, they have neglected to tell us the stages by which the majority of us—well, of civilized peoples, at any rate—have succeeded in losing the natural capacity for Swimming. For Swimming is a *natural* capacity and not an acquired art as is so commonly supposed, so that its lack of popularity is really a matter of wonderment.

-EDWIN TENNEY BREWSTER, *Swimming*

Another important consideration is the swimmer's center of gravity. Ideally the body should skim across the surface with most of its weight in front, propelled along as much as possible by the arms and hands. Although your whole body works as it swims, most of the propulsion comes from your arms. The kicking of your legs mostly helps keep your body stable, on an even keel in the water. This is true in just about every stroke except the breaststroke. That is one reason why a swimmer's legs stay lean and long. A strong swimmer's kick keeps your body riding and gliding high in the water, where there is the least amount of resistance. The lower you lie in the water, the more resistance your body meets as it moves.

But unless you plan to swim in the next Olympics, your own body shape and size don't really matter. You won't be swimming against fanatically trained competitors in do-or-die races. The fact that you are not shaped like Mark Spitz or Diana Nyad is important only in that comparing your body to theirs will help you to know what parts will be getting more exercise than others. Unlike jogging and bicycling, which primarily work out the legs, swimming primarily works on the upper half of your body. But it does not do this exclusively. Your bottom half—lower back and hip and leg muscles—also get used. In this way swimming is a more demanding, and more rewarding, fitness alternative.

NOT FOR WOMEN ONLY!

If you are a woman who plans to get serious about swimming as a fitness exercise, or maybe is already doing a little swimming and wants to step up the intensity of workouts, you might be put off by all this talk about added strength and muscles. All women like to feel physically fit, but some avoid exercising for fear of getting excessively muscular. For example, some may have an image in their minds of athletes like the women who competed on the East German swimming team in the 1976 Olympics. They were large, broad-shouldered women who were products of one of the most grueling training programs in the world, and who, some have claimed, took drugs such as male hormones and steroids to enhance their muscle development.

This is not likely to happen to you for two reasons. First of all, you will not be training at Olympic levels and won't be pushing your body with nearly the same intensity. Even if you did, it is genetically impossible without steroids to develop the heavily muscled look of a well-conditioned man. A man has those rippling biceps and chest muscles in part because of male hormones (which is one reason some suspect the manlike bodies of some female athletes to be achieved with the assistance of drugs). Women's hormones limit the size to which muscles can grow, and, for better or worse, women naturally have a slightly thicker layer of fat on their

bodies, called adipose fat, which will cover those stronger muscles, giving a woman's body sleeker, smoother lines.

As was mentioned before, swimming may or may not help you lose weight, but it will make you slimmer. Areas of the body that sag from poor muscle tone will firm up. Problem areas such as thighs, hips, and buttocks become less of a problem as swimming burns off the fat stored there. The stomach will become firmer and flatter as a result and, depending on which stroke a woman uses in swimming, she may even notice some breast development. After exercising a while, a woman's chest muscles will develop, and as a result her breasts will appear firmer and higher. Finally, that mysterious "cellulite"—actually excess body fat—will diminish as the body burns up more calories and fat. For these reasons alone, no woman has to fear looking too strong. She has nothing to lose but excess bulges.

Lowered cholesterol. Not all the fat you might be losing is visible. The President's Council also found that swimming lowers the body's serum cholesterol, which has been implicated as a cause of one of this era's greatest killers, heart disease. The exact reasons why this happens aren't known, but it does happen; in studies with both men and women, investigators found that people who made it a daily habit to swim 1,000 yards showed a dramatic drop in their cholesterol after they had exercised.

Water pressure for better breathing. Another feature of being in water is that the pressure of the surrounding liquid helps the lungs draw in more air as you exercise. In a way, just being in the pool forces better breathing habits on you. The water pressure around you, as slight as it is, applies a gentle push that makes you draw just a little more air into your lungs. The pressure is subtle but strong enough to make a difference.

MEASURING THE BENEFITS

Scientists are often frustrated when trying to compare swimming to any other exercise because of the unique and elusive nature of the sport. To study a runner's body in action, doctors can put him on a treadmill and let him run. To study a bicyclist working, they can have him sit on a stationary bicycle and pedal to his heart's content. Even with various monitoring attachments stuck to their bodies, the runner or cyclist can perform more or less normally. This is not true of the swimmer, which makes it very tricky to make exact studies of the body at work in the water.

Sport physicians have tried different methods. First they got in a rowboat and coasted alongside of the swimmer as he moved along in open water. In time they moved their observations indoors and used swimming pools with underwater windows to study the body movement of the swimmer. More recently, they tried attaching a harness around the swimmer's waist and rigging a rope from the harness to a pulley system; the other end of the rope was connected to a series of weights. By measuring how much weight the swimmer could lift, doctors were able to get a rough idea of how much work he was doing.

The problem with this system was that the harness-and-weight system usually interfered with the swimmer's stroke, and so what scientists were getting was not a true measurement of the swimmer's normal body movement.

Finally they came up with a better method, something called the flume. Essentially it's a very large bathtub with water flowing at a steady current from one end to the other. It's the swimmer's equivalent of a treadmill. Once a swimmer is in the tank, the investigators can test his strength and endurance by speeding up the flow of water. As one sports expert put it, the swimmer is "like a salmon swimming upstream." With this new method, they've been able to discover a good deal about how the human body operates in water.

There are certainly many ladies who possess sufficient courage to venture into the sea; but it is amusing to see them dallying with the rope of the bathing machine, struggling and splashing in an unsightly garment that seemingly holds each fair nymph in bondage, when her limbs should be free and gracefully gliding in healthful exercise through the freshening water.

–Life and Adventures of Professor Robert Emmet Odlum, 1885

BATTLES OF THE SEXES

To no one's surprise, studies have turned up a few differences in how men and women swim. One is that because women generally have smaller bodies than men, they also have smaller hearts, smaller lung capacities, and less blood (and therefore less oxygen stored in the blood.) This all means that a woman doesn't have to swim as far or as fast as a man to get the same kind of aerobic fitness. There is a kind of reverse sexism at work here.

On the other hand, women do not do as well as men in the short swim events, called sprint races, because they are less muscular. As their name indicates, sprint races involve quick bursts of speed. In a sprint the human body isn't in action long enough for the oxygen it breathes to be used and processed by the muscles. This is called exercising anaerobically, or without oxygen. Power here depends not so much on how your body can use oxygen but on how much energy is stored in the muscles. The more of the right kind of muscles you have, the more potential you have for anaerobic exercise, for those short bursts of speed. Since men tend to be more muscular than women, they can maintain those bursts longer and at higher intensities.

Things can change over distances. Studies of women's bodies as swimming machines found that in many ways they are superior to men. First of all, since a woman's body is smaller, there is less water resistance as she swims. But that advantage is balanced out by the smaller amount of muscle on a woman's body. Beyond that, however, is the fact that the woman's body is more buoyant. Women are naturally endowed with a slightly thicker layer of fat tissue on their bodies than men. This helps keep their bodies afloat more efficiently and also means that they ride higher in the water and meet less resistance as they swim.

What this means in practice is that if you pitted a man against an equally trained woman who had the same amount of muscle and the same oxygen-using capacity as the man, she would swim as much as 50 percent faster than the man. In the water, the man's body is much heavier, less buoyant, and generally tougher to push around. In a race over a long enough distance, this fact would take its toll on a male swimmer. And so, swimming experts says, over distances of more than 10 kilometers (roughly 6 miles), women start to gain the advantage in spite of their lower oxygen-using abilities. The efficiency of their bodies in the water starts to balance out the power and larger lung capacity of the male swimmer. This is one reason women make good distance swimmers.

THE SINGLE BEST EXERCISE

Is swimming really all that special? Does it have things to offer that no other aerobic exercise does? The answer to both questions is yes. For openers, swimming can be as social or as solitary an exercise as you want to make it. Swimming pools tend to be social magnets even for people who don't swim that much. If you find the idea of exercising alone a little grim, the odds are that you will probably enjoy swimming for this reason alone. It's always pleasant to have someone there to talk to while you're resting during exercise intervals, for example, especially if you're swimming like an Olympian that day. At the very least, it gives you a small audience for your workouts as you whip through your Mark Spitz fantasies in your mind.

Anyone can do it. More concretely, swimming is a highly adaptable exercise. The Red Cross has known this for years and accordingly sponsors and teaches swim programs for people who because of one physical disability or another can't do other exercises. The low-stress, low-gravity world of the pool is ideal for people who couldn't exercise otherwise. The pool's low gravity also protects, shielding bodies from injury, acting almost as a cushion surrounding them.

Fat floats. The beauty of swimming for someone who has more pounds than he or she needs is that the natural buoyancy of the water supports the exercising body. In fact, the more fat a person has on his body, the more easily he floats. In this one sense, being overweight may even put a beginning swimmer at a slight advantage. You have to admit there's a lot to be said for an exercise that literally supports the overweight and out-of-shape and makes those who are in shape work harder. Thin people don't float nearly as well as fat people.

A fat man or woman must be both extremely cowardly as well as clumsy, to get drowned at all, if not injured when falling in.

–J. A. BENNETT, *Art of Swimming*, 1846

You're never too old. Another advantage of swimming over other exercises is that, practically speaking, it has no age limit. Long after friends have hung up their squash or tennis rackets or handball gloves, the swimmer can keep on exercising, his ligaments and joints still injury-free and working smoothly. In this way swimming is unique. As long as you can move your arms and legs, or even just your arms, you can continue to swim.

Best for total fitness. After making a study of the sport, the President's Council on Physical Fitness and Sports managed to add a few more things to this list of advantages. In a chart the council made to compare various exercises ranging from bowling to skiing, swimming was given the highest possible point rating for building up the body's stamina, and it tied with jogging as the exercise that does the most for the body's muscular endurance. And the Council found swimming second only to calisthenics in enhancing the suppleness and flexibility of the body.

The Council noted studies done on women swimmers that indicated an increase in strength in the swimmers' legs, calf muscles, upper back, lower back, and abdominal and chest muscles. Thus swimming delivers more total fitness than running or bicycling, which primarily develop the leg muscles and do little for upper-body strength.

Get it together! Swimming also is a way to tune up your coordination. Few other sports involve as complex and intricate a series of body movements as swimming. To be an efficient athlete in the water you have to time everything—from how you turn your head to when you move your arms and kick your feet—with split-second accuracy for the most benefits. Swimming is a pat-your-head/rub-your-stomach test of coordination that keeps your mind as well as most of your body totally involved.

DIFFERENT STROKES, DIFFERENT TRIMS

Both men and women face the same challenge when they swim, regardless of body shape: water resistance. It's both an enemy and friend. On the one hand, you should learn how to orient and use your body so it forms the most streamlined shape you can assume as you slip through the water. On the other hand, without that resistance you wouldn't be working your body, speeding up your heart rate, increasing your oxygen uptake, and increasing your body's endurance. In the chapter entitled "Strokes and Style," you'll find out the best way to streamline yourself during various strokes to get the most out of your pool time.

The principal idea is to lie as flat as possible in the water, with your legs as close to the surface as you can get them, and with as little wiggle in your hips as possible when you kick. With each stroke there are certain muscles you'll be using, and by learning how to increase the power of your strokes, you'll find out how to work your muscles in the most efficient way rather than wearing them out unnecessarily.

Since the basic strokes all require different kinds of coordination, the effects they have on your body will vary. Certain muscles get worked more than others with each kind of stroke. Depending on your body's weak and

strong points, you can adopt the stroke that suits you the best. Here's a rundown of what you can expect from each stroke.

The Sidestroke. This is a more relaxing and therefore less demanding way to get through the water. The arm action of the sidestroke primarily works on your trunk or abdominal muscles, and the scissors kick, like the flutter kick, works on slimming both the front and back of your thigh muscles. It has a stretching, elongating effect on your waist and leg muscles.

The Crawl (Freestyle). This is probably the best overall conditioner of the various strokes. It stresses your triceps—the muscles on the back of your upper arms—and your back, chest, and abdominal, or trunk, muscles as well. In addition, the flutter kick you use with it stretches your quadriceps muscles—the "quads," those muscles on the front of your thigh—and your hamstring muscle, the large muscle on the back of your thigh. If you run as well as swim, you may find your legs feel a little tight when you first start out, because running tends to overstress and tighten up your hamstring muscles, making your legs less flexible in the water. Swimming will help to stretch some of these tight muscles. And one last benefit for those who like to wear tight designer jeans: the crawl works wonders on tightening up your gluteus maximus muscles, better known as your derriere.

The Breaststroke. Aptly named, this stroke primarily benefits the pectoral muscles, the ones supporting the breasts. Except for the triceps muscles on the back of your arms, the breaststroke stresses your arm and shoulder area, firming and rounding your biceps and deltoid muscles. It also works on (and shrinks the fat off) your stomach muscles. Because of the special nature of the frog kick, only the inner part of your thigh gets much of a workout and benefits from the slimming effect of this stroke. One precaution in using the frog kick: Be careful if you are prone to what is known as runner's knee, in which the kneecap rubs painfully against the thigh bone. This kick aggravates that condition and in fact causes a similar condition among competition swimmers called, logically enough, swimmer's knee or sometimes breaststroker's knee.

The Backstroke. The backstroke is just a gentle way to travel through the water if you swim in the elementary style, and therefore it has minimal benefits for your body, basically just exercising your trunk muscles and toning up the muscle on your inner thigh. For the most benefits from a backstroke you have to adopt the surging, reaching style of the racing backstroke. Done vigorously

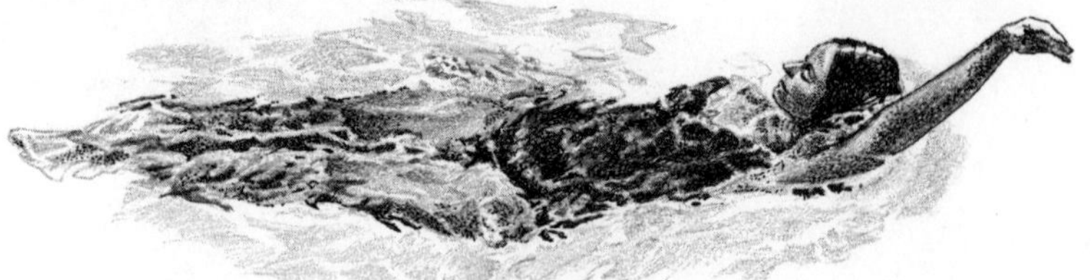

enough, the racing backstroke has most of the benefits of the crawl without the problem of getting a mouthful of water now and then. It is especially good for developing chest muscles and slimming thighs, arms, and shoulders. Just about the only area of the body the racing backstroke doesn't stress is the triceps muscle, the one on the back of your arm.

The Butterfly. This is a power stroke usually done by those who have already achieved a high level of fitness in the water. Probably the simplest way to think of it is as a more grueling version of the breaststroke. It is extremely fast, second only to the crawl, but taxing to do because you move through the water in jerky, bobbing surges that work your shoulders, arms, and back harder than any other stroke. Also, the dolphin kick peculiar to this stroke puts an equally large strain on your legs, especially the front and back of your thighs. If you're really looking for a rugged workout that will build up your upper-body strength, especially chest, shoulders and back, this is the stroke for you.

A QUESTION OF STYLE

One last point to remember as you begin your swimming fitness program: Take the time to learn the correct way to do your strokes. Concentrate on your technique. More than running and bicycling, swimming is a sport that requires some skill and finesse in the way you perform. To get the most out of it, you have to turn your body into an automatically-functioning swimming machine, one that can do lap after lap smoothly and effortlessly for 20 minutes or more at a time. Many of the benefits of swimming come only after you've been working out steadily over a period of time. In order to do that, you have to have your basic swimming skills and conditioning already in hand. Part of that conditioning starts even before you get into the water, which is why you should take a close look at the next chapter before you get wet.

Getting Set, Tuning Up

Once you've adopted swimming as your fitness exercise, you'll find your body consciousness will be raised to a whole new level. For one thing, you will simply be more aware of your body and how much better you feel—stronger and more energetic. For another, you will probably be more concerned with how you care for it and keep it in tune.

Doing that is a lot simpler than you may think. Basically it's a matter of fueling yourself the right way with what you take in at mealtime and taking a few minutes each day to stretch and shake loose your muscles so you can enjoy your swims even more. By themselves, these stretching and toning exercises are tremendously effective ways to relax, and you may find yourself using them for that purpose as well.

But first, we'll discuss the subject that has generated more confusion and disagreement than peace in the Middle East: nutrition. There is a tremendous amount of information about food and nutrition, and a tremendous interest in it. Cookbooks and diet books are perennial best sellers, and all kinds of cults have sprung up around just what it is you should put on your plate at mealtime. Out of this barrage of facts and half-facts and sometimes dietary craziness come all kinds of garbled nutritional messages—carbohydrates are bad for you; protein is good; cholesterol will kill you; brown food (brown sugar, brown rice, brown bread) is healthier than white food; the more vitamins you take, the better off you are; natural is good, artificial is bad, and on and on.

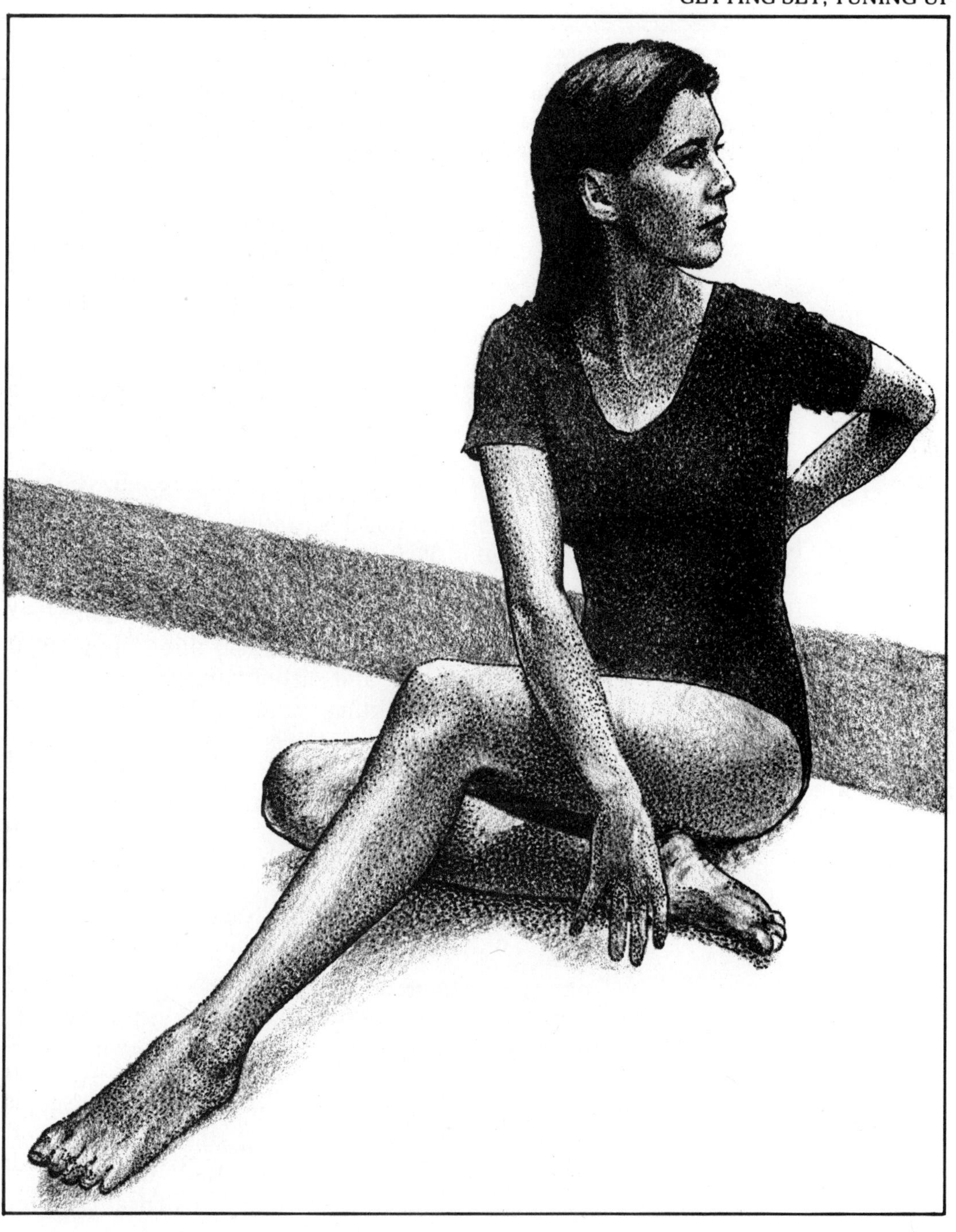

ATING TO SWIM

With a more athletic and probably hungrier body, you will no doubt want to feed it the right things. But what are the right things? Forget, or at least try to ignore for the moment, whatever you've remembered reading in articles and books on fad diets. There are no magic foods that offer you a new lease on life or nudge you in the direction of immortality. If you're the average eater there are probably no deficiencies in your diet. In fact, if you're the average American, dietarily speaking, you may be taking in more than enough of some of the foods your body needs. Now that you have become a little more athletic, you might take stock of your diet and decide whether or not it suits the new, more active you.

What about your muscles? Are you doing right by those? Feeding the muscles is often one of the big concerns of athletes. To find out what muscles need, it might help to cover just what goes on in them when you swim, or do any other aerobic exercise. To develop and work properly, your muscles chiefly need three things from your diet: protein, fat, and carbohydrates.

Protein is the building material for muscles, the raw stuff of which your tissue is made. Proteins consist of a basic group of chemicals—amino acids—which specialized cells in your body transform into everything from the hair on your head to eye tissue. Scientists estimate that about 60 percent of your body (exclusive of water) is protein. In itself protein is not a prime source of energy for your body, but it is a prime source of body material.

Your prime source of fuel for energy is the food component known as carbohydrates. Your body breaks it down from the food you eat and stores it in your muscle and liver in the form of glycogen, the body sugar. A backup source of energy to this is fat, which your body stores in the muscle and under your skin. Obviously your body can store just so much energy fuel. An endurance, long-distance exercise like swimming will drain off your fuel reserves after a while, a feature that is to your benefit. The more you exercise and use up your body fuel supplies, the more efficient the tissues get at storing fuel.

But do you need a special diet to do this? Every time a marathon is run, for example, articles appear about carbohydrate loading—eating a carbohydrate meal the night before the race. Sports magazines are full of articles about the benefits of one kind or another of dietary supplements. The temptation is to worry too much about special foods now that you're getting more use out of your body.

THE WALL AND BONKING

One of the reasons for this concern about diet is what is usually called the "wall" of exhaustion. Typically mentioned in connection with marathon running, "hitting the wall" can happen to anyone participating in any endurance event, including marathon swimming. Essentially what happens is that the muscles that work the hardest run out of their glycogen stores. Although there may be plenty more in other parts of your body, they are not transferable. When the glycogen level is down, the muscle feels tired and it takes more willpower to keep moving. This doesn't mean you're out of energy. Once glycogen goes, you start burning fat, and then the sugar in your bloodstream starts getting used up. And if you still keep going, you start draining off your muscle tissue. Once your body has hit this wall, you can't recover, at least not while you're exercising. Your body will need a few days to assimilate and store a new supply of muscle glycogen.

Another problem distance athletes have is called "bonking." This happens when the glycogen stored in your liver runs out. You may start to feel lightheaded and dizzy, because the brain has run out of sugar. Bonking is different from hitting the wall, because you can recover from it fairly quickly by eating or drinking some high-sugar foods. (If you don't do this, however, there is no

The following summary of a day's work for a man in full Training for a swimming match, based in all essential particulars on the system so successfully pursued by the celebrated Captain Barclay, will, if so modified as to suit age, locality, and previous mode of life, fairly indicate the method to be adopted by one who wishes to attain for any specific purpose a maximum condition of health and strength.

5 a.m. Rise. Either plunge at once into cold water, or have a sponge bath; be well rubbed down with a dry, coarse towel; dress quickly, and eat a hard biscuit, or small piece of stale bread.
5:30 a.m. Walk a mile briskly, then run up hill for half-a-mile as rapidly as possible; afterwards walk four miles at a moderate pace.
7 a.m. Breakfast. Rump steak or mutton chop, underdone, without fat, and stale bread. Note: rest, or take very gentle exercise with dumb-bells, for the remainder of two hours.
9 a.m. Walk two miles at a moderate pace; swim sharply for a quarter-of-an-hour or twenty minutes; quickly and thoroughly dry with a coarse towel; dress, and walk three or four miles at a moderate speed.

(Continue on right)

way you'd be able to coordinate your body well enough to finish your event.)

They sound pretty horrible, don't they? Fortunately, unless you plan to begin marathon swimming, or something on that scale of effort, these are not problems you are likely to face in your exercise sessions. According to sports physiologist Dr. Hemming Atterbom of the University of New Mexico, you'd have to swim steadily for at least an hour, more likely an hour and a half, before you would experience anything like hitting the wall. For that reason you don't have to worry about any swimmer's wall or about loading with any special kind of food.

NECESSARY NUTRIENTS

All you should concern yourself with is whether or not your body gets its share of the more than 40 nutrients it needs to function smoothly. You've already read about three of the food substances—protein, carbohydrates, and fat—that contain some of these nutrients. There are three others you should know about.

Water. Even without exercise you are constantly losing water vapor, in your breath for example, that has to be replenished. There's a good reason why you may feel thirsty after a hard swim. Even though you may have been surrounded by fluid, your body will lose more during exercise. Your body needs water for your cells to metabolize nutrients and get rid of waste, for a stable blood volume, and to drain off toxic substances from your body in the form of urine.

Minerals. Usually found in fruits and vegetables, minerals are necessary components in the chemical interactions with vitamins to get energy out of the food you eat, to build new tissue, and to synthesize chemicals your body needs. Also by themselves many of the minerals are needed for the kind of nerve activity that controls muscle contractions, from your heartbeat to when you flex your

(from previous page)

12 midday. Undress, and lie down in bed for half-an-hour. On rising, take a glass of old ale or sound sherry, and eat a hard biscuit.
1 p.m. Walk four miles.
2 p.m. For one hour and a-half occupy oneself with such athletic exercises as are calculated to develope the muscles of the arms and the trunk.
3:30 p.m. Rest for half-an-hour.
4 p.m. Dinner. Rump steak or mutton chop, or a slice or two from a joint of beef or mutton, underdone, free from fat; stale bread, one or two mealy potatoes, and a little greens; no pastry or cheese.
4:30 p.m. Rest till five.
5 p.m. Walk a mile sharply; run half-a-mile at the top of one's speed; and walk four miles at a moderate rate.
7 p.m. A half-pint of old ale, or wine-glass of sherry, and hard biscuit. Gymnastics for the arms and chest till eight.
8 p.m. Rest, and amusing conversation or light reading till nine.
9 p.m. Body to be well rubbed down with coarse towels, then to bed till five next morning.

-CHARLES STEEDMAN
Manual of Swimming, 1867

bicep, and they play an important role in controlling how much water your body can store.

Vitamins. There are a couple of things you should remember about vitamins. The first is that while you may need more food when you exercise, you usually do not need more vitamins. Those requirements stay the same for the most part. You really don't gain much by taking more vitamins than before. And if you substitute them for foods in your diet, you could do yourself a nutritional disservice. Vitamins act on other nutrients, making up parts of enzymes, for example, and are involved in various biochemical processes. There is no firm scientific evidence that anyone who has nutritionally sound eating habits gains anything by taking in extra vitamins. Most excess vitamins get expelled as waste products, and some vitamins taken in too high dosages can do you some harm.

You should be concerned about vitamin supplements only if the advice to take them comes from your doctor. Women on the pill, for example, sometimes take vitamin-mineral supplements to balance out the vitamin B6 depletion that the pill can cause. Also, people on a vegetarian diet—no animal or dairy products—may be shortchanging their system of vitamin B12 and may have to take vitamin supplements to even the nutritional score. Aside from special circumstances like these, you should not have to worry about investing in a medicine cabinet full of pills if you have a balanced diet.

And what's that? Well, without going into specific day-by-day recipes, you can get all of the six nutrients your body needs by following what's come to be called the Four Food Plan. During World War II, U.S. Department of Agriculture researchers devised a nutritional guideline for eating which, if followed every day, would satisfy your RDA, or Recommended Daily Allowances of nutrients. They found that by including foods from four general groups in your daily diet you were more than likely to satisfy your nutritional needs. Exclude one of these groups and you may be gypping yourself nutritionally.

THE FOUR FOODS

The four groups are: fruits and vegetables; cereals and grains; high-protein foods; milk and milk products. Although each group satisfies a chief nutritional need, each also offers other nutritional plusses as well. First of all, fruits and vegetables are low-calorie, high-food-bulk sources of basic carbohydrates, vitamins, and minerals. As you probably already know, your body cannot store vitamin C, for example, and must get it from foods like oranges or orange juice. Fresh fruit belongs in everyone's daily diet and is one of the best alternatives you have to a junk-food snack.

The second group, cereals and grains, includes breads and other baked goods as well as whatever cereals (not those chocolate and marshmallow breakfast snacks) you eat at breakfast. The better whole-grain flours, cereals, and the products made from them are rich in proteins, carbohydrates, and minerals.

Third is the high-protein group, which includes meat, fish, eggs, nuts, and legumes such as peas, string beans, soy beans, and other common beans. This is one of the more controversial food groups, because some of the high-protein foods, such as red meats and eggs, also have a high fat content, and most nutritionists agree that we are eating more than our share of these.

The fourth group, milk and milk products (mostly cheese), contain large amounts of calcium, protein, and riboflavin, or vitamin B2.

As a general rule you'll do a decent job of feeding your body if each day you have four healthy servings of something from the fruits and vegetables group and the cereals and grain group, and two good-sized servings of food from the protein group and the milk and milk products group. You can improve a little more on your

Better athletic performance should be accomplished through physical and psychology training, not through excessive eating, special supplementation, or other food fads.

-JAMES COUNSILMAN
Competitive Swimming Manual

Four Food eating habits by cutting down on other foods.

Red meats. The good news about them is that they are high in protein. The bad news is that they are also high in fat, an excess of which can be a contributing factor in heart disease. It's better to develop a habit of eating lean meats such as veal (if you can afford it), and chicken, or another high-protein source that is low in fat, such as fish.

Eggs, butter, and whole milk. All are also high-fat foods and can load up your bloodstream with the dreaded cholesterol, a risk factor, again, in heart disease. If you limit your egg intake to about three or four per week, and substitute skim milk for whole milk, and corn oil margarine for butter, you can minimize your cholesterol overload. This doesn't mean your body doesn't need cholesterol. It does. Cholesterol is key to many body processes—building hormones, insulating nerves—but too much of it can settle out in your blood vessels and contribute to atherosclerosis.

Sugar. Sugar, the kind you sprinkle on your cereal or stir in your coffee, is a simple carbohydrate, and as far as food scientists and nutiritionists know, is the one we need the least and seem to get the most. If you cut out all the sugar in your diet you would probably still get the carbohydrates you need from other food sources—complex carbohydrates like vegetables, for example. A starch food such as the potato has calories, but it also has vitamins, minerals, and protein. Simple sugars, on the other hand, are empty calories—no vitamins or nutrients of any kind. Simple sugar also seems to raise fat levels in the blood and the risk of heart disease right along with it. Finally, it runs your hormonal system ragged, especially your pancreas. When a dose of simple sugar hits your bloodstream, your pancreas overreacts, pulsing a huge surge of insulin into your system. The result is a drop in your blood sugar level, and your hunger switch gets thrown.

There is no appreciable difference among simple

sugars. As far as your system is concerned, white sugar is the same as brown sugar, honey, or liquid sugar such as corn syrup which is added to food. Even when you try, it is hard to avoid sugar because it is sometimes buried in some of the most unlikely places, from catsup to supposedly nonsweetened breakfast cereals. Read the list of ingredients the next time.

Salt. According to the Public Health Service, we take in much more salt than we need, as much as 12 times (or more) our minimal daily requirement. Habitually eating salty foods or dumping a lot of salt on foods that don't have it can be a way to court hypertension and heart disease.

CALORIES

One last word about calories. Your caloric needs are independent of your nutritional needs, which remain fairly constant. Caloric needs vary with how active you are. If you consume more calories than you use, you'll end up carrying them around as excess weight. Now if you're wondering what new calorie needs you're generating when you're swimming, check this chart for your favored stroke and read across to the speed that fits you best. The swimming speeds are given here in miles per hour. One mph is roughly equal to 29 yards per minute, or if you're swimming in a 25-meter pool, one length per minute.

Stroke	**Calories Burned Per Hour**		
	1 mph	1.6 mph	2.2 mph
Crawl	420	700	1600
Breaststroke	410	490	850
Backstroke	500	800	2000
Sidestroke	550	1200	3000

RE- AND POST-SWIM EXERCISES

It may seem a little redundant to spend time doing exercises on land in addition to the time you spend in the water, but there is a sane reason for it. Even when you're in the peak of physical condition—*especially* when you're in the peak of physical condition—you have to take the time to flex and prepare your body so you can get the most out of your swimming session in the pool.

For one thing, as you get older your body loses some of the natural suppleness you had in your youth. One reason is that as you grow, your bone structure naturally gets bigger. With this may come more strength, but you may lose some of your former flexibility. The bulk of bone interferes with the free and easy movement of muscle. And that's why thin, small-boned men are usually, by nature, more flexible than huskier men. That's also why women, with their thinner skeletal frames, are usually more supple than men. This doesn't mean that a man can't be as flexible as a woman or a husky man can't be as nimble and loose as one with thinner bones. They can—it just takes a little more work, that's all.

UNTYING THE KNOTS

Another variable that affects how loose your body is has to do with your muscles. Like rubber bands, muscles have a natural elasticity that lets you move around with a certain freedom. One of the by-products of exercising routinely and flexing your muscles during your workouts is that they tend to get tighter and harder. This may be good for your muscle tone and strength, but if you don't do something about it, your well-developed body can become its own strait jacket, restricting how you use the power and endurance you have been so carefully building up in your swimming sessions.

As you can tell from your own experience in the water, the swimmer needs a great deal of flexibility in certain muscle groups and body areas. Flexible ankles, for ex-

A stretched muscle is more efficient and responsive than an unstretched muscle.

-DAVID ARMBRUSTER
Swimming and Diving, 1968

ample, are tremendously important for a powerful, stabilizing kick as you move through the water. When you swim the crawl and backstroke, you also need a wide range of movement in your shoulders to do the strokes smoothly and with a minimum of effort. According to swimming coach and expert on swimmers' physiology James Counsilman, freestyle swimmers with shoulders that are too tight will have to rock the body from side to side more in order to clear the arms out of the water. They might also develop an awkward recovery stroke that will increase the drag in the water and slow them down.

Of course, he's talking about Olympic caliber swimmers who win or lose races by hundredths of seconds. Just the same, it makes sense to think about your body's flexibility. Having the right amount of suppleness means that you will be a lot more efficient in the water and basically will have to work less hard to swim the same distance. From this point of view it's a lazy man's way of making exercise just a little bit easier.

Just as important is keeping your body free from injury. If your muscles are too tight and you haven't taken the time to loosen them up at all, you could injure yourself when you exercise, wiping out all the good healthy reasons for doing exercise in the first place.

SWIMMER'S SHOULDER

For example, there's an ailment called swimmer's shoulder that plagues some competition swimmers, especially those who compete in freestyle, butterfly, and backstroke events. It seems to be more common among swimmers in the speed events, such as sprints, than among those who swim distances. One reason, doctors think, is that high-speed swimmers put a greater amount of stress on the shoulder joint with the explosive surges of muscular effort they put into every stroke. Distance swimmers, who have to conserve their energy for the long haul, aren't as intense and explosive in their swimming style. Swimmers also get one-sided versions of this ailment. They may develop a sore shoulder on their breathing side or on the side where muscles may not be as well developed, if their bodies are unevenly muscled.

In serious cases, where a swimmer's career may be at stake, doctors may even perform surgery, but typically they recommend cutting down on distance and using heat packs. Finally, they recommend doing flexibility exercises before every workout.

Although you are not likely to have any problems with this ailment, it's not a bad idea to keep this in mind as a reason for developing and following a series of flexibility exercises. After all, swimming is a heavy upper-body exercise, one that will have you working your shoulder joints hundreds of times a week in your pool sessions. Taking the time to do a little flexing now might save you a few days of agony in the future.

Most professional athletes recognize the value of a loose body. It minimizes injuries. Flexibility exercises are the perfect way to warm up or simply relax a little. Best of all, they feel great—after they're over.

LIFTING WEIGHTS

Another type of exercise you should consider as part of your extra-pool conditioning is strength exercising. Although it does involve working with weights, this program is nothing like a Mr. Universe course in building a bigger biceps. It is based on the experience of swimming coaches who have been able to relate their swimmers' performances to the kinds of exercises they do outside of the pool. Many of these exercises involve using barbells or some system of weights. Not heavy weights, just enough to stress certain muscles.

This is based on the common-sense notion that if you continue to work certain swimming muscles when you're out of the water, your body will perform a lot better once you're in the water. By doing a few simple exercises at a moderate pace, using nothing more elaborate than a couple of heavy books, you can get your body in peak swimming condition at home. The prime value of these exercises, you should remember, is not endurance but brute strength. Endurance you get from swimming itself. You also get added strength from the sport, but you can speed up this effect with the strength workouts.

WARMING UP

Before you get going on any of these exercises, you should remember one last bit of advice: Always warm up. As you begin swimming you'll notice a little tightness in your arms and legs. Part of the reason is that circulation hasn't been stepped up yet to supply your muscles with the blood they need. And until your muscles get warm, they are still a little tense. Push them too hard too quickly and you might injure yourself. As you begin your stretching and flexibility exercises, choose the easier ones first and do them slowly, stretching various parts of your body in a smooth, even pull. Don't jerk or bob your muscles. It won't do you any good and may do you some harm. The same holds true for strength workouts. Begin slowly and increase the intensity of the exercise as you feel your muscles come alive. And lastly, when you swim, take an easy lap or two if you feel you need one. Pick a relaxing stroke such as the sidestroke to start, and after a few minutes switch over to your more serious practice stroke.

Are you that Beowulf who contended with Breca, competed in swimming on the broad sea, where for foolish pride you explored the water, and for foolish boast ventured your lives in the deep? There you embraced the sea-streams with your arms, measured the-sea ways, flung forward your hands, glided over the ocean; the sea boiled with waves, with winter's swell. Seven nights you toiled in the water's power.

-Beowulf
c. 720 A.D.

TAKE A BREATHER

It's a good idea to ease into your exercise session. The best way to do this is with a short breathing exercise that will not only give you a little time to relax but will also remind you of what is the best—that is, the most efficient—way to breathe.

Stand relaxed, with your feet comfortably apart and your hands, placed fingertip to fingertip, on the last one or two ribs of your rib cage. Now start to inhale as though you've just stepped outside on a rain-washed spring morning and are drawing in the day's rich perfumes. As you inhale, press gently against your lower ribs and feel your stomach expand. Do your inhaling slowly and evenly, counting to 10 as you do it. Count to 10 as you exhale, letting the air come out in a quiet sigh. Notice how your abdominal muscles draw in and tighten as you do this. Repeat this little exercise five or six times to help you get a sense of how it's done and also to give you a little time to relax.

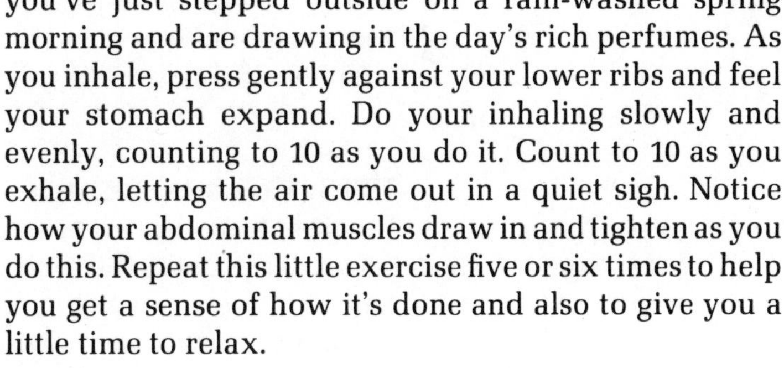

LOOSEN UP

In the following pages you'll find four groupings of exercises designed to flex and stretch specific areas of your body. Try to do them at least once a day, ideally when you get up in the morning, and, if possible, again before you take your swim or at night before you go to bed. They're not complicated, and they're not hard. They basically involve stretching a particular muscle or muscle group for a certain number of seconds or for a specific number of repetitions. If you find you can't do a certain exercise for the length of time or the number of times suggested, experiment until you find what's comfortable. Then gradually work your way up to the suggested level.

Make it a habit to set aside a certain time each day for these workouts. And don't rush through them. You won't need much time—10 to 15 minutes at the most. You'll get the most benefit by stretching slowly and smoothly.

Finally, glance through what follows on these pages to see how the exercises are done. Experiment a little. You'll find some easier to do than others. Remember to vary your repertoire of exercises so you can avoid getting bored while you do them. It also helps if you exercise to a favorite record or while watching TV.

A clock or watch with a sweep second hand will come in handy for the timed stretch exercises. The important thing is to make your flexing a daily habit.

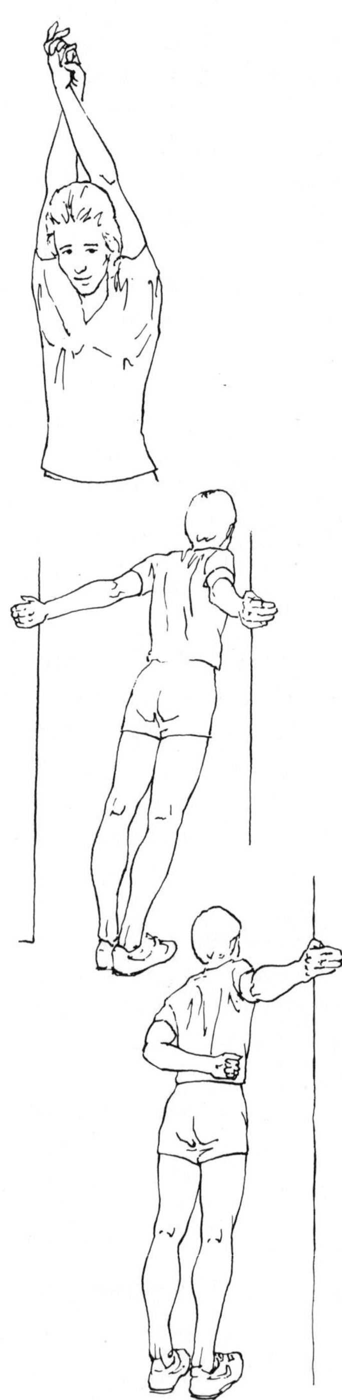

Group I. For arms, shoulders, and upper back. Do the Twisting Arm Reach and at least two other exercises of your choice.

TWISTING ARM REACH
Purpose: Stretches and loosens the muscles in your upper arm, especially the triceps muscle on the back of your arm, shoulders, and upper back muscles.
Getting set: Intertwine your arms like two embracing serpents, as shown, and clasp your hands together.
Exercising: Simply stretch up as high as you can go. Hold for 20 seconds. Then relax.

BUTTERFLY STRETCH
Purpose: Excellent flexing for shoulder and upper-arm muscles, especially the back of the arm.
Getting set: Simply stand in an open doorway and grab the two sides of the frame with your hands at shoulder height, or as close to it as possible.
Exercising: Lean forward. Let the weight of your body do the pulling. Hold for 30 seconds.

ONE-ARMED BUTTERFLY
Getting set: This is basically a one-sided version of the Butterfly Stretch.
Exercising: Curl your nonexercising arm behind your back and reach back with your free arm to grab the doorframe. Lean forward and hold the tension for 15 full seconds. Repeat with the other for 15 seconds.

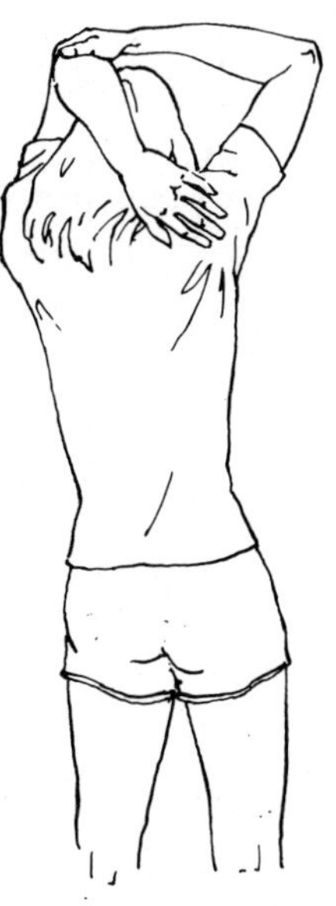

BACKSCRATCH

Purpose: Mainly to stretch your shoulder muscles.
Getting set: Reach back as though you were going to scratch your right shoulder with your left arm. Cup your left elbow in the palm of your right hand.
Exercising: Gently push down on your elbow and try to hold it in its tense position for 30 seconds. Do the same with your other arm.

ROTATING TOWEL

Purpose: Loosens the shoulder muscles that limit full arm movement (and make you prone to swimmer's shoulder) and stretches your chest (pectoral) muscles.
Getting set: Get a towel (or a broomstick) and grab one end in your right hand, the other in your left. Stand up straight with your feet comfortably apart. Pull the towel taut between your two hands.
Exercising: Raise your arms, the towel still taut, up and over your head, rotating both arms behind your back. Then reverse that move, bringing arms and towel back over your head to your starting position. Try to do 12 of these rotations in one minute. If you find you can do that easily, bump it up to 15.

BACKSLIDER

Purpose: This does a good job of stretching your upper arms and your upper back.

Getting set: Sit down on the floor with your feet comfortably stretched out in front of you. Place your hands on the floor behind you as shown, palms down, fingertips pointing away from your body.

Exercising: Let your hands slide backward slowly as far as they will comfortably go. Try to hold that position for at least 5 seconds and up to 15 seconds. Don't push yourself on this, or you might get a cramped muscle.

II **Group II.** For your abdomen and mid-torso (hips and buttocks). Always use the Total Stretch to help relax after a particularly strenuous workout.

LAZY TWIST

Purpose: This is a prime stretcher and conditioner of your abdominal muscles.

Getting set: Lie on your back, your head resting in the palms of your hands, your feet stretched out in front of you.

Exercising: Cross your left leg over your right and, keeping your back as flat against the floor as possible, twist or rotate the lower half of your body to the left. Hold it in this position for up to 20 seconds. Return to starting position. Now cross your right leg over your left leg and twist your lower body to the right for 20 seconds.

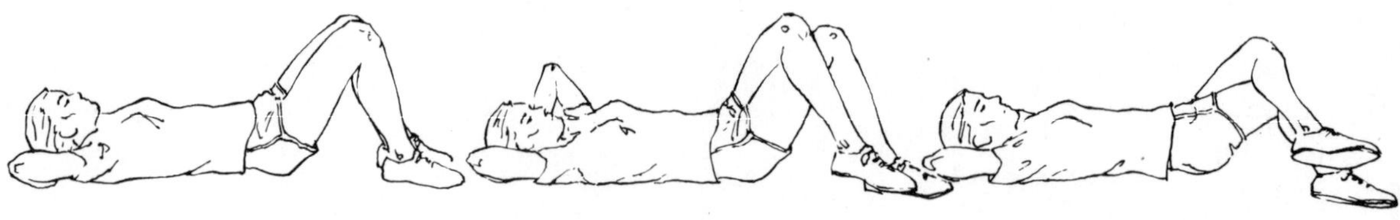

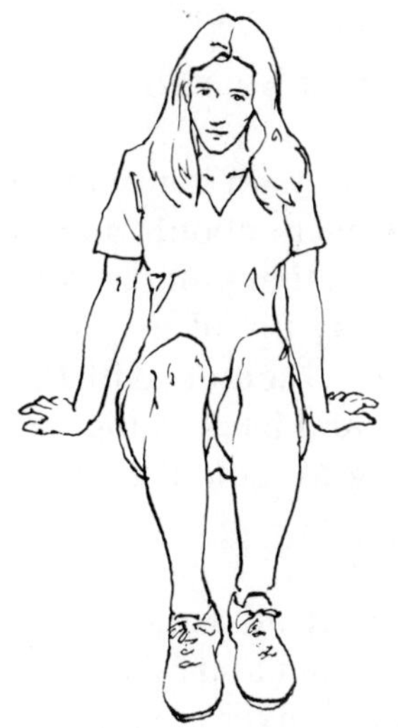

TWO-WAY TWIST

Purpose: The beauty of this exercise is that it simultaneously stretches neck, waist, and hip muscles.

Getting set: This is a more elaborate version of the Lazy Twist. To begin, sit up on the floor with your knees bent and your hands placed to either side of your body. This is a two-sided exercise. To begin with one side, drop your right leg to the floor and cross it under your left leg; at the same time shift your left foot as far to the right as possible. Now grab your ankle with your left hand.

Exercising: Now that you're in position, put your right hand in the small of your back and twist your body and head as far to the right as you can go, so that you end up looking over your right shoulder. Now twist to your left, draping your right hand over the outside of your left thigh and steadying yourself with your left hand placed behind your back. Twist your body a total of 10 times, 5 times to each side.

SPINE CURL

Purpose: This will stretch the muscles in your abdomen, as well as in your neck.

Getting set: Lie face down on the floor with your hands placed palms down as though you were about to do a pushup. Keep your legs close together, toes pointed, and push just the upper part of your body up off the floor. Leave the lower half of your body in full contact with the floor, but lift your head, shoulders, and back as high as you can, as though you were trying to look at a point directly above.

Exercising: There are three simple steps.

1. Bend your right leg and turn your head as far to the right as you can. Lower the leg to the floor and raise your left leg, turning your head to the left. Lower the leg.
2. Bend both legs up simultaneously and turn your head first to the right and then to the left.
3. Lower both legs and return to your getting-set position. Try to repeat this sequence five times.

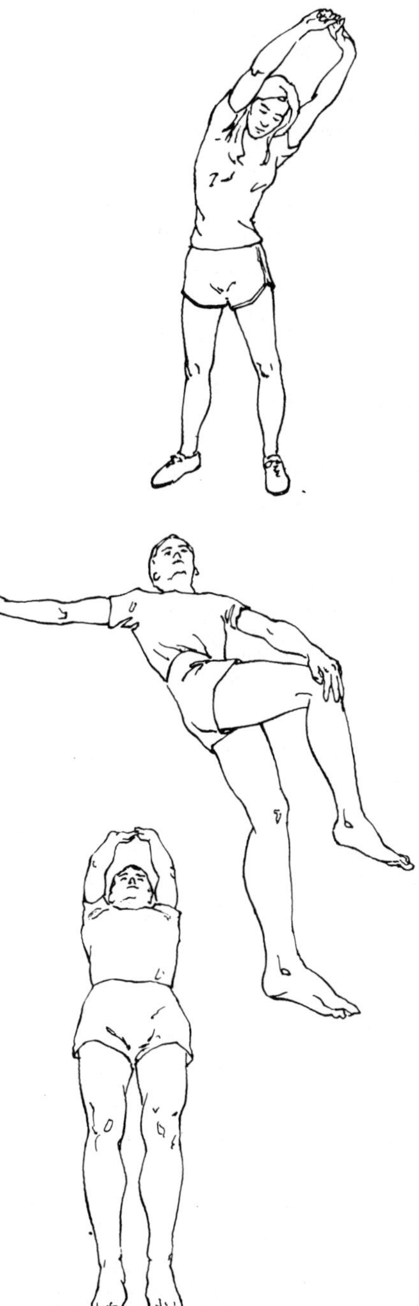

SIDE STRETCH

Purpose: This will firm and trim up your waist, as well as side muscles and hips.

Getting set: Put your hands straight up over your head and clasp them together. Space your feet about your shoulders' width apart.

Exercising: Bend to the right as far as you can. Hold this for 15 seconds. Now bend to the left. Hold again for 15 seconds.

LEG TWIST

Purpose: This firms and stretches your abdomen, the back of your upper thighs, and your buttocks.

Getting set: Lie on your back with your feet stretched out below you. Let your arms rest comfortably by your side.

Exercising: Flip your right leg over your left leg as far to the left as possible. Press your right leg down toward the floor as shown in the illustration. Keep your back as flat on the floor as possible. Hold for 20 seconds. Switch over and do the same thing with your left leg and right arm. Hold for 20 seconds.

TOTAL STRETCH

Do this at the end of Group II exercises.

Purpose: This is a total-body relaxer, although it works very well in limbering up your back and abdomen.

Getting set: Lie on your back with your arms loosely stretched out on the floor above your head and your legs lying on the floor as shown in the illustration.

Exercising: Now s-t-r-e-t-c-h as far as you can for 5 seconds. Relax. And do it one more time.

III **Group III.** For your legs. Do the Bend and Crouch and three other exercises of your choice. For full benefit, as you stretch go slowly. Don't bounce.

YOGA STRETCH TRIPLET

Purpose: The first and third parts of the exercise stretch muscles and tendons in your groin area and tone your abdominal muscles. The second part firms and tones your thighs and buttocks.

Getting set: This three-part series has only two distinct positions. First, sit with the soles of your feet touching. Hold them in place with your hands. This is done for the first and third parts of the exercise. For the second part, sit on the floor, lean on your right hand, cross your right leg over your left, outstretched leg, and look directly to your right. There is a second part to this pose which is basically its mirror image. Lean on your left hand, cross your left leg over your right, and look to your left.

Exercising: 1. Grasp your feet in the first position, bend forward as far as you can. Hold for 10 seconds.

2. As you lean on your right hand and turn to the right, simultaneously lean on your cocked left knee with your left elbow as shown in the drawing. This will force your body to twist a little more. Hold for 15 seconds. Then switch to your left side and do the same thing.

3. Repeat the first step for 10 seconds.

SPLIT AND REACH

Purpose: This is especially good for inner thigh muscles, lower back, and abdominal muscles.
Getting set: This is one for someone who is already fairly supple. Try to do as much of a split as you can, facing forward with your legs spread apart.
Exercising: While you are in this position, lean forward as far as possible and try to hold that position for a full minute. Set a minute as your goal.

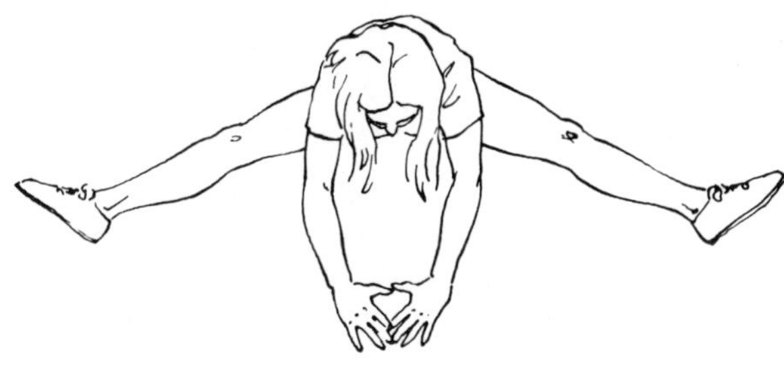

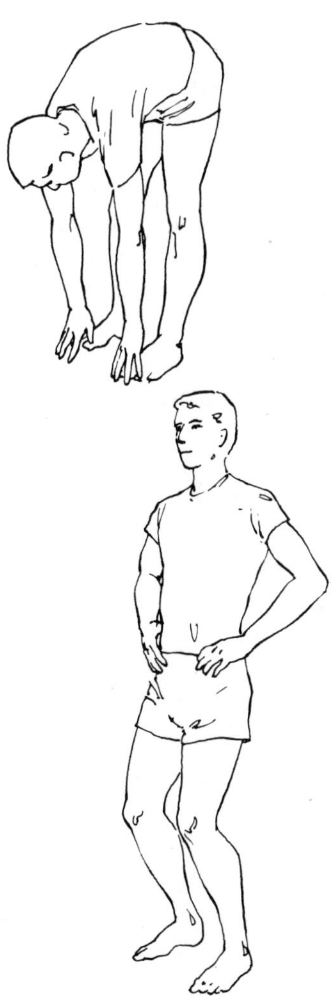

BEND AND CROUCH

Purpose: The first and third parts of the exercise are especially effective in stretching the hamstring muscles on the backs of your thighs and limbering up the tendons around your knees. The second exercise works principally on the front of your thighs.
Getting set: There are two simple positions, both standing. In the first, keep your legs straight and bend over, reaching for the floor. In the second, stand with hands on hips, knees slightly bent.
Exercising: 1. Keep your legs straight and your feet a comfortable distance apart. Bend from the waist and reach for the floor. If you can reach it, fine. If you can't, don't worry. It doesn't matter. The important thing is to bend as far as you can and hold for 10 seconds.
2. Place your hands on your hips and dip your body in a slight crouch with your knees bent just a little. Hold this position for 30 seconds
3. Repeat the first exercise.

ACHILLES STRETCH

Purpose: The first part of the exercise is especially good for stretching your Achilles tendons, which run down the back of your lower legs to your heels.

Getting set: The only equipment you need is a wall. Lean against it as shown in the illustration with your right foot back about 4 feet from the base of the wall and your left foot much closer, about a foot from the wall. Keep the right leg stiff, but you can cock the left one. You will also be doing a reversal of this with the left leg back and the right leg placed close to the base of the wall. The second position is essentially the same, but whichever leg is farther from the wall should have a slight crook or bend in it.

Exercising: 1. Lean against the wall and extend your left leg as far back as it will go. Keep the leg straight and keep leaning for 30 seconds. Hold for 30 seconds. Now relax the left leg, move it close to the wall, and stretch back your right leg. Hold that for 30 seconds as well as you lean.

2. Do the same thing, slightly bending your outside leg. Hold for 30 seconds on each leg.

IV **Group IV.** For your back. If you have back trouble, check with your doctor first. If you just want to do one of these, do the Back Kicks. Do not continue any exercise if you feel pain.

BACK ROLLER

Purpose: This is as close to a total back massage as you can give to yourself.

Getting set: Sit on the floor and hug your knees tightly.

Do this on a soft surface such as an exercise mat or a carpeted floor.

Exercising: Knees hugged close to your chest and head bent between your knees, slowly roll until you have rocked back to your shoulders and your feet are up in the air. Roll back to your starting position. Do this four to six times.

THE PLOW

Purpose: The Plow serves the double purpose of stretching your lower-back muscles and stretching the hamstring muscles on the backs of your thighs.

Getting set: Lie on your back and then prop your body up as though you're about to do bicycle exercises. Let your legs, held straight, continue to fall overhead and try to touch the ground with your toes.

Exercising: There is no movement, just the effort necessary to hold this position for up to 30 seconds.

STRAIGHT-LEGGED BACK ROLLER

Purpose: A great way to soothe a tense and tired back in much the same way as the Back Roller does.

Getting set: Bend your legs back straight as you're lying on your back and grab your legs near your ankles as shown in the illustration.

Exercising: Slowly roll your back down toward your buttocks one vertebra at a time. Do this slowly, taking about 30 seconds to roll all the way.

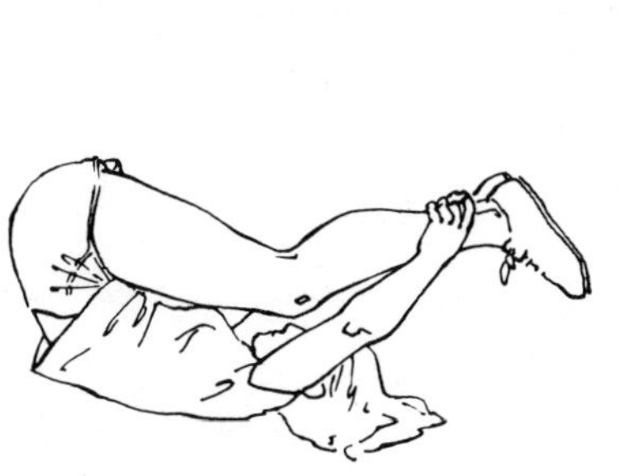

BACK KICKS

Purpose: This limbers up and stretches your lower-back muscles.

Getting set: Lie on your back with your legs extended.

Exercising: Cock your right knee up to your chest, clasp it in your hands, and hold it there for about 10 seconds. Lower that leg to the floor and cock your left leg to your chest, holding it there, again for 10 seconds.

STRENGTHEN YOUR BODY

As was mentioned before, this moderate weight training series is not designed to turn you into a muscle-bound hulk, but merely to give you an edge by flexing your swim muscles while you're out of the water. You do need equipment for this, but it's not elaborate. Get something that fits comfortably in your hands and that weighs about 2 pounds. A couple of books the same size should work fine. If you happen to have a set of weights, even better. As you get more involved in your exercises you may want to invest in a set of dumbbells. The advantage they offer is that they are adjustable. It's a lot easier to add weights than juggle books.

There are a few simple rules to remember before you begin work with your weights. First, schedule your workouts for every other day. Your muscles are going to need some time to recover from a weight session, especially if it's been a while since you've done anything like this. Second, always warm up first. A cold muscle, like a cold car, isn't going to run smoothly if you don't give it a chance to get warm. It might be a good idea to put your weight sessions after one of your daily flexibility series of exercises. Third, start slowly and start small. As mentioned before, 2 pounds is a good starting weight for each hand. If that feels too light, move up a pound or two. As a general rule, though, don't begin with more than 5 pounds. You may wear yourself out too quickly, not be able to do the full series of repetitions, and get discouraged. As you get stronger, you can always add weight. It's not the weight that's important so much as the repetitive exercise. Settle on your own personal rhythm as you work out, beginning with a deliberately slow version of the exercise and stepping it up slightly as your muscles warm.

Repetition is the key to all these exercises. To get their full benefit, you have to do them over and over again in sets with a brief three- or four-minute breather. Always do three sets of exercises, and as you get stronger, increase the number of repetitions per set. Start with 8 repetitions and, as you feel stronger, move up to a maximum of fifteen. Once you've reached that maximum and want to increase the challenge, start increasing your weight about 1 pound per hand. And don't get caught up in the "heavier is better" trap. If you feel that one exercise isn't challenging enough, add another to your workout.

The exercises that follow are clustered into groups that benefit certain strokes, or rather the muscles that are used to make those strokes. Look through them. Try out the ones for the stroke that appeals to you, and begin with a routine of at least two upper-body exercises for your stroke and two for your legs. As you get stronger you may want to add more, but keep things simple at first.

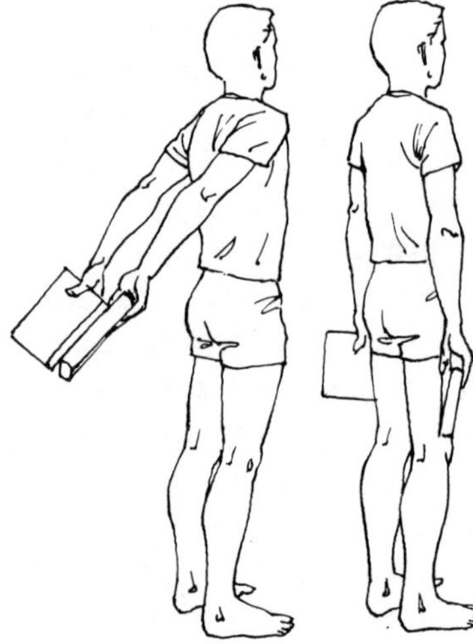

BACKWARD ARM LIFT (For All Strokes)
Purpose: Develops the muscles at the back of your shoulders and in your upper back.
Getting set: Stand comfortably with your feet about shoulder-width apart. Hold your weights with your palms facing backward.
Exercising: This is a two-count exercise. On the first count, raise your arms as far up and back as they will go. On the second count, slowly lower them to your side. Keep your head and body erect as you do this.

STANDING ROW (For All Strokes)
Purpose: This is especially good for your shoulders as well as your chest and upper back.
Getting set: Stand with your feet shoulder-width apart, your hands hanging in front of your thighs, your palms facing the rear.
Exercising: Keeping your palms facing the rear at all times, simultaneously raise both weights to your chin and lower them back to your starting position.

PRONE ARM LIFT (For All Strokes)
Purpose: This works your shoulders and back muscles.
Getting set: Lie flat on your back with your legs together and your arms sticking straight out from your shoulders. Hold the weights with your palms facing the floor.
Exercising: Simultaneously raise both arms as high off the floor as you can. Then slowly lower them to the floor again.

ROWING (For All Strokes)
Purpose: This develops the front of your upper arms, your chest, and your upper back.
Getting set: With your feet comfortably apart, bend from the waist until your upper body is parallel with the floor. Let your arms down naturally.
Exercising: Work the arms in an alternating motion. Raise your right elbow and hand straight up, bringing the weight to your right shoulder. Lower it back down. Now lift your left hand with its weight to your left shoulder. Lower it back. Keep your knees bent slightly.

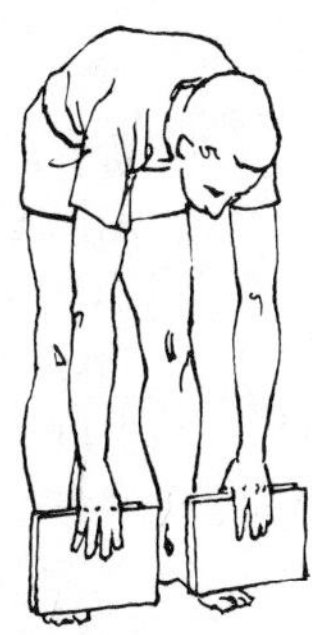
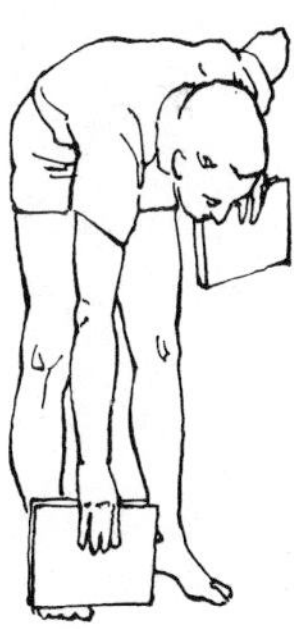

FORWARD ARM LIFT (For Backstroke, Breaststroke, and Crawl)
Purpose: This develops your shoulders and chest.
Getting set: Stand with your feet about shoulder-width apart and your arms hanging at your sides, the palms of your hands facing your thighs.
Exercising: Keeping your arms straight, raise them forward and up until they are parallel with the floor. Now lower them slowly back to the starting position. Keep your head completely erect as you do this.

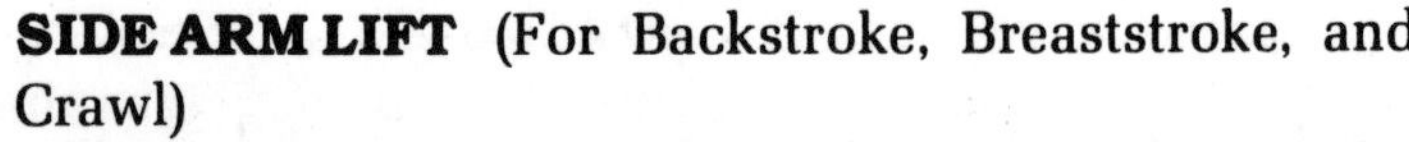

SIDE ARM LIFT (For Backstroke, Breaststroke, and Crawl)
Purpose: This is chiefly a shoulder exercise working the outer muscles of your shoulders.
Getting set: Assume the same position as the Forward Arm Lift—hands hanging by your sides and palms facing your body.
Exercising: Keep your arms straight and raise them straight out to your side until they are parallel to the floor. Slowly lower them back to your sides.

WEIGHT ROTATION (For Backstroke, Breaststroke, and Crawl)
Purpose: This will develop both the front and back of your shoulders.
Getting set: Lie on your back with your arms straight out from your shoulders and bent at the elbow in a stick-'em-up pose. Your palms should be facing up. You can lie either with your legs flat on the floor or with your knees bent up and your feet on the floor.
Exercising: This is a two-part exercise. First, without raising your upper arm or elbow from the floor, lift the weight in your right hand, rotating it up and forward until it is again resting on the floor near your waist. Now reverse this movement, rotating the weight back to its starting point. Second, do the same with the weight in your left hand, rotating it down and back. Each movement should be smooth and uninterrupted. Do not pause between the up and down rotation.

PERPENDICULAR ARM LIFT (For Backstroke, Breaststroke, and Crawl)
Purpose: This is good for your shoulders and chest.
Getting set: Lie on your back with your arms stretched straight out from your shoulders. Hold the weights with your palms facing up.
Exercising: Keeping your arms straight, raise them straight up so they are perpendicular to the floor. Then slowly lower them to the floor.

BENT-OVER SIDE RAISE (For Backstroke, Breaststroke, and Crawl)
Purpose: This does a particularly good job of working your upper shoulder and back muscles.
Getting set: Stand with your feet comfortably apart and bend over at the hips, keeping your legs straight. Let your arms hang straight down so they are roughly parallel with your legs.
Exercising: Keeping your arms straight, slowly raise them until they are straight out from the sides of your body. Now slowly lower them. Keep the upper part of your body parallel with the floor as you exercise.

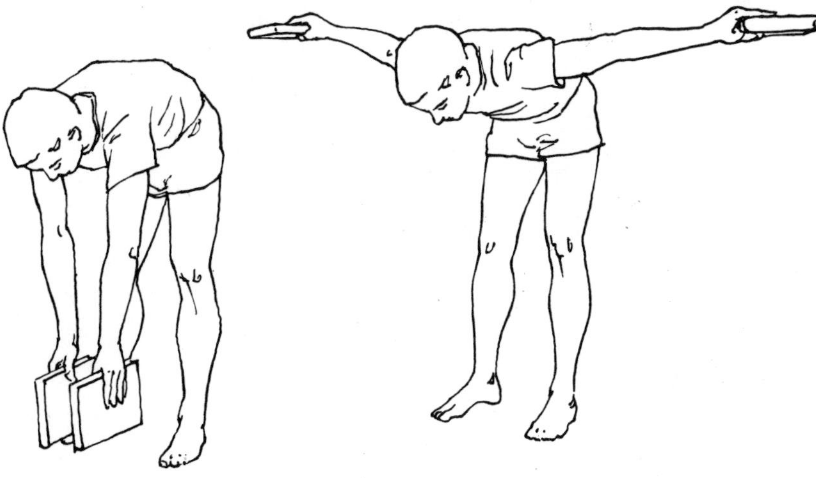

TRICEPS FLEX (For the Breaststroke)

Purpose: This is an excellent workout for the triceps muscle on the back of your upper arm.

Getting set: Do this one standing with your feet shoulder-width apart, and your hands, palms facing in, holding the weights straight over your head.

Exercising: Slowly lower the weights behind your shoulders. Use your elbow as a pivot point. Elbows should be pointed straight up in the air after you lower the weights. The second part of the exercise is just raising the weights back to the starting position.

BICEPS CURL (For the Backstroke)

Purpose: As its name suggests, this primarily works on your upper arm muscle, the biceps.

Getting set: Stand, feet at shoulder-width, with your palms facing in, up against your shoulders.

Exercising: This is a two-part sequence. First, lower your right arm slowly until the arm is straight and the back of your hand is almost touching your thigh. Return slowly to the starting position. Do the same with the left arm.

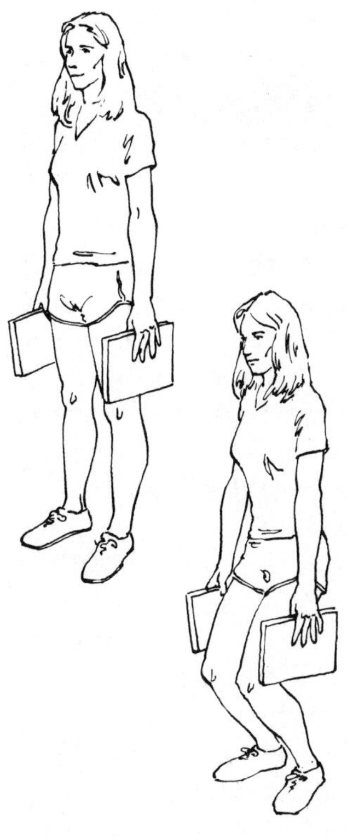

RAISED SQUAT (For Your Kicking Muscles)
Purpose: This helps work your thigh muscles and tightens up your buttocks.
Getting set: Put two thick books under your heels (it helps your balance) and space your feet shoulder-width apart. Let your arms hang at your side, your palms facing in.
Exercising: Squat until your thighs are parallel to the floor. Keep your back straight. Straighten up and repeat.

GIANT STEP (For Your Kicking Muscles)
Purpose: You'll feel it in your thighs and hips.
Getting set: Weights in hand, let your arms hang down by your sides, your palms facing in.
Exercising: Keeping your left foot in place, take a giant step forward with your right. Bend both knees as you do this. Return to your standing position and reverse. Try to keep your back and neck as straight as possible during this exercise.

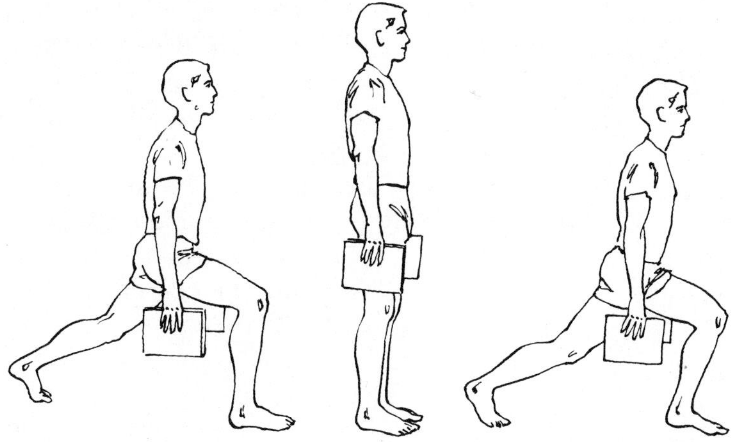

Aquametrics

Virtually all sports training makes ample use, as mentioned in previous chapters, of both anaerobic and aerobic exercise. The first produces the ability to perform at low oxygen levels. The second gives endurance. There are also two reasons why many people run out of steam when they begin a swimming regimen. First, the pressure of water on a submerged body makes breathing more laborious. The initial effect, if you haven't been swimming, is to run out of oxygen long before you would have expected to "be out of breath." You have performed an anaerobic exercise without being totally prepared for it. The second cause of sudden weakness is the weight of the water you must push against in order to go forward. When you first start swimming, the buoyancy you gain in the water (where you experience a relative loss of 90 percent of your weight) is overwhelmed by the resistance of water to your movements. This suddenly added work load (moving from land to water exercise) further taxes the muscles and their oxygen supply. As a result, without having gone very far or done very much you have suddenly spent your energy.

And this is why it is essential to build up strength and endurance carefully and systematically. You can do so with Aquametrics.

Aquametrics is a specially developed program of *in the water* physical conditioning exercises. It is the best conceivable strengthener and toner for swimming, as well as an all-around conditioning program.

Aquametrics makes use of the same elements which made you suddenly weak, and turns them to your advantage. It employs the weight and resistance of the water to give you added strength and muscle tone. It

uses your buoyancy when submerged in water to permit you to relax and tone your body with stretching and flexibility exercises. And it uses the weight of the water to vastly increase your lung power and oxygen capacity.

Because of the buoyancy factor, Aquametrics are for *everyone*. It is important to remember that these exercises are useful for swimming and just plain great for all-around conditioning and tone.

Alternate Toe Touch
Waist-to-chest deep water.
1. Raise left leg, and bring your right hand toward your left foot. Extend left hand rearward.
2. Recover to starting position.
Repeat 10 times.
3. Reverse position.
Repeat 10 times.

Side Straddle Hop
Waist-to-chest deep water.
Hands on hips, feet 6 to 8 inches apart.
1. Jump so that your feet are approximately 2 feet apart.
2. Jump back to starting position.
Repeat 10 times.

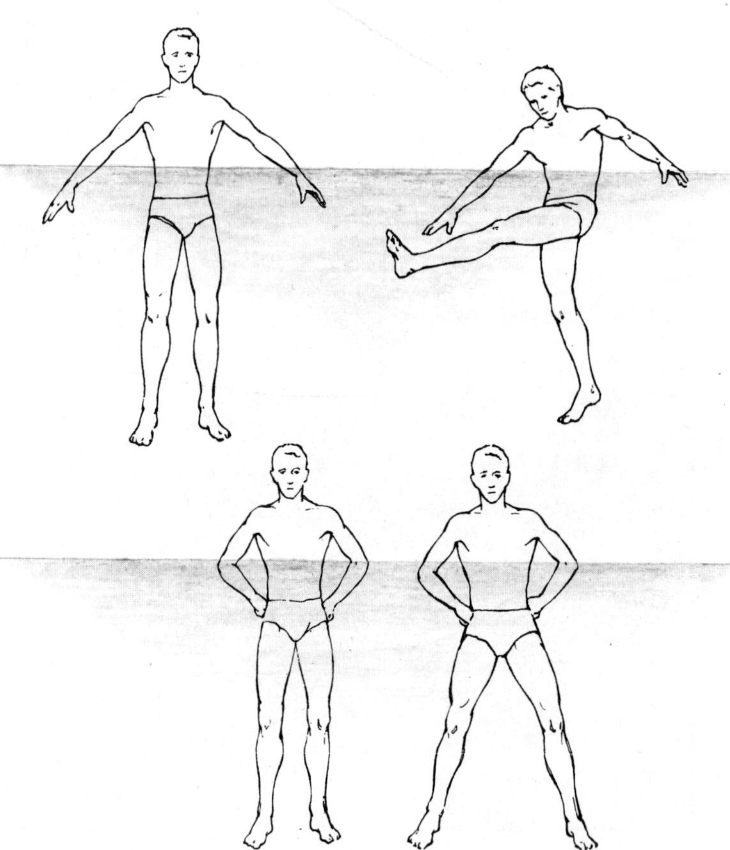

Toe Bounce
Waist-to-chest deep water.
Hands on hips, feet together.
1. Spring high by pushing up from your feet. Point your toes as you rise. As you come down, land toe first.
Repeat 10 times.

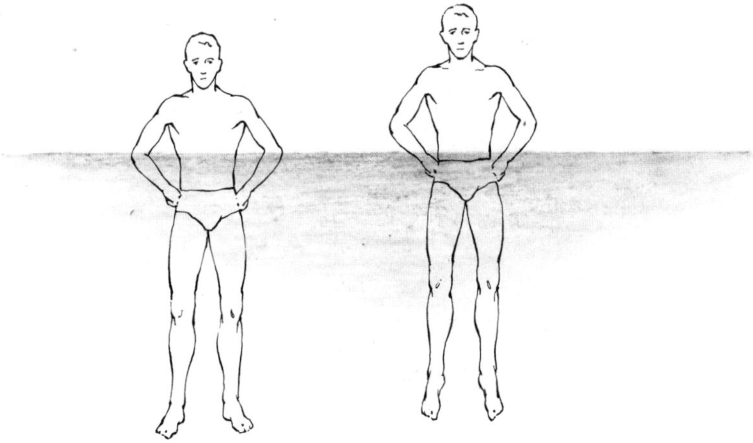

Stride Hop
Waist-to-chest deep water.
Hands on hips, feet in stride position, right leg forward.
1. Jump, changing to left leg forward, right leg back.
Repeat 10 times.

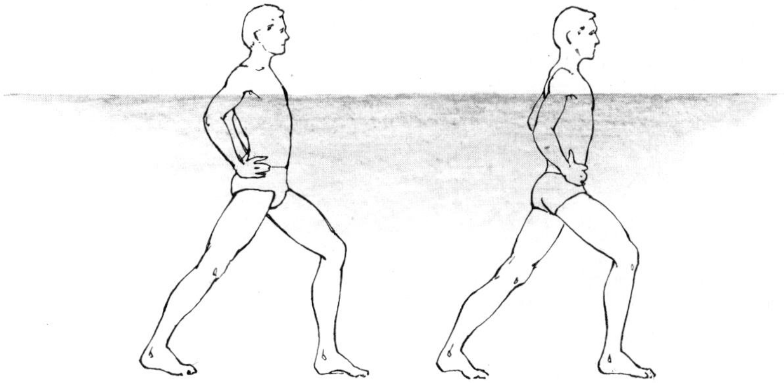

Side Bender
Waist-deep water.
Left arm at side and right arm overhead.
1. Stretch right hand high overhead. Bend slowly to the left.
2. Recover.
Repeat 10 times.
3. Reverse to right arm at side and left arm overhead.
Repeat 10 times.

Standing Crawl
Waist-to-chest deep water.
Bend slightly at the waist.
1. Simulate the overhand crawl stroke. Reach out with the left hand, pressing down into the water. Pull, bringing the left hand through to the thigh.
2. Reach out with the right hand, etc.
Repeat 10 times.

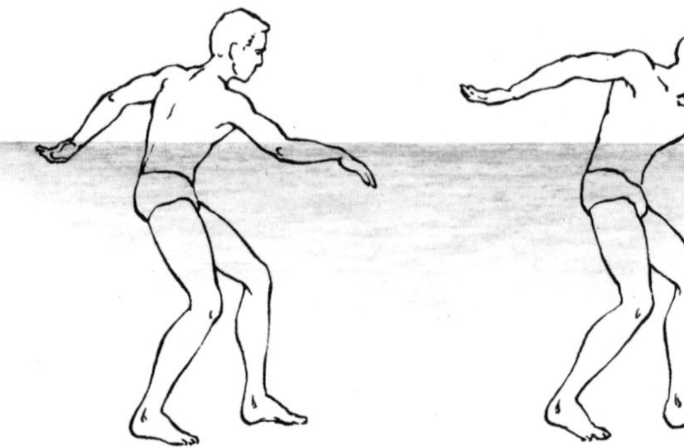

Step Twists
Waist-to-chest deep water.
Fingers laced behind neck.
1. Step forward, raising knee up high. Twist and bend from the waist to touch knee with opposite elbow.
2. Reverse.
Repeat 10 times each side.

Bouncing
Chest-deep water.
1. Bounce on left foot while pushing down vigorously with both hands flat, causing the upper body to rise.
2. Bounce on right foot while pushing down with both hands.
Repeat 10 times each foot.

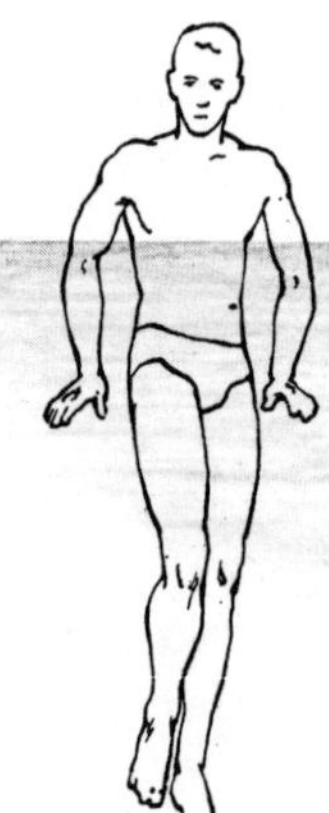

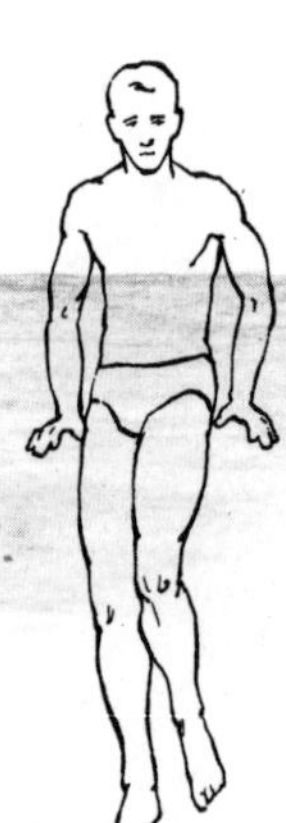

Bouncing in Place with Alternate Arm Stretches

Waist-deep water.

1. Bounce in place with high knee action; right arm stretched far forward when left knee is high, the left arm and hand stretched behind you.

2. When right knee is high, stretch the left arm and hand forward, with the right arm and hand behind.

Special Note: When the position of the arm and hand are reversed, pull down and through with your hand simulating the propulsion of the crawl stroke. When reversing arm position, drag hands and forearms through water.

Repeat 10 times.

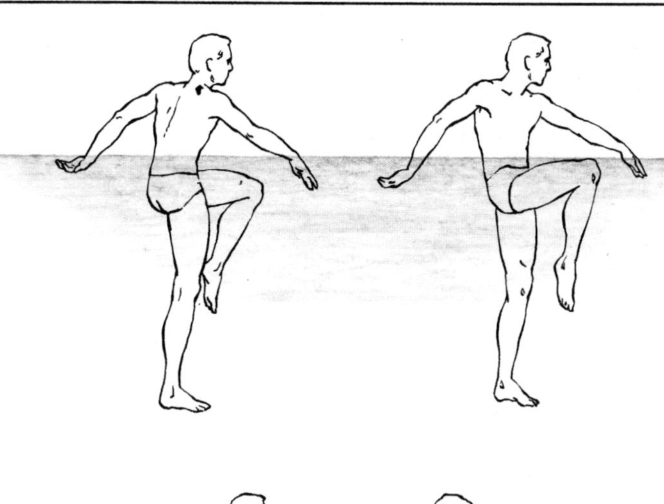

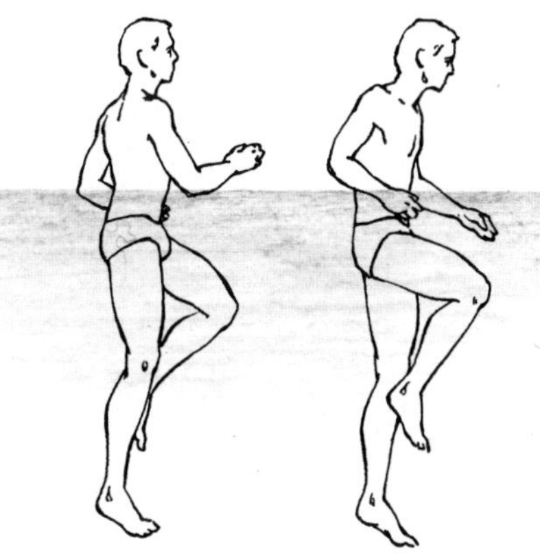

Jogging in Place

Waist-deep water.

Arms bent in running position.

1. Jog in place.

25 to 50 times.

Stretch and Touch

Chest-deep water.

Face the wall, arms extended and fingertips approximately 12 inches from wall.

1. With shoulders underwater, twist left and try to touch the wall with both hands.

2. Twist right and try to touch the wall with both hands.

Repeat 10 times.

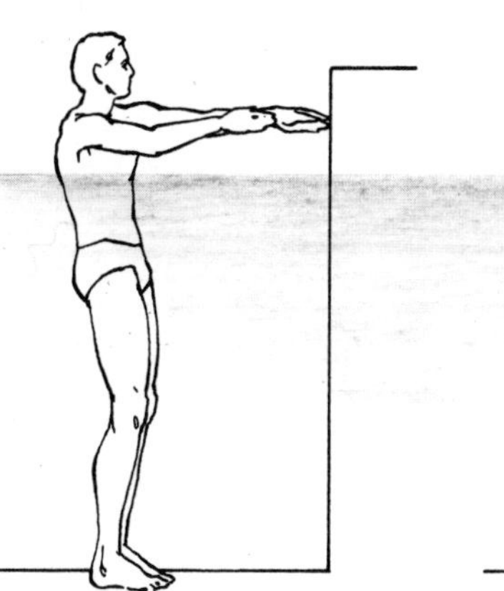

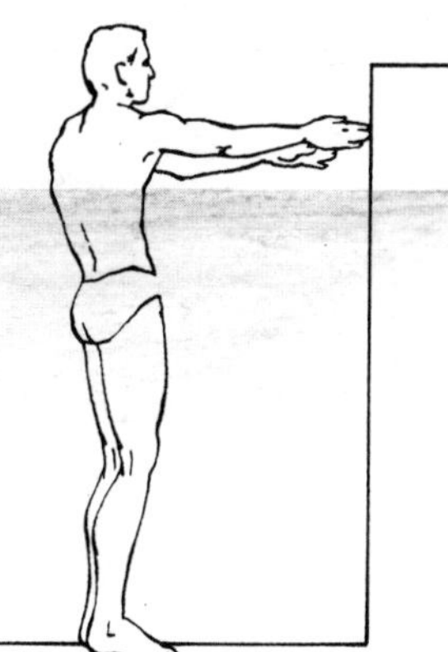

Flat Back
Waist-to-chest deep water.
Back against side of pool.
1. Press the small of your back against the wall, by pulling your stomach in. Hold for six counts.
2. Relax.
Repeat 10 times.

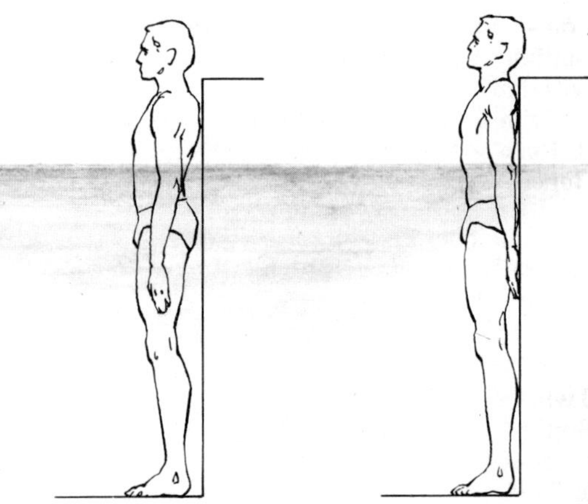

Leg Out
Chest-deep water.
Back against pool wall.
1. Raise left knee to chest.
2. Extend left leg straight out.
3. Stretch leg.
4. Drop leg to starting position.
Repeat 10 times.
5. Reverse to right leg.
Repeat 10 times.

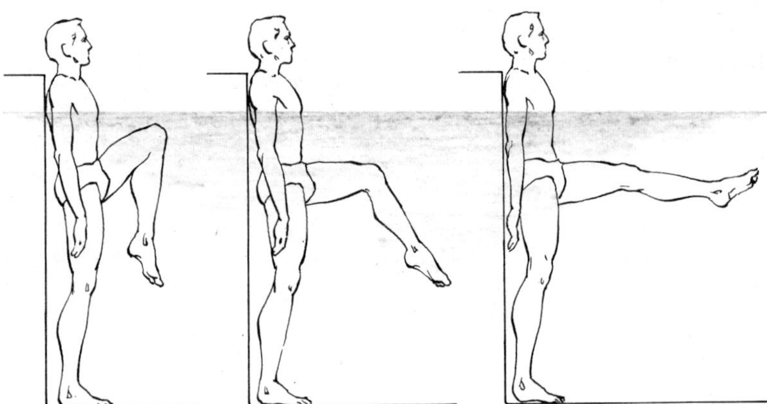

Pull and Stretch
Waist-to-chest deep water.
Back against pool wall.
1. Raise left leg, clasp calf with both arms, and pull leg tightly into the chest.
2. Hold for a count of three, return leg to starting position.
3. Raise right leg, clasp calf with both arms, pulling leg vigorously to the chest.
4. Hold for a count of three.
Repeat five times each leg.

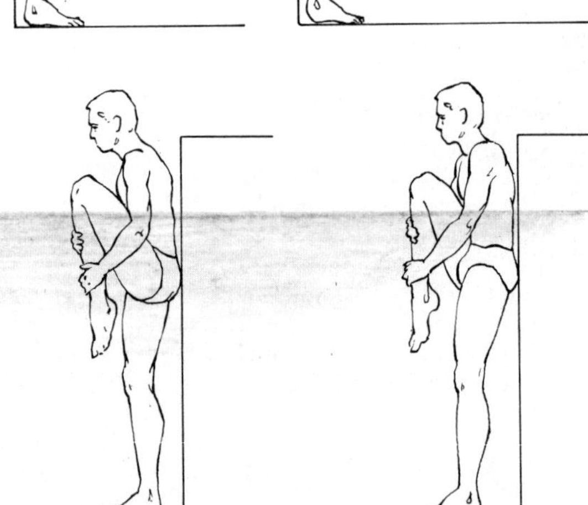

Pool-side Knees Up
Supine, holding pool gutter with hands, legs extended.
1. Bring knees to chin.
2. Recover to starting position.
Repeat 10 times.

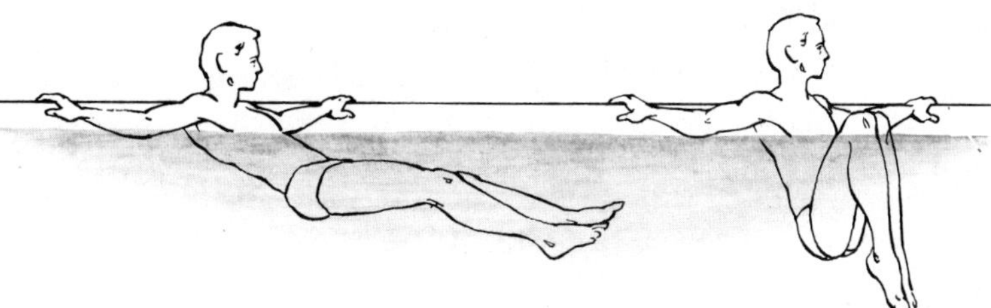

Twisting Legs
Supine, hold pool gutter, legs extended.
1. Twist slowly to left.
2. Recover.
3. Twist slowly to right.
4. Recover.
Repeat 10 times.

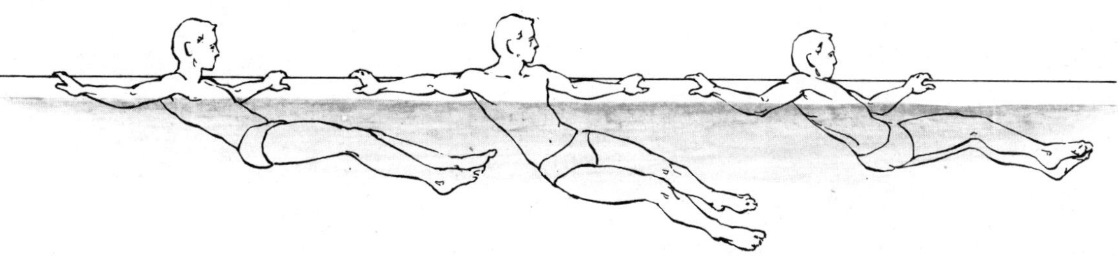

Knees Up Twisting
Supine, hold pool gutter, knees drawn up to chest.
1. Twist slowly to left.
2. Recover.
3. Twist slowly to right.
4. Recover.
Repeat 10 times.

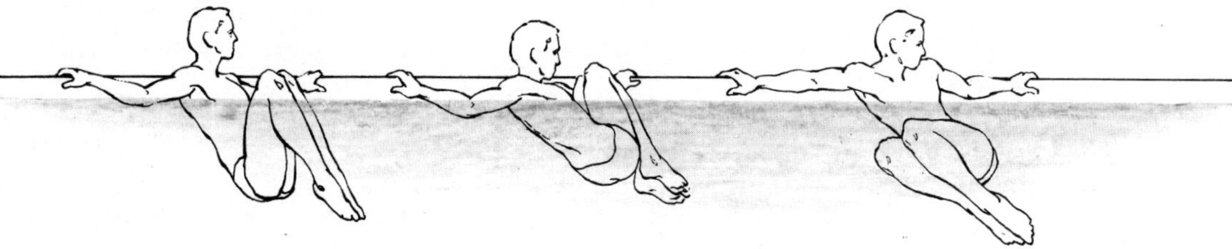

Leg Crosses
Supine, hold pool gutter, legs extended.
1. Swing legs far apart.
2. Bring legs together, crossing left leg over right.
3. Swing legs far apart.
4. Bring legs together, crossing right leg over left.
Repeat 10 times.

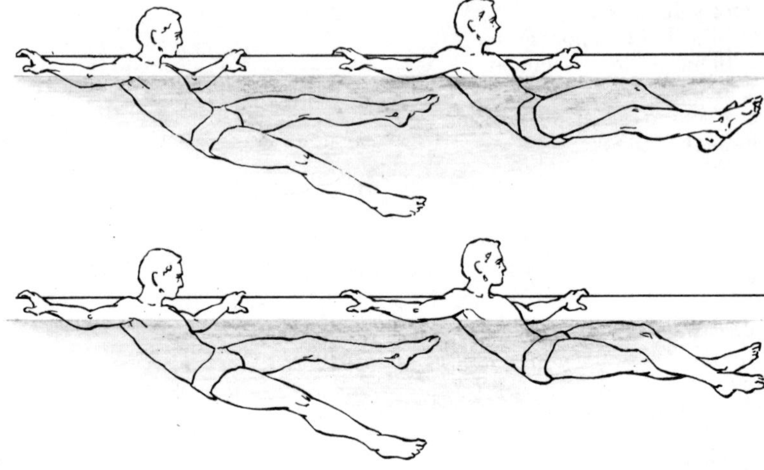

Alternate Raised Knee Cross-overs
Chest-deep water.
Stand, holding pool gutter with hands, back to wall.
1. Lift left knee and cross it over. Twist to the right.
2. Recover.
3. Lift right knee and cross it over, twisting to the left.
4. Recover.
Repeat 10 times.

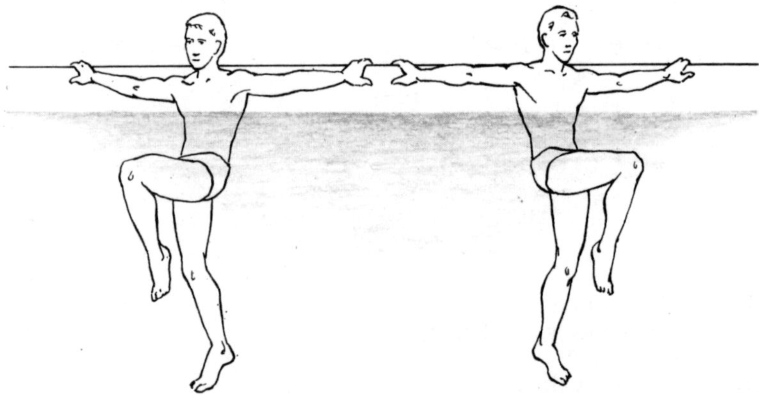

Leg Stretch (Back)
Supine, hold pool gutter with hands. Keep legs together and extended about 6 feet under water.
1. Spread legs apart as far as possible.
2. Pull feet and legs vigorously together.
Repeat 10 times.

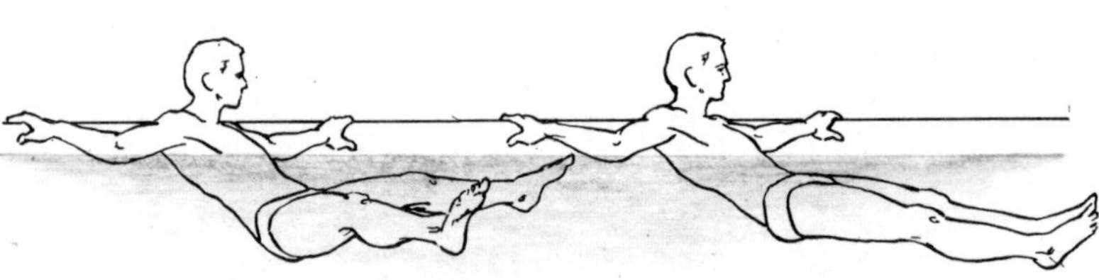

Leg Stretch (Front)
Prone, hold pool gutter with one hand, the other flat on the wall to push your legs out. Keep feet together.
1. Spread legs apart as far as possible.
2. Pull feet and legs vigorously together.
Repeat 10 times.

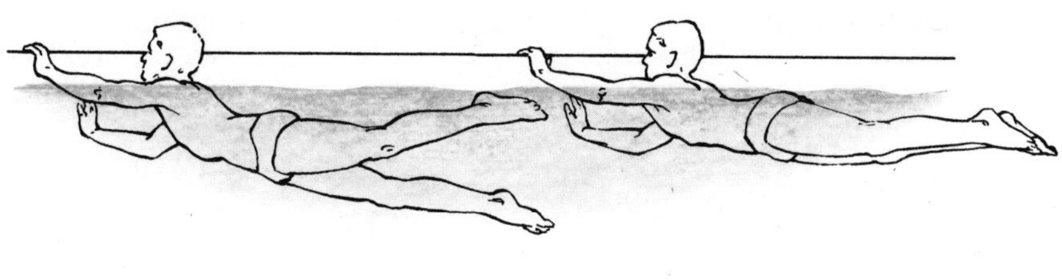

Circle Legs
Prone, hold pool gutter with one hand, the other hand flat on the pool wall to push legs out.
1. Circle legs outward left.
Repeat 10 times.
2. Reverse to right.
Repeat 10 times.

Leg Swing Outward
Chest-deep water.
Stand with back against pool side, hands sideward holding gutter.
1. Raise left foot as high as possible with leg straight.
2. Swing foot and leg to left side.
3. Recover to starting position by pulling left leg vigorously to the right.
Repeat 10 times.
4. Reverse to right leg.
Repeat 10 times.

Circle Ankles
Prone, hold pool gutter with one hand, the other hand flat on the pool wall.
1. Circle ankles left.
Repeat 10 times.
2. Reverse to right.
Repeat 10 times.

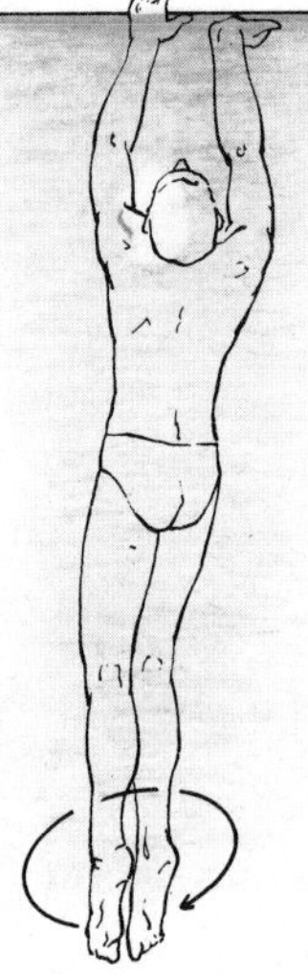

Climbing
Hands in pool gutter, face pool side and put feet flat against side, approximately 16 inches apart.
1. Walk up side, taking six short steps.
2. Walk down side to starting position.
Repeat 10 times.

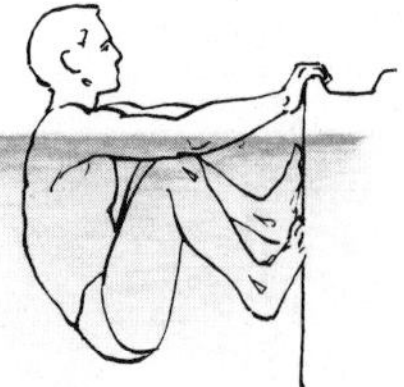

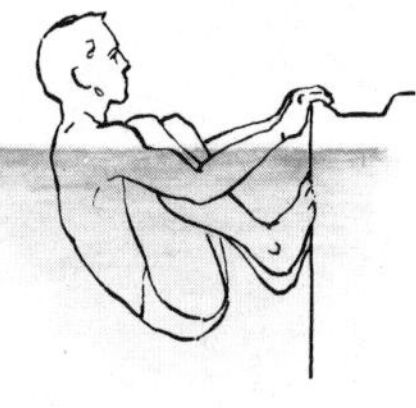

Front Flutter Kicking–Lie prone, holding side of pool with hands. **1.** Do the flutter kick, toes pointed back, ankles flexible, knee joint loose but straight on upbeat, bent on downbeat. *Sustain for 30 seconds.*

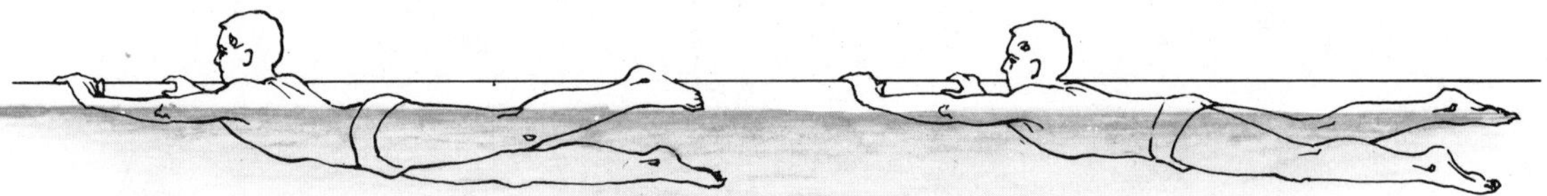

Back Flutter Kicking–Lie supine, holding side of pool with hands. **1.** Flutter kick. *Sustain for 30 seconds.*

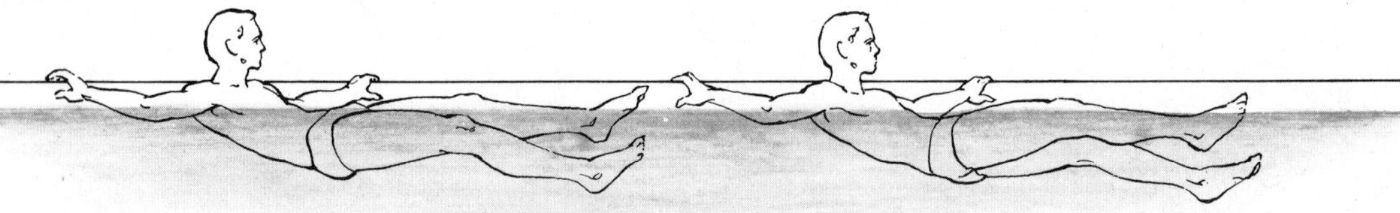

Left and Right Side Flutter Kicking–Lie on left side, holding side of pool with right hand, left side braced on pool wall. **1.** Flutter kick. *30 seconds.* **2.** Reverse to left side. *30 seconds.*

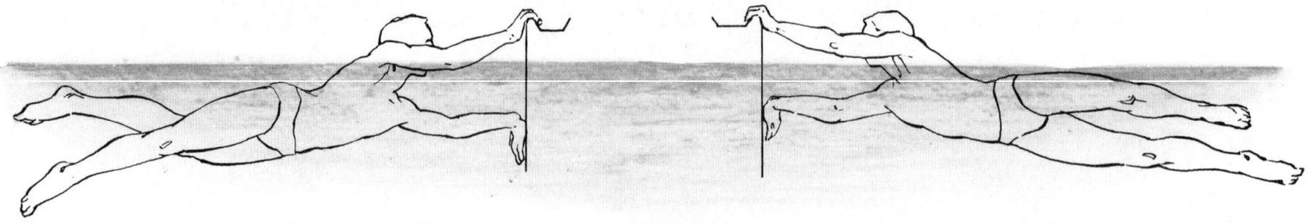

BOBBING

This is an excellent water conditioning activity. In bobbing, you push your head and shoulders out of the water much as a cork held under water bobs up when released. Some experts say that if you had *only* 5 minutes for exercise each day, it would be best to spend that time in one of four ways: 1. high bobbing, 2. trampolining, 3. skipping rope, or 4. running. During bobbing you place great demands on your breathing. Breathing itself is an exercise, especially the quick inhaling and forced exhaling required for bobbing. Maximum exertion depends upon maximum respiration, and bobbing gets your breathing muscles in shape. You can feel the stimulus of forced heavy breathing after advanced bobbing for 5 minutes (approximately 100 to 125 times). Because you need strong breathing for swimming, about 20 percent of Aquametrics is devoted to bobbing.

Elementary Bobbing
Chest-deep water.
Stand straight up.
1. Inhale.
2. Submerge in a squat position with feet on the pool bottom. Exhale during 2. and 3.
3. Shove up off the bottom and regain a standing position.
4. Inhale with head out of water.
Repeat 10 times.

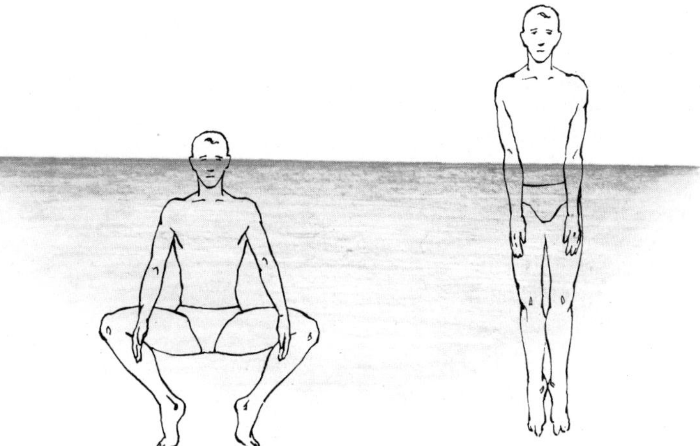

Alternate Leg Rearward Bobbing
Chest-deep water.
Stand straight up.
1. Inhale.
2. Submerge with left leg squatting forward, right leg extended rearward. Exhale during 2. and 3.
3. Shove up from bottom, reversing position of legs. Inhale when head is out of water.
4. Submerge with right leg squatting forward, left leg extended rearward. Exhale.
Repeat 10 times.

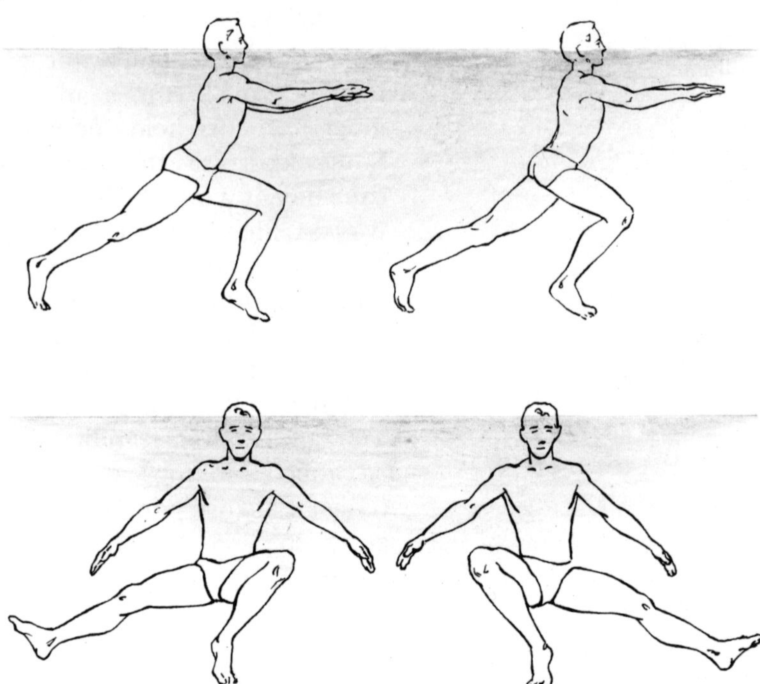

Alternate Leg Sideward Bobbing
Waist-to-chest deep water.
Stand straight up.
1. Inhale.
2. Submerge with left leg in a full squatting position, left foot on pool bottom, right leg extended sideward. Exhale during 2 and 3.
3. Shove up off bottom, reversing legs, inhaling when head is out of water.
4. Reverse, submerging with the right leg in squat position, etc.
Repeat 10 times.

Advanced Bobbing
Treading in overhead water.
1. Assume a vertical position, hands extended outward from sides, just under surface of the water, palms turned down. Legs are drawn up in preparation for a frog or scissors kick.
2. Execute kick as hands are pulled to thighs. The head and shoulders rise out of the water. Take a deep breath.
3. As the body sinks, stretch the arms overhead and exhale.
Repeat 10 times.

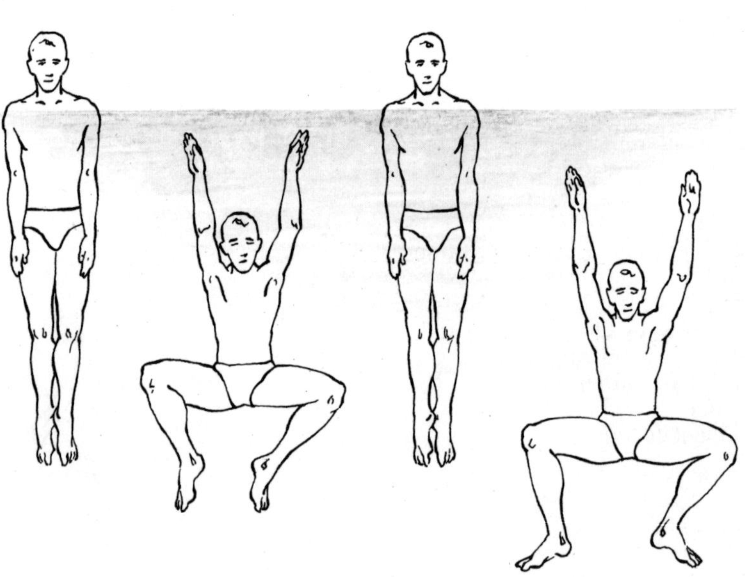

Left Right Leg Bobbing
Standing or treading in overhead water.
1. Inhale.
2. Submerge in a tuck with right leg drawn up, left foot on pool bottom, arms extended forward.
3. Push up off left leg, pushing down with both hands. Exhale during 2. and 3.
4. Inhale with head out of water.
Repeat 10 times.
5. Reverse to right leg.

Progressive Alternate Leg Bobbing
Chest-deep water.
Standing.
1. Perform action described in Alternate Leg Rearward Bobbing: alternate legs, bob progressively, and move forward the length of the pool or a specified distance.

High Bobbing
Overhead water.
1. Extend hands outward from side, palms turned down. Legs are drawn in position for frog kick.
2. Simultaneously pull hands sharply to thighs with legs executing frog kick.
3. Inhale at peak of height.
4. Drop with thrust of arms downward, palms turned upward, until feet reach bottom of pool, and tuck to squat position. Exhale throughout this action.
5. Jump up with leg thrust, pull arms in breaststroke down, head and shoulders rising out of water.
6. Inhale.
Repeat 10 times.

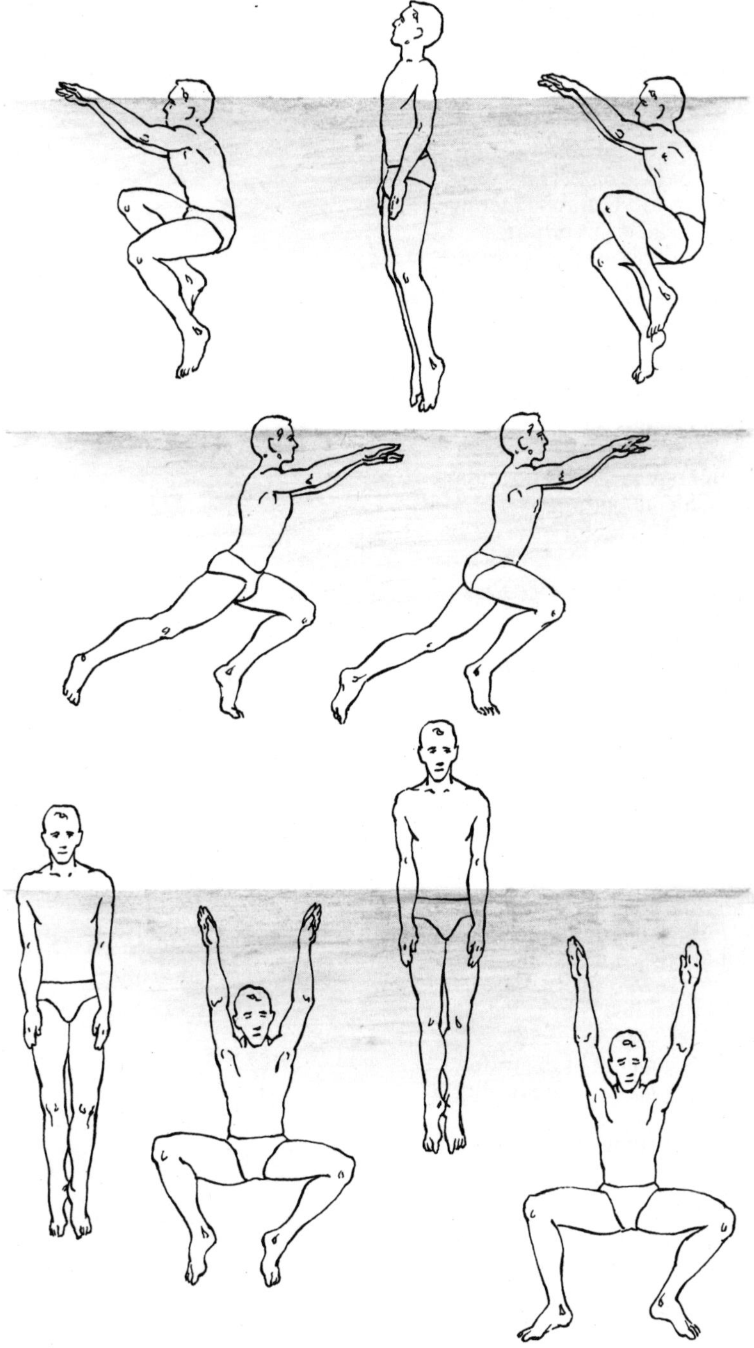

Legs Astride Bobbing
Waist-to-chest deep water.
Stand straight up.
1. Inhale.
2. Submerge with legs astride, left leg forward, and right leg back. Exhale on 2. and 3.
3. Shove off bottom, inhaling when head is out of water.
4. Submerge with legs astride.
Repeat 10 times.

"Bunny Hop" Bobbing
1. Inhale.
2. Submerge in tuck position, feet on pool bottom.
3. Push up and forward off bottom. Exhale during 2. and 3.
4. Inhale with head out of water.
Repeat, pushing forward the length of the pool or a specified distance.

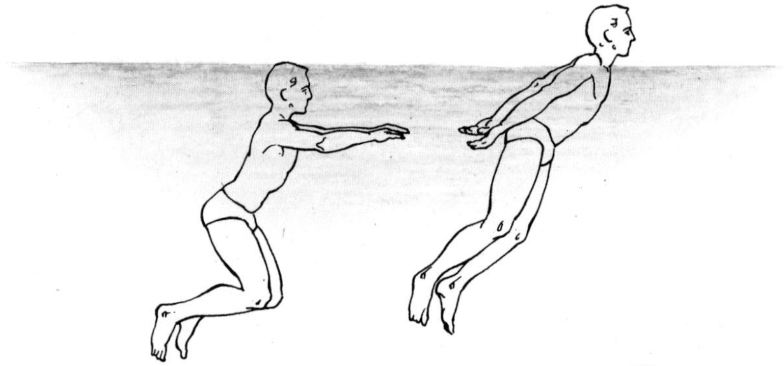

Power Bobbing
Overhead water.
1. Follow instructions for High Bobbing except that at the top of the upward thrust, the hands scull vigorously as the legs flutter kick.
2. Rise high out of the water, exposing all of the body above the hips.
Repeat 10 times.

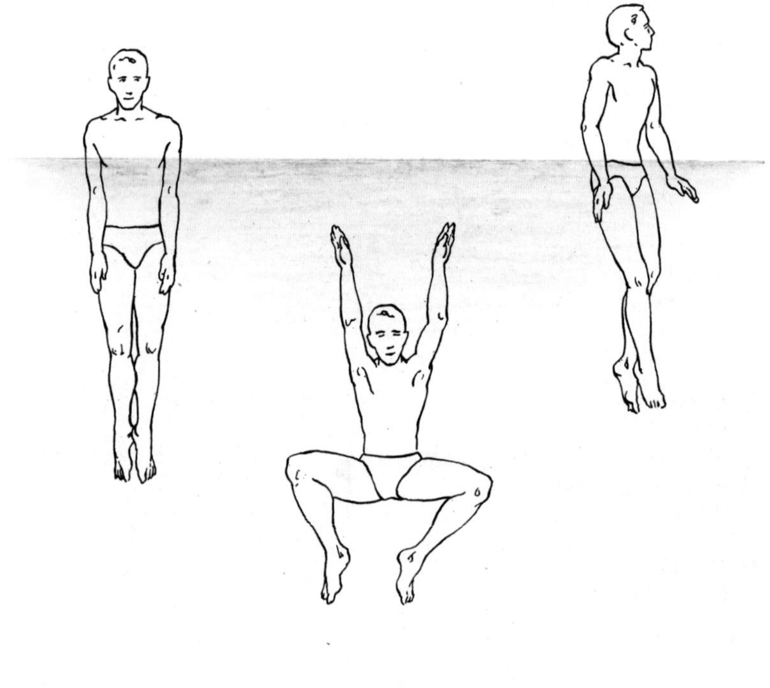

SCULLING, TREADING & EXTENSIONS

Controlled breathing is important to the following exercises. You should try to inhale through the mouth and exhale through the nose. And maintain a steady breathing rhythm.

"Extension" exercises are largely dependent upon sculling ability. Hand action is basically the same, regardless of the position of your body, and provides lifting power or combined lifting and propulsion power. Keeping your hands flat, fingers together, rotate your wrists, bringing your palms forward. Then, roll your wrists to turn your palms slightly backward and push back. Downward pressure should be constant throughout the movements.

One Hand High Treading
Overhead water.
1. Kick bicycle, scissors, or frog style holding one arm straight up, the other hand held shoulder high.
2. Reverse arms.
Repeat 10 times.

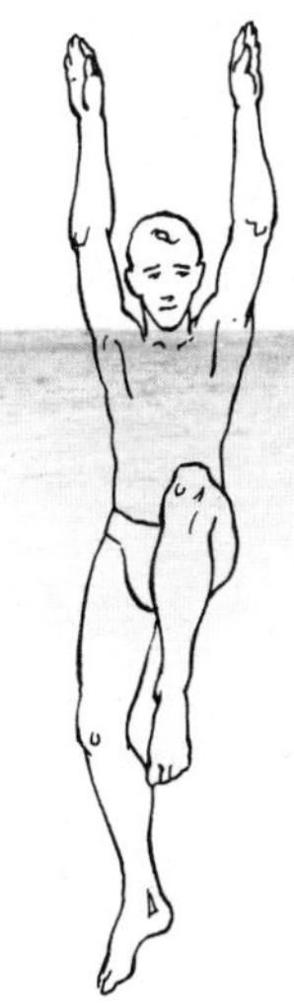

Two Hands High Treading
Overhead water.
1. Kick bicycle, scissors, or frog style, holding both arms straight up out of water.
Hold at least 3 minutes.

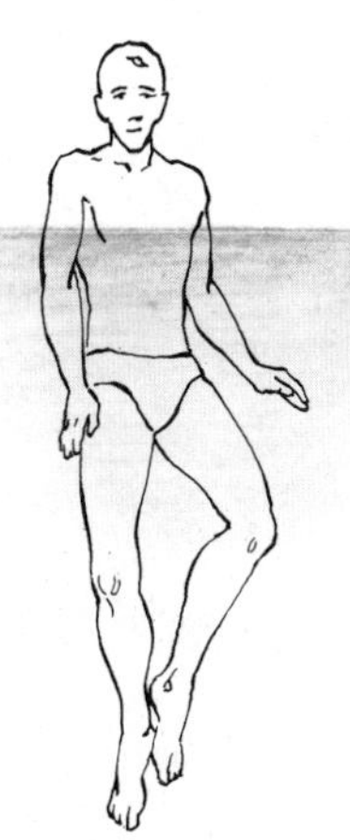

Look-Out Treading
Overhead water.
1. Kick vigorously while thrashing the water by sculling.
2. This action should keep the shoulders and chest high out of the water.
Maintain for 30 seconds.

Sculling
Sculling is done by arm and hand action. The use of the hands in sculling is the same regardless of the position of the body or the direction you're going. Sculling provides lifting power or combined lifting and propulsion.
1. Begin by pushing down on palms, with arms sideward. Hands are flat, fingers together, and thumbs close to forefingers.
2. With thumbs up, rotate wrists, bringing palms forward, then turn palms down and back.
3. Lifting power comes as the hand pulls to the front and side.

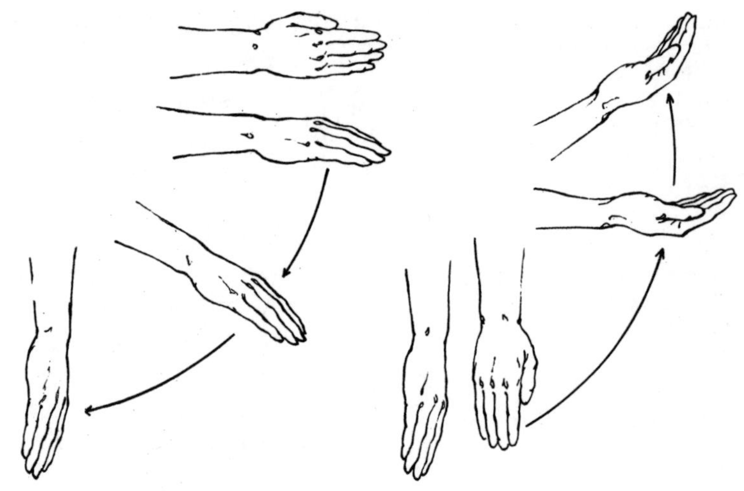

Left Knee Up, Back
Supine.
1. Scull, drawing left knee up to chest, right leg extended, toes of right foot out of water.
2. Scull, straightening left leg, returning to starting position.
Repeat 10 times.

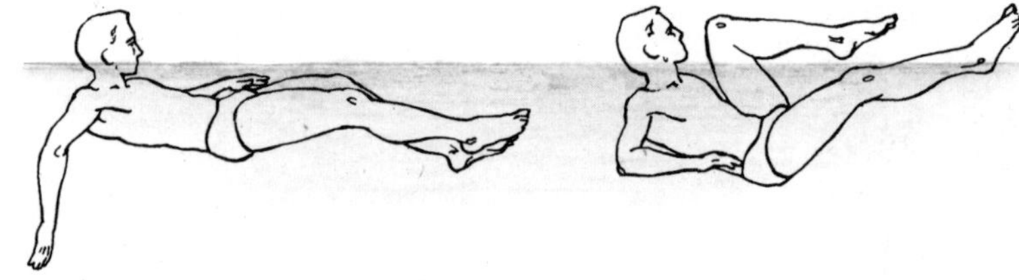

Right Knee Up, Back
Supine.
1. Scull, drawing right leg up to chest, left leg extended, toes of left foot out of water.
2. Scull, straightening right leg, returning to starting position.
Repeat 10 times.

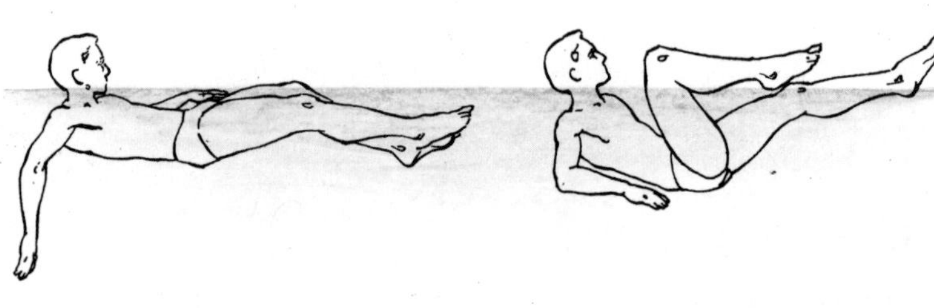

Knees Up, Back
Supine, legs out.
1. Scull, drawing knees up to chest.
2. Scull, shoving legs forward, returning to starting position.
Repeat 10 times.

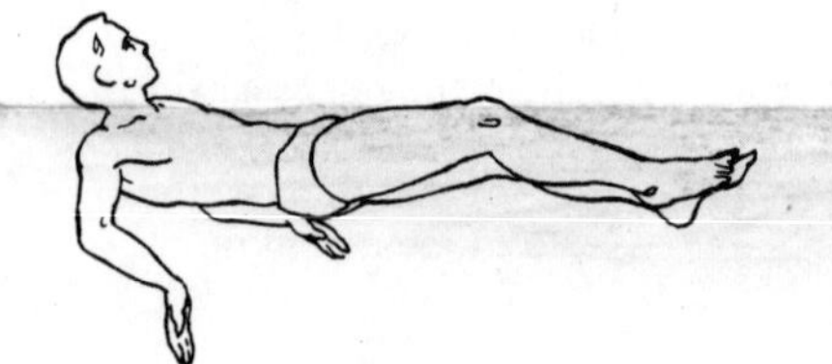
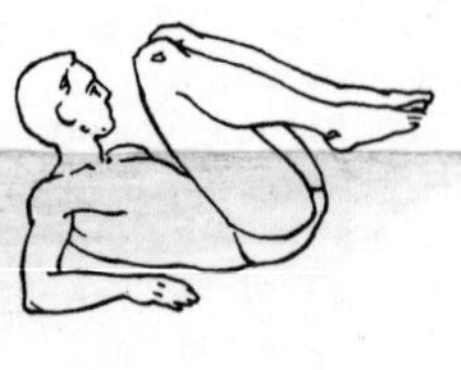

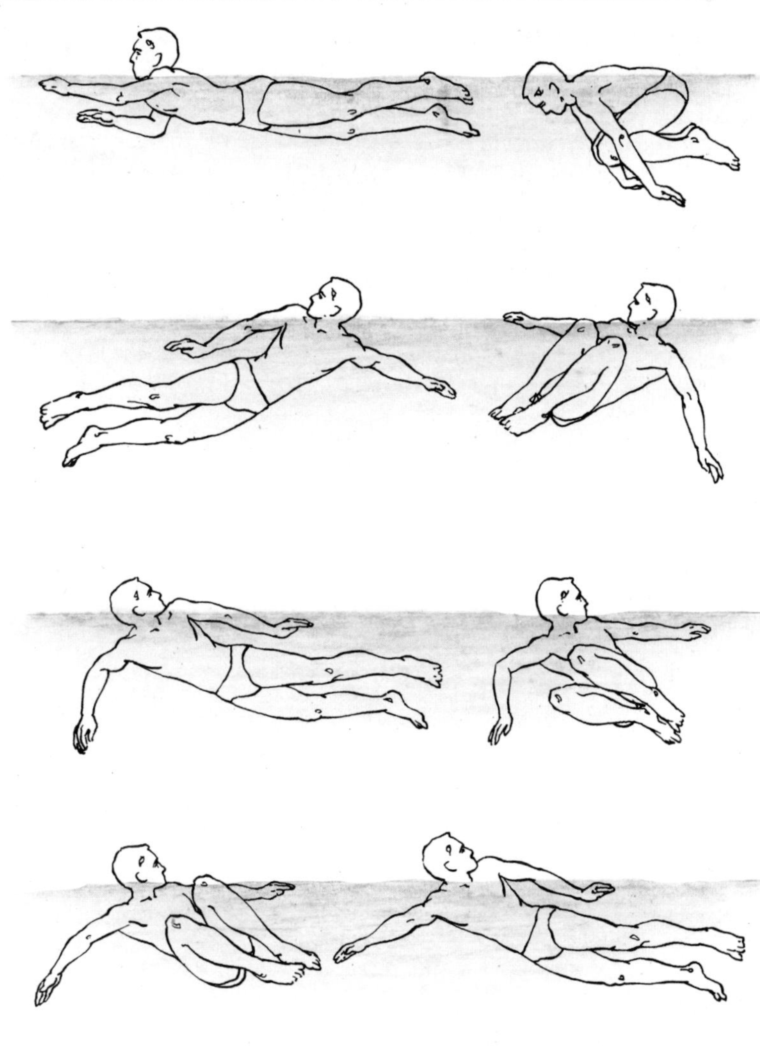

Knees Up, Front
Prone, legs out.
1. Scull, drawing knees up to chest.
2. Scull, pushing legs backward, returning to starting position.
Repeat 10 times.

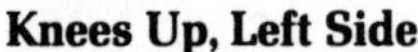

Knees Up, Left Side
Left side stroke position.
1. Scull, drawing knees up to chest.
2. Scull, shoving legs to the right, returning body to starting position.
Repeat 10 times.

Knees Up, Right Side
Right side stroke position.
1. Scull, drawing knees up to chest.
2. Scull, shoving legs to the left, returning body to starting position.
Repeat 10 times.

Reverse Sides Extension
1. Scull, drawing knees up to chest, shoving legs to left side, causing body to be in a right side stroke position.
2. Scull vigorously, drawing knees up to chest and reversing position, shoving legs to the right side, shifting body to a left side stroke position.
Repeat 10 times.

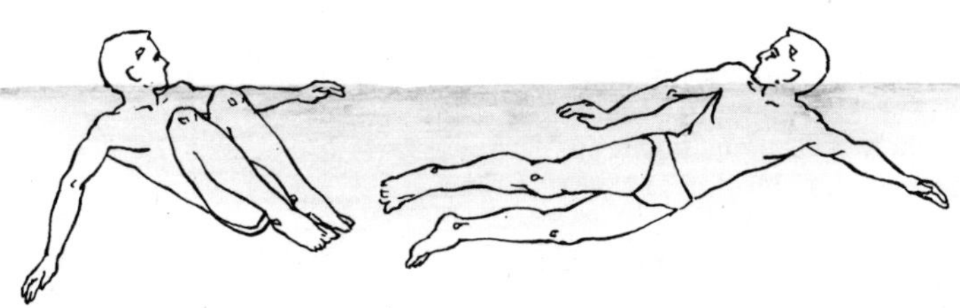

Around the Clock Extension
1. Scull, drawing knees up to chest, shoving legs forward to a back-lying position.
2. Scull vigorously, drawing knees up to chest, shoving legs to left side, causing body to be in a right side stroke position.
3. Scull, drawing knees up to chest, shoving legs outward to a prone position.
4. Scull, drawing knees up to chest, shoving legs to right side, causing body to be in a left side stroke position.
Repeat 10 times.

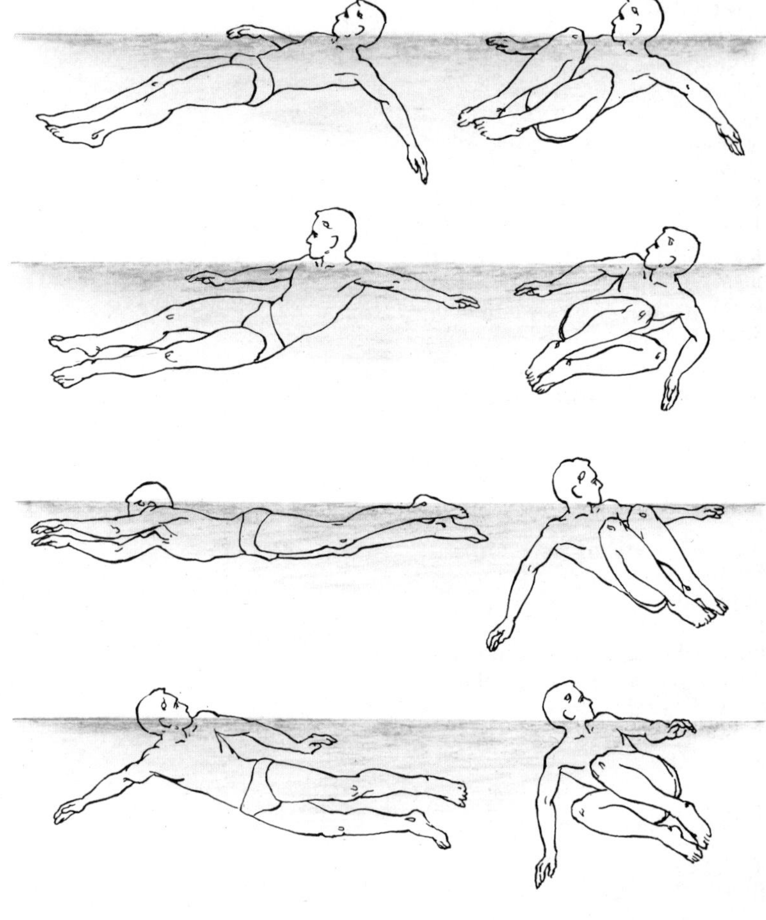

Rub-A-Dub-Dub
Supine.
1. Bring knees to chest with knees and toes together.
2. Spin in a circle using an opposite sculling motion of the hands.
3. After one full turn, reverse.
Repeat 10 times.

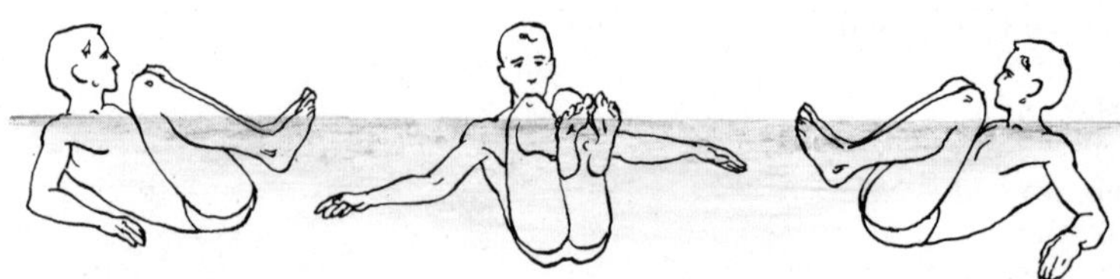

Left Leg Raiser
Supine.
1. Scull continously, bringing the left knee to the chest until the lower leg is nearly parallel to the surface of the water.
2. Scull, straightening the left leg so that it is perpendicular to the water.
3. Return the left knee to the chest.
4. Return to starting position.
Repeat 10 times.

Right Leg Raiser
Supine.
1. Scull continuously, bringing the right knee to the chest until the lower leg is nearly parallel to the surface of the water.
2. Scull, straightening the right leg so that it is perpendicular to the water.
3. Return the right knee to the chest.
4. Return to starting position.
Repeat 10 times.

High Sculling
Vertical with knees up to chest, heels close to hips.
1. Scull, making a figure 8 pattern, using your arms only.
2. Raise the upper body as high as possible out of the water.
Maintain for one minute.

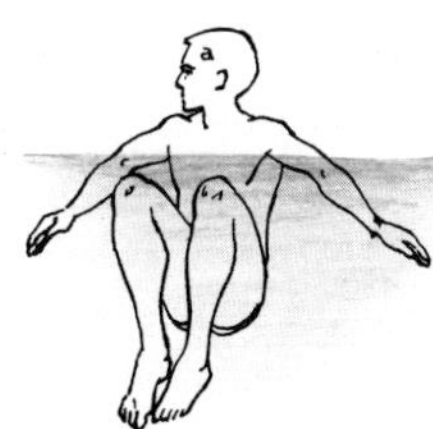

Sculling V Sit
Supine.
1. Lower your hips, raising both feet out of the water with your legs together.
2. Scull in the direction you're facing.
Maintain for one minute.

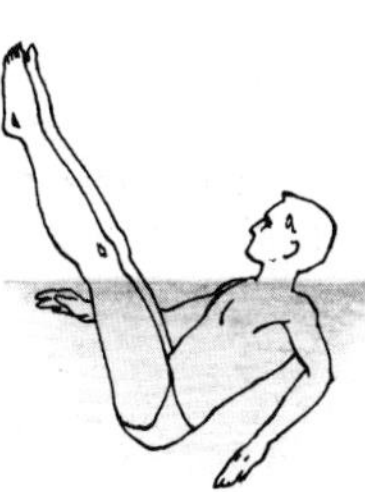

Alternate Leg Raiser
Supine.
1. Scull continuously, bringing the left knee to the chest until the lower leg is nearly parallel to the water.
2. Scull, straightening the left leg so that it is perpendicular to the water.
3. Bend the left knee into the chest.
4. Lower the leg to the starting position.
5. Scull continuously, bringing the right knee to the chest until the lower leg is nearly parallel to the water.
6. Scull, straightening the right leg so that it is perpendicular to the water.
7. Bend the right knee into the chest.
8. Lower the leg to the starting position.
Repeat 10 times, alternating left and right legs.

Double Leg Raiser
Supine.
1. Scull continuously, bringing both knees up to the chest until the lower legs are parallel to the water.
2. Straighten both legs up until they are nearly perpendicular to the water.
3. Return both knees to chest.
4. Lower both legs to the starting position.
Repeat 10 times.

Alternate Sculling and Treading
Overhead water, vertical position.
1. Tread water with hands held shoulder high.
2. Shift to sculling action of the arm and hands. Pull the knees up with the feet under the hips.
3. Return to treading water with the hands held shoulder high.
4. Resume the sculling action with bent knees.
Repeat this alternating pattern 10 times.

Under and Up
Prone.
1. Swim four breaststrokes under water.
2. Surface and breathe.
Repeat 10 times.

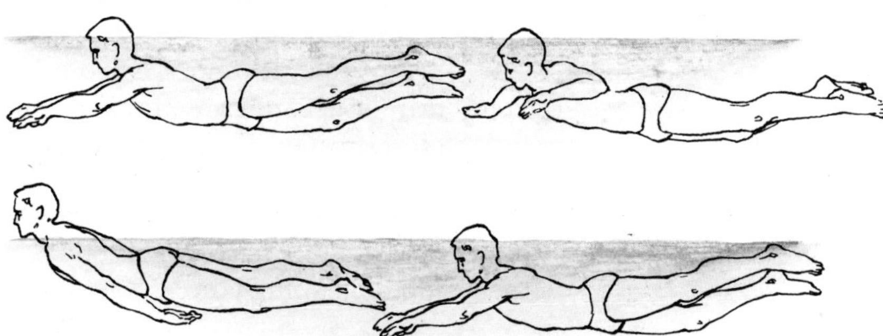

SwimProofing

Few sports are more minimal in their equipment needs than swimming. All you need is your body and a bathing suit to cover it, and sometimes even the suit is optional. This is not to say there is no other equipment you can or maybe even should buy, but most of you will probably be able to get along with your basic body and suit.

SUITS

Your suit should be anything that closely resembles your skin in its fit and feel. The choice is fairly simple for men. Any brief swim suit made of a smooth, quick-drying fabric such as nylon is fine. It lowers your drag in the water and satisfies the laws of public modesty. Baggy shorts should not be a man's first choice unless he wants to use the added resistance and drag of the suit as some kind of training aid. Besides, a closer-fitting suit is a good incentive to get your body in shape and keep it that way.

For women the problem of picking a suit can be a little more complicated. For one thing, many of the designer suits now sold are more for show than for use. Diving into the water, or even just swimming too swiftly, may separate swimmer and suit. The suit should be close-fitting and cut so as not to hinder your movements, but it should be substantial enough to stay on your body as you exercise.

Fortunately there are a couple of companies that make attractive and functional swim suits. Made of slick, close-fitting lycra, they are cut high near the thighs to allow maximum leg movement. They fit close to the chest, so they don't trap water at the top, and they have comfortable narrow shoulder straps that do an efficient job of keeping your suit up but leave your arms free for

> Bathing is best performed when quite naked, but, as in the bathing establishments in large towns and cities, and in thickly-settled parts of the country, decency forbids entire nudity, a kind of short drawers is worn.
>
> -EDWIN T. BREWSTER
> *Swimming*, 1910

any stroke. They cost no more—usually less—than most designer suits. If you're serious about swimming, such a suit is well worth the investment.

CAPS

Most women and some men wear bathing caps as they swim. Besides the obvious advantage of keeping hair dry, the caps reduce water drag and resistance. (As an alternative to the cap, some male swimmers shave their heads before competition, a much more drastic alternative.) If you plan to buy a cap, just remember that the simpler the better. Forget about caps with a rubber lily pad attached to the top or any other decorations. A plain white tight-fitting stretch swimmer's cap, which usually costs just a couple of dollars, is all you'll need.

GOGGLES

If the chlorine-treated water in the pool irritates your eyes, invest in a pair of swim goggles. Don't skimp on these, because a cheap pair will probably never fit you very well, and water will leak in, giving you the same eye-irritation problems as before. In general, buy goggles with shatterproof glass lenses. Plastic lenses scratch too easily. If you do much of your swimming in an outdoor pool, you might also want to consider getting goggles with lenses that are tinted (gray is the best color) to cut the glare. Finally, if you wear glasses, you can even have prescription goggles especially made for you. One company that does this is Aqua Optics, 575-B 6th Street, San Pedro, CA 90731. Write the company for a brochure and price quotation.

Be sure to try goggles on before you buy them if you can. If they feel comfortable but tend to leak a little on your first or second time in the water, don't worry too much. If you bought a good pair, you'll find that they will shape themselves more closely to the contours of your face the more you use them.

If you don't like the tunnel-vision effect of the goggles

but still want to shield your eyes from pool water, you could invest in a swimmer's mask, a single piece of transparent material that covers your upper face. Again, try the mask on before you buy it.

PLUGS AND CLIPS

Ordinarily you should not need nose clips unless you've found that you are prone to sinus infection when water goes up your nose. A couple of dollars will buy you a decent pair. An added bonus of wearing the clips, if you must, is that they force you to breathe through your mouth and so they can be a training aid.

No one recommends ear plugs for swimmers, for a number of reasons. First of all, if you wear them when you dive, the added pressure of the water could force them farther in and injure your eardrums. Second, no one has yet come up with a watertight ear plug. They all leak. If you are having ear problems, try the suggestions given later in this chapter. If you still want to wear something to protect your ears from the water, wear two bathing caps and pull them tightly down around your ears.

TRAINING AIDS

If you're interested in developing your upper-body strength as you swim, there are a few body add-ons you can try. A favorite tool of some swimming coaches is a small inner tube, sometimes called a *trainer tube*, that twists around your ankles. It does three things. First and most obviously it immobilizes your legs, forcing you to use only your arms to get through the water. Second, it creates some drag for you to struggle against as you swim. Third, it does all this while keeping the bottom half of your body up on an even keel with your front so you are lying flat in the water. It's a relatively inexpensive item costing from five to ten dollars.

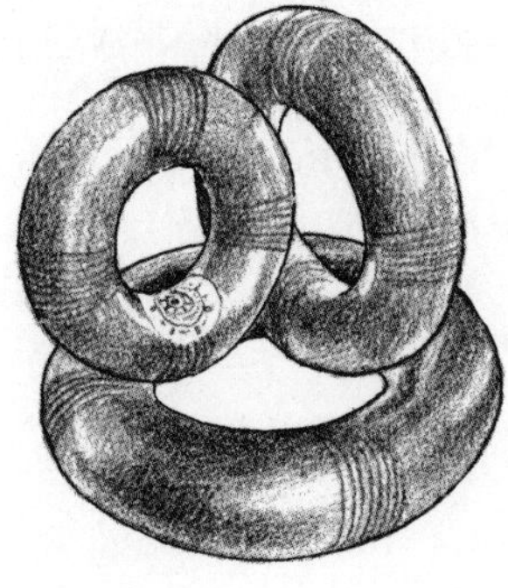

Another upper-body developing tool is the *hand paddle*, basically just a flat piece of plastic, usually the

size of a spread hand, with loops on its back for your hands and fingers. The paddle is a way of increasing water resistance as you move your hands through the water. This makes your shoulders and arms work harder and eventually strengthens them. Again, these are fairly inexpensive, costing about three or four dollars. One word of caution: If you suffer from any kind of shoulder problem, it might be better to leave these off your equipment list, since they may aggravate your ailment.

As a total-body conditioner, you could try a *drag belt*—a nylon web belt with a series of cups or scoops strung along it, their openings facing your direction of swim. As you can probably figure out, the cups or scoops snag the water and slow you down with the resistance they create. You can vary the amount of resistance by the number of scoops you string on it. Another training aid with a similar effect is the pull buoy, essentially a small float you tow behind you as you swim. It too increases your water resistance and makes your muscles work harder. None of these aids is very expensive; they cost anywhere from 5 to 20 dollars depending on how complicated they get.

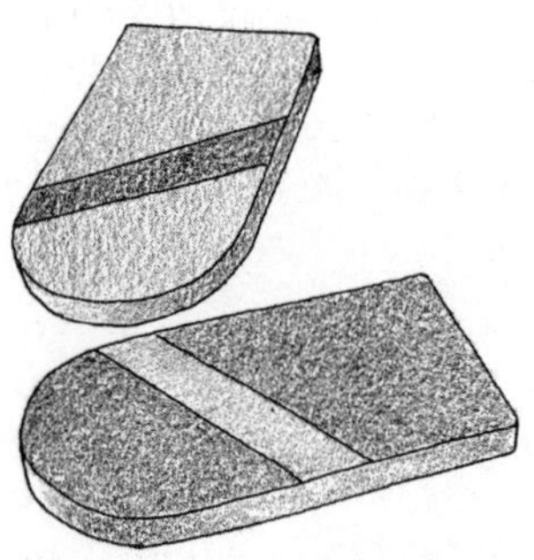

If you just want a little drag in your workouts and you're a woman, you can increase water resistance by wearing two bathing suits when you swim. If in time you feel you need more, maybe that's when you should spring for the resistance equipment.

To work on your kicks you can always hang onto the side of the pool and flutter away, or, if you need the satisfaction of moving through the water as you kick, you can invest in a lightweight styrofoam *kickboard*. This typically costs less than 10 dollars. To get the most out of using it, make sure you hold it with your arms straight and as low on the board as possible to create enough water resistance and also to make sure your body "planes" correctly as you move along.

There are, of course, more elaborate training devices

you could invest in, but unless you have hopes of an Olympic gold medal or a record marathon swim, they are not likely to be worth your while.

BAD NEWS, GOOD NEWS

There is no such thing as an injury-free sport, but swimming, it is safe to say, is certainly kinder to your body than most sports. Most of your problems, if you have any, will tend to be minor and can be taken care of fairly easily.

Hair and skin are sometimes affected by chlorinated water. If you have delicate or dry hair you may find it thinning as a result of your swimming. All that time in the water can further dry already dry skin. Taking care of your hair is usually just a matter of wearing a bathing cap and/or using a hair conditioner with your shampoo to keep it from getting too dry and brittle. Rubbing a moisturizer as basic as baby oil on your skin after you shower will restore some of the skin oils you have lost.

Slightly more irritating is the problem known as athlete's foot. It is a fungus that grows on the skin and often itches. Usually you pick up the fungus infection by walking on wet shower floors. The fungus settles in between your toes, most commonly between the fourth and fifth toe. The condition gets aggravated when your feet are wet or perspire in hot weather.

Usually you can treat the condition with a commonly available nonprescription cream or ointment containing the medication tolnaftate. Daily application of this will clear up your problem in a couple of weeks. You can keep it from recurring by drying your feet carefully after showering and using a foot or body powder to help keep your feet dry. Changing your socks frequently and wearing loose-fitting shoes, especially in hot weather, will also help.

If you let your athlete's foot go unchecked, it can turn

into a painful bacterial infection that may require the attention of a dermatologist and more powerful medication.

EYE PROBLEMS

Eye irritation can also be a problem to the pool swimmer. What happens to your eyes is that the chlorinated solution you swim in irritates the cornea, the clear membrane that covers the eye surface. As a result your cornea may lose some of its surface cells, and you may find that after you've been swimming a while your eyes may be sensitive to bright light or may get bloodshot, a problem called pink eye. Neither problem is serious; both usually clear up overnight. If your eyes feel irritated after a swim, rinse them out when you shower, using shower water and your cupped palm as a crude eye cup.

If you want to avoid this irritation completely, get a good pair of goggles and wear them when you swim. It's that simple. One last precaution, however: Don't get in the habit of wearing other people's goggles. For one thing, they probably won't fit you as well as your own and will leak water; but more important, there is a virus that you can catch from an infected swimmer's goggles that will give you a particularly nasty case of red eye along with a few other unpleasant symptoms such as a fever and sore throat.

NOSES AND EARS

Sinus problems that plague some swimmers can be avoided fairly easily by spending a dollar or two on a set of nose clips. If the problem persists even after you've taken this precaution, then maybe it's time to see your doctor.

Swimmer's ear, or, in medical terms, external otitis, is one last common problem among swimmers. It usually develops because of moisture that remains in the ear after a swim. Some of the skin cells there start to fall away, and the tissue is temporarily less resistant to infection. This is more apt to happen to those who swim in fresh water, because, sports physiologist Dr. Hemming Atterbom suspects, the fresh water leaches out some of the salt in the skin tissue, making the ear more vulnerable to the bacteria and fungus that cause the infection. The result is that the ear canal swells up and starts producing pus.

Treatment is simple. A prescription drug called Cortisporin, available as ear drops, will clear up the problem in two weeks or less. With these ear drops you can continue to keep swimming. Most doctors think being in the water may help clear up the condition a little, since the water rinses out infected debris from the ear canal.

If you are prone to this infection, taking preventive measures is easy. First of all, forget about ear plugs. They eventually will leak and do nothing to keep this from happening. Instead, before a swim, put a dab of ordinary petroleum jelly in each ear and smear it around. This will protect the tissues from the water much more effectively than any ear plug.

After you swim, shake out any water that has settled in your ear. Then take an eyedropper and fill it with ordinary rubbing alcohol. Squeeze two or three drops into each ear and let the alcohol evaporate. This will dry out your ear tissue and practically eliminate the chance of an infection.

Jerry swam out to the big barrier rock, adjusted the goggles and dived. . . . Now he could see. It was as if he had eyes of a different kind—fish eyes that showed everything clear and delicate and wavering in the bright water.

-DORIS LESSING
"Through the Tunnel"

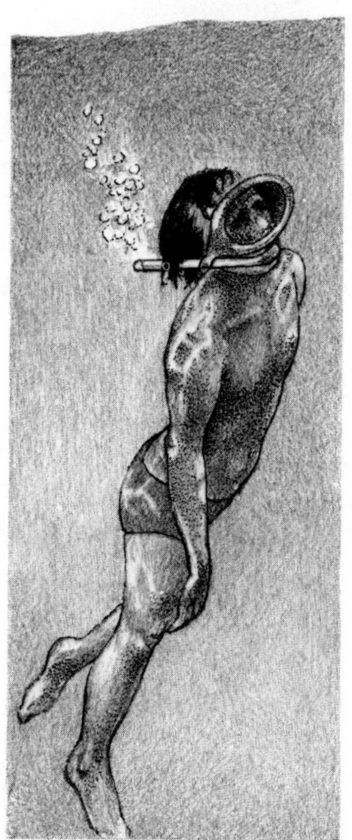

Strokes & Style

Swimming is a highly personal sport, perhaps the most individual there is. How you swim and even what stroke you choose is a highly individual matter determined by, among other things, your body shape, your experience as an athlete in general and as a swimmer in particular, and even by personal whimsy.

As a result a swimmer will develop a style to suit individual variables. And to get the most out of your strokes, you should get to know your body better. Experiment with some of the guidelines and insights you'll find on the following pages. Let your body tell you what feels right and what doesn't, but above all don't force yourself to extremes. You should do all exercise, including your swimming, at a realistic pace.

Throughout this section you'll find suggestions on breathing, hand positioning, developing kick power, and upper and lower body coordination. Always remember that these are not all rules — some are just suggestions. Use what you feel is helping to improve your stroke ability. Discard what doesn't work. Only you can be the ultimate judge of what suits you best.

By using this section as a guide, you will soon find that your skill as a swimmer is constantly improving, reason enough for keeping this available for reference. And as you develop additional stroke finesse, it's not a bad idea to come back and check on yourself to see where your technique has improved and where it is slipping. Even world-class competition-level swimmers need a coach to tell them where they are going wrong. This section offers you a chance to be your own coach. What you'll get out of it is the ability to swim well — that is, with efficiency and strength, with greater ease and grace, and, most important, with greater enjoyment.

CRAWL (Freestyle)

For speed and total conditioning, no stroke can compare with the crawl. It's the fastest, most demanding stroke in a swimmer's repertoire. It's the one that you'll probably use the most. In the competition event known as the freestyle, swimmers can execute with any stroke. Since most prefer the crawl because of its high speed—a strong swimmer can hit 5 mph—the term "freestyle" has become synonymous with the crawl.

Because the crawl is a complex stroke demanding a good sense of coordination in timing body movement and breathing, and because it places tremendous demands on your stamina, the keys to a smooth, almost effortless stroke are practice and attention to detail.

UPPER BODY

Most of the power for the crawl comes from your upper body: back, shoulders, upper and lower arms, and hands. And it's those parts of your body that demand much of your attention as you swim. The stroke, however, involves much more than just movement.

You begin the stroke by correctly positioning your body in the water. Wasted motion cuts down severely on swimming efficiency. You have to concentrate on keeping your body aligned and as square as possible when you move. Make a conscious effort to minimize rocking and swerving in the pool as you swim. If you don't keep your body on an even plane in the water, you will do more work than is necessary and be an inefficient swimmer.

These problems disappear as you gain control over the stroke. To do the crawl well you need to think of your arms and legs in mechanical images. Your arm motion is critical. It should have the steady synchronized beat of alternating hinged oars with your flat hands serving as the blades. Naturally it's not that simple, but it's a way to put oneself into the right frame of mind.

The arm stroke starts at the shoulder. Roll your right shoulder (assuming you're beginning with your right arm) up to about ear level — and at the same time extend your arm out in front of you. You should be reaching to a point that lines up between your nose and your shoulder.

As your hand enters the water your fingers should be together and your palm should be slightly cupped and facing out to the side. You cut into the water with the thumb side of your hand, your fingers pointed down at a slight angle so that the tip of your index finger hits the water before your thumb does. It's almost as though your hand is making its own mini-dive. This way the hand leads your arm in with only minimal water resistance, sparing your energy for the important part of the stroke, the pull.

As your hand cuts into the water your elbow should be slightly bent and raised, putting your arm in position to immediately begin your pulling action. (This is not possible if you keep your arm completely straight.)

Once your hand is fully in the water, turn it so that your fingers are pointing down and your palm is coming into position facing directly toward the rear. Your hand is now in position to begin the pull. At this point you should be able to make the maximum use of your shoulder muscles. You should be positioned so that your forearm is sloping downward with your wrist above your hand, your elbow above your wrist. You should enter the water in this order: hand, wrist, forearm, elbow, and upper arm.

As your hand digs into the water you'll feel it "catch"—that is, you'll begin to feel the pressure of the water against your hand. You'll sense this when your hand is about 8 inches below the surface. At this point, as you begin pulling with your hand and forearm, in-

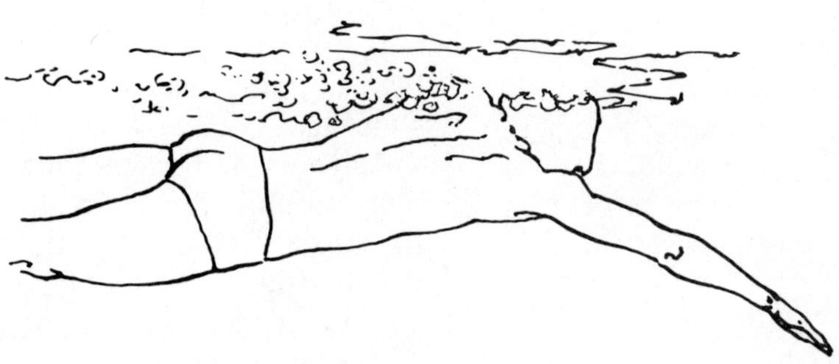

crease the bend in your elbow. This will maximize the initial power of the pulling action. Make sure that the plane of your hand (your fingers should be close together at all times) is perpendicular to the bottom of the pool and your palm is facing rearward.

If you were to watch a skilled freestyle swimmer from the bottom of the pool as he or she stroked overhead you'd see the full hand motion of the stroke scribe a kind of lazy flopped-S route underneath the swimmer's body.

Still using the right arm as the stroking example, what happens is that the right hand slides slightly out to the right as it pulls into the stroke. But by the time the arm has drawn to a point directly below the shoulder, your hand, which has now begun to angle back slightly from right to left, has moved directly under the center of your body. During this motion your elbow is bending more and more. When the pulling hand is directly under your body the elbow should be bent at its sharpest angle, about 90 degrees.

This is a critical point in the pulling stroke. You can't

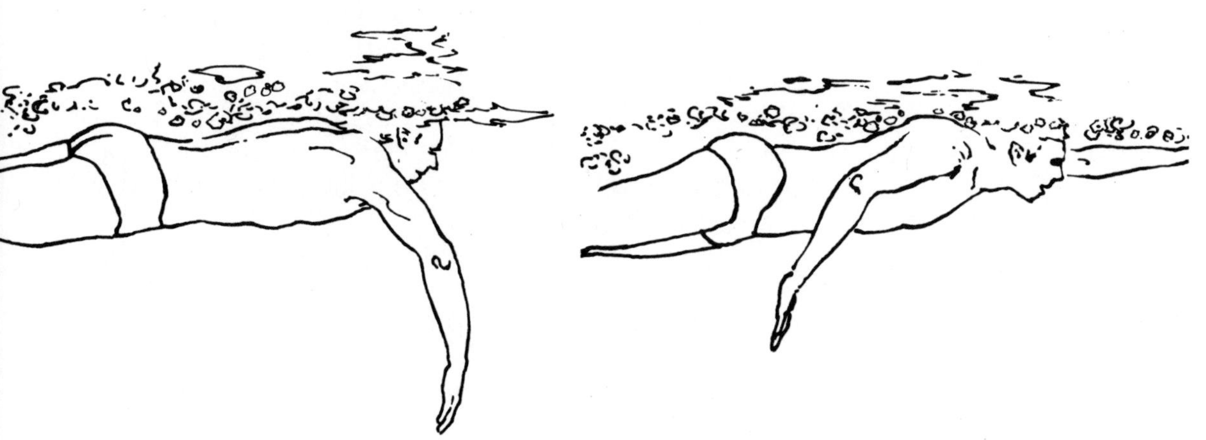

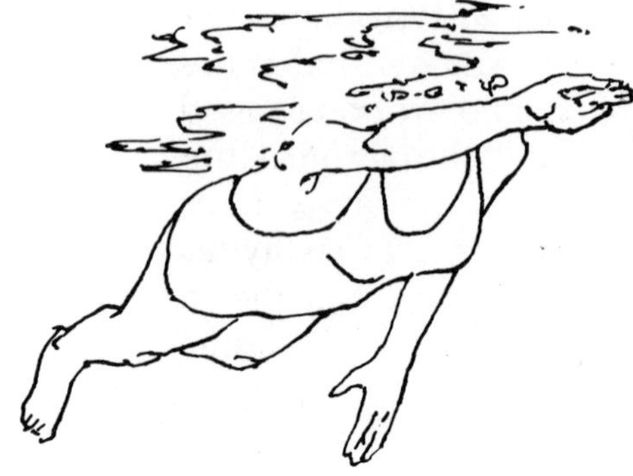

let your hand and forearm cross the centerline of your body. If this happens, your body will have a tendency to roll. To correct this motion your legs, which are already working to keep your body stable in the water, would be forced to work even harder.

Be careful not to overcompensate for this tendency by letting your arm slide too far to the outside of your body. Your hand should never move farther out than your shoulder. If it does you will dissipate much of the power you are getting from your shoulder.

The next part of the stroke comes as your hand passes through the midpoint. As mentioned earlier, your elbow should be bent at a right angle and it should be pointed out to hold your hand in the most efficient position. Don't let your hand or elbow drop or you'll lose some of your stroke power. Ideally at this midpoint your hand should still be perpendicular to the bottom of the pool. To continue the stroke, push your hand back toward your thigh, gradually extending and straightening your arm in the process, and keeping your hand perpendicular to the pool bottom as long as possible. Your hand should end the stroke by brushing lightly past the outside of your thigh.

At the end of the in-water stroke, as your hand moves past your thigh you must bend your wrist in order to keep your hand moving backwards. As you complete the stroke your upper arm leads the rest of your arm out of the water. Finally, just as the hand is ready to come out of the water you should rotate it, facing the palm inward toward your body so your hand exits the water little finger first.

To prepare yourself for the recovery — the above-water phase of the stroke — roll your shoulder and make sure your elbow is up high. Use your elbow to lead the recovery, letting the forearm swing naturally in front of the elbow as you sweep your whole arm for-

ward. In order to not waste time and motion, keep your hand low above the water—no more than 2 or 3 inches off the surface. Also, make it a point to keep your hand moving forward as close to your body as possible. Swinging your arm too wide will make you rock in the water, throw your hips out of line, and ruin the hydrodynamic profile of your body. At no point in the recovery phase should your hand ever be higher than your elbow.

Finally, let this part of the recovery be a relaxed, easy motion, not forced or rushed. Once you get into the rhythm of a steady, even stroke, the movement comes more naturally and effortlessly. You'll be concentrating your power on the pull-push motion of your in-water arm. There's nothing to be gained by straining the recovery arm.

In summary, your stroke will come in an in-water, out-of-water rhythm on each arm. Always keep the pressure firm and constant on your hand throughout the pull-push. And keep your wrist sensitive to the movement of your hand, bending it to maintain the force throughout the in-water phase.

Points To Remember

- Let your shoulders roll as you stroke. When one shoulder is involved in the in-water stroke, the other should be riding high, carrying your free arm through the recovery.
- Don't drop your elbows during any part of your stroke.
- Except at the beginning and the end of the in-water stroke, your elbows should be bent.
- During recovery, keep your hand close to your body and low to the water.

HEAD POSITION AND BREATHING

Many people succumb to the temptation to let the head roll from side to side too much throughout the crawl because they think it's a logical approach to the stroke. In fact, there should be a minimal amount of head motion in this stoke, even when taking a breath.

How you maintain the position of your head in the water when you're not taking a breath is important to your entire water posture. You should be looking forward with your head tilted down into the water at an angle of about 45 degrees. With your head positioned this way the waterline should just meet the top of your forehead. Of course, you have to turn your face away from the water in order to breathe. The side to which you turn is entirely up to you. There was a time when coaches told their swimmers that if they were right-handed they should breathe on the right, and if left-handed on the left. They now tell swimmers to breathe on whichever side feels the most comfortable, which is exactly what you should do. Experiment a little and in time you'll find that one side feels more natural.

Time your breathing on that side so that you turn your head for a breath when the same-side arm is pulling out of the water beginning the recovery. Your opposite arm should be just entering the water. As a general rule, try breathing during every other same-side recovery stroke. And do it by rolling your head as slightly as possible. If you turn your head during each

breathing-side recovery, or rotate it too far back during your breath, you'll break your rhythm and slow yourself down. Finally, try not to dip your opposite shoulder as you take your breath. You should be turning only your head, not your upper body. And get your face back into the water as quickly as possible after taking a deep breath.

Try to hold your breath until just before you are ready to come up for another breath. Exhale at the last moment, just prior to rolling your head to the breathing position. This helps prevent water from getting into your mouth and also gives you added buoyancy through most of the stroking sequence.

LOWER BODY

Your arms deliver most of the power in the crawl stroke. Your legs keep your body raised in the optimum position to use your upper-body power efficiently. Of all the kicks you may learn, the crawl flutter kick is the most efficient. But even this is no match for the pulling power you get from your arms. For that reason you have to kick your legs many more times than you stroke to add any real power to your swimming motion.

If you're not certain about the efficiency of your kick, or if you feel something is wrong with your basic form, you can practice easily enough by hanging onto the side of the pool and kicking away. Or you can work out with a foam-molded kickboard, which is usually more satisfying.

As you kick, you can think of your legs as two flexible shafts that whip up and down, bending only slightly. Your true power source is in your upper legs. To execute a good flutter kick, extend your legs with your toes pointed straight out. As you kick, whip the tip of your foot down 12 to 18 inches beneath the surface, with a sharp snapping motion. At the same time your other leg should be rising to a point just beneath the water's surface, in preparation for the next kick.

As you do this you will feel a slight rocking, or oscillation, in your hips. Try to minimize this as much as possible. The kick should come from the hip joint. You will also have to fight the temptation to let your hips roll as you stroke through the water — if you don't, you're simply wasting energy.

As you kick with each leg your toes should be pointed and there should be just a slight flexing in your knees. If you find that during a swimming session or during a kickboard workout you just aren't getting anywhere very quickly while kicking your legs off, you are probably bending your legs too much. Failing to keep your toes pointed also reduces the power gained through the kick.

Another sign of an inefficient kick style is heavy water turbulence. A decent flutter kick should leave only the slightest wake, and certainly shouldn't break through the water. In general you can let your heels and soles come close to the surface, but don't break through the water. Even experienced swimmers frequently make this mistake when they begin to take their kick form for granted.

Your kick should be tight and fast. It makes sense to aim for a tempo of six kicks for each full left-right arm stroke cycle. If this seems to be too rapid a pace, try two kicks per cycle and work your way up. Most swimmers maintain six beats per cycle, but experiment until you find a tempo that works for you.

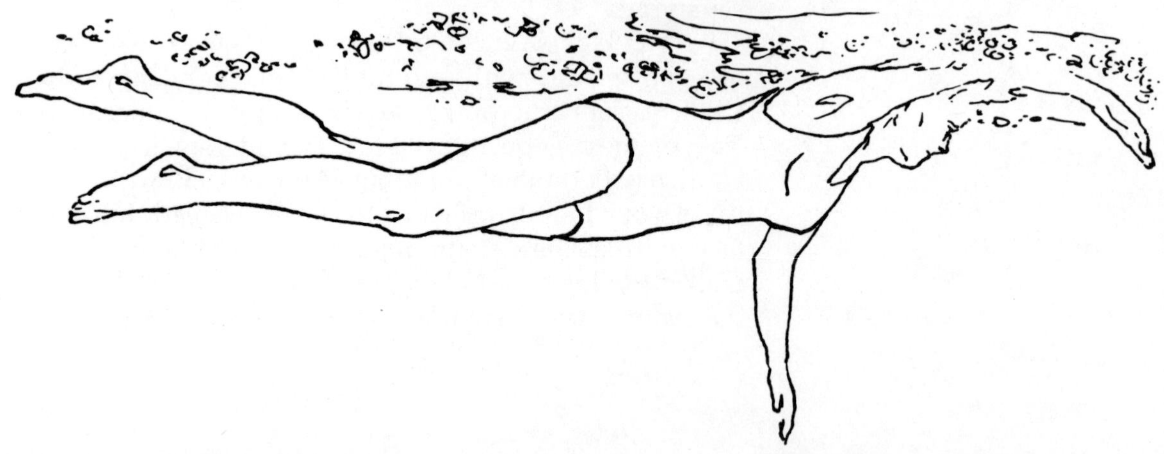

The secret to using a kickboard effectively is to hold it on the side without leaning on it. Don't press down. Just keep it stretched out in front of you. The idea is to keep your body riding horizontally in the water with your shoulders as low as possible. This helps approximate the position you assume while doing the crawl. Start out slowly, kicking until you get a whipping, snapping action in your legs with your toes pointed, your knees slightly flexed. As you get the hang of it, speed up your flutter kicks. You'll soon be able to do a six-beat kick rhythm with little effort.

Points To Remember

- Keep your legs moving, from the upper thigh.
- Bend your knees only slightly.
- Keep your ankles loose and stretched throughout the kicking sequence.
- Consistency and steady rhythm, not pure muscle, count in kicking. Concentrate on consistency.
- Strive for a six-kick-per-stroke cycle.
- The downbeat is the most forceful part of the kick. Emphasize it when you kick.

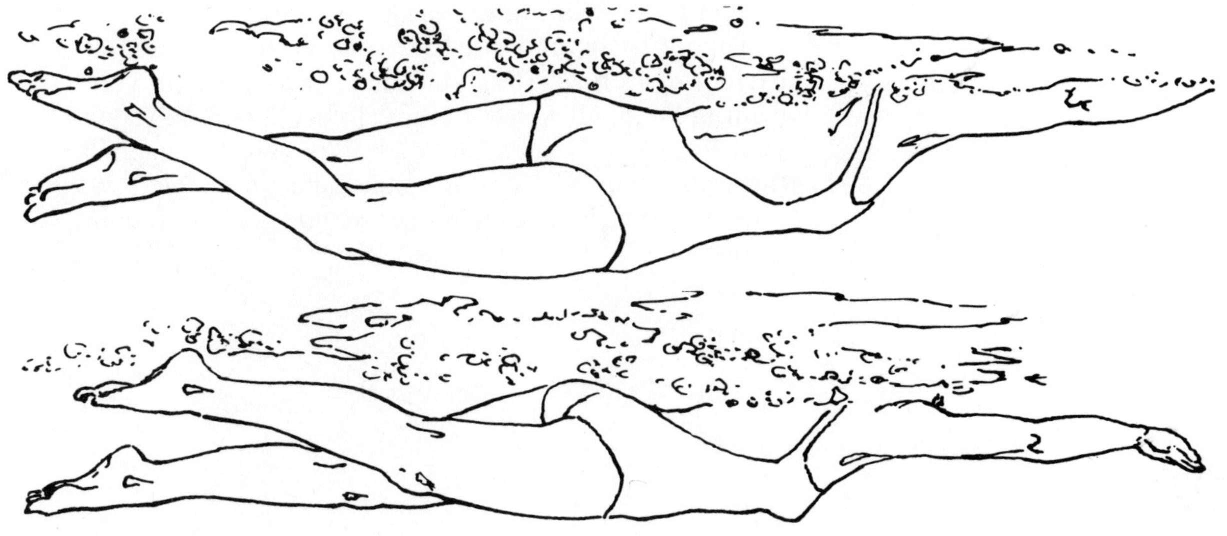

THE TURNS

The quickest turn you can make from the crawl stroke is the flip turn. This is a combination surface dive, somersault, spin, twist, and pushoff. It takes some practice to handle it properly but once learned, it's fun to do.

You need some distance, approximately a full body length, between you and the wall to do this. Practice is the only way you'll learn to gauge it correctly. Once you figure it out (by trial and error), start your turn by dropping your head while pulling directly up with your in-water stroke hand. This starts you into an underwater somersault.

Tuck your legs up to your chest as you begin to drop down into the water. The tighter the tuck, the better. This should accelerate you in spinning head over heels in the water onto your back. During the somersault you should twist a quarter-turn onto your side to begin regaining the proper body position, and place your feet, knees still cocked, in position against the wall. As you push off with your legs, continue turning your body another quarter turn so you begin your glide on your stomach. Extend yourself into a streamlined stroke position and glide away from the wall until you slow down to your swimming speed.

A more basic, and simpler to learn, turn is the fallback or open turn. Here you touch the wall with your leading hand, allow your elbow to bend, and, drawing your legs up, swing around and place your feet against the wall. Push off into the open water from this position and straighten yourself out as you glide into your next stroke.

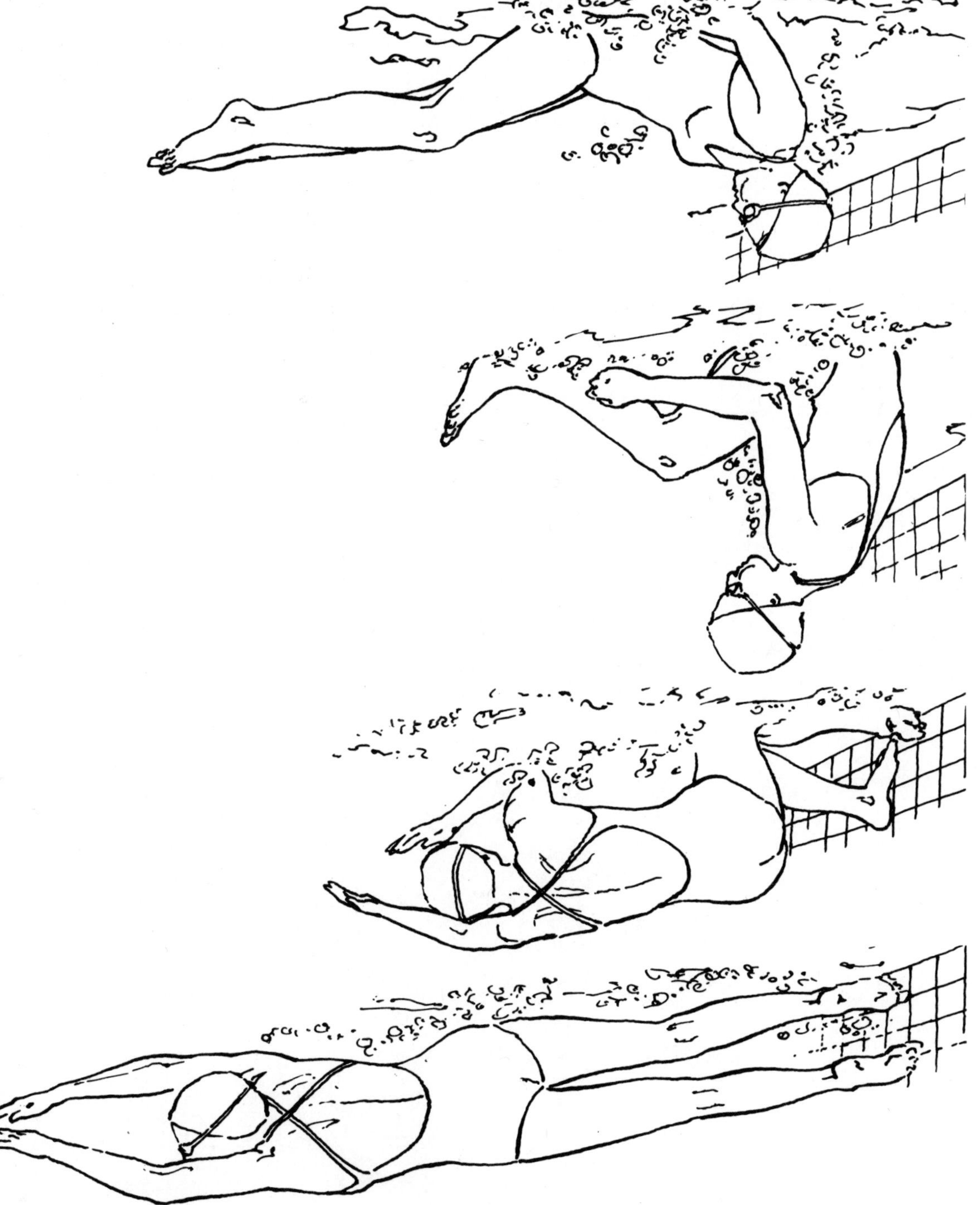

BACKSTROKE

The backstroke is an extremely fast way to move through the water. It also poses a problem, for it puts you in the unique position of seeing where you've been — not where you're going. This takes a little getting used to, but once you're comfortable you'll experience the backstroke as swimming at its purest and most enjoyable.

Half the secret of this dramatic and challenging swimming style is having the right water position. Once you attain the proper backstroke water "posture," the rest should come easily. And after you have the knack, you may find as many serious swimmers do, that this is one of your favorite workout strokes.

UPPER BODY

Form follows function in the backstroke. You should be riding high in the water, to minimize drag and to be able to move as smoothly and easily as possible. Keep your hips riding up just beneath the surface by arching your lower back slightly.

Head position is also critical. Your head should be as still as possible and tilted slightly up out of the water so that you are staring straight toward your toes. The water should meet the back of your head 2 to 3 inches below the center of the crown.

Don't consider your arm strokes as individual movements. Rather, they are changing elements in a larger continuous fluid motion. Each stroke is more than a simple arm movement. It involves your whole upper body. For the sake of an example, let's suppose your initial stroke is made with the left arm. The stroke really begins with your left shoulder and works its way out toward your hand.

Begin by rolling your shoulder over and back, keeping your arm extended but relaxed. Your head should be steady. Your upper body, however, will swivel slightly to the left as you do this. This is where flexibility in the shoulder is important. The shoulder and arm movement should be easy, graceful, and without extraordinary strain.

As you roll your shoulder, your arm and hand will descend toward the water. Your hand should cut through the water's surface, palm out, like a karate chop: the leading edge of your hand entering the water with your small finger hitting the water first. Your hand should cut into the water in line with your shoulder.

Once your arm and hand are in the water you begin your pull. At this point your entire arm, about to resemble roughly a hinged oar, will be primarily responsible for pulling your body along. As mentioned, you'll find that your upper body rolls naturally over toward your left side as you really start to dig in and draw yourself through the water. This will help increase the depth and power of your stroke.

Once your hand drops about a foot below the water's surface, make sure you allow your arm to begin bending. To increase your power, let your elbow drop and bend your arm to approximately 90 degrees. Throughout the major portion of the stroke your elbow serves as a fulcrum. Continue the movement. After the midpoint your hand and arm begin to push rather than pull. And your arm begins to extend. The stroke should be done as a single swoop.

As you finish this movement your arm should be fully extended—the hand finishing the stroke approximately mid-thigh. And your other arm and hand (in this example, your right) should already be cutting into the water. A poorly coordinated stroke cycle is one of the most frequent mistakes made by swimmers. One arm and hand should be entering the water as the other is in the final stages of the stroke. Also, as you move through the stroke, keep your shoulder relaxed. Your shoulder is a pivot point and is there to add power to your arm. Let it roll naturally.

The recovery part of this stroke is done by lifting your arm from the water straight up into the air, carrying through with the momentum of the stroke. Your wrist should be relaxed as your arm reaches out of the water. The only difference between entry and exit is that your hand breaks out of the water thumb edge first.

To maintain a fluid and even movement the timing of your pull/push and your recovery is important. Perhaps the most important thing to keep in mind throughout the backstroke is that you reach for a vertical plane during the recovery phase and position your forearm on a horizontal plane throughout much of the underwater pulling/pushing phase.

Points to Remember

• Keep your arm straight as you reach up and back.

• Keep your wrist slightly bent and your palm facing out as your hand enters the water.

• Relax and roll your shoulders and involve your entire upper body in the stroke.

• During the underwater phase of the stroke, maintain strong and even pressure on your hand.

• Let your hand sweep through on the pull/push movement.

• Complete the stroke forcefully by giving your hand a sharp, whipping motion. And get your arm up and out of the water for the recovery.

• Your hand should come thumb first out of the water—your palm facing inward.

• Keep your recovery arm straight and perpendicular to the surface. Roll your shoulder.

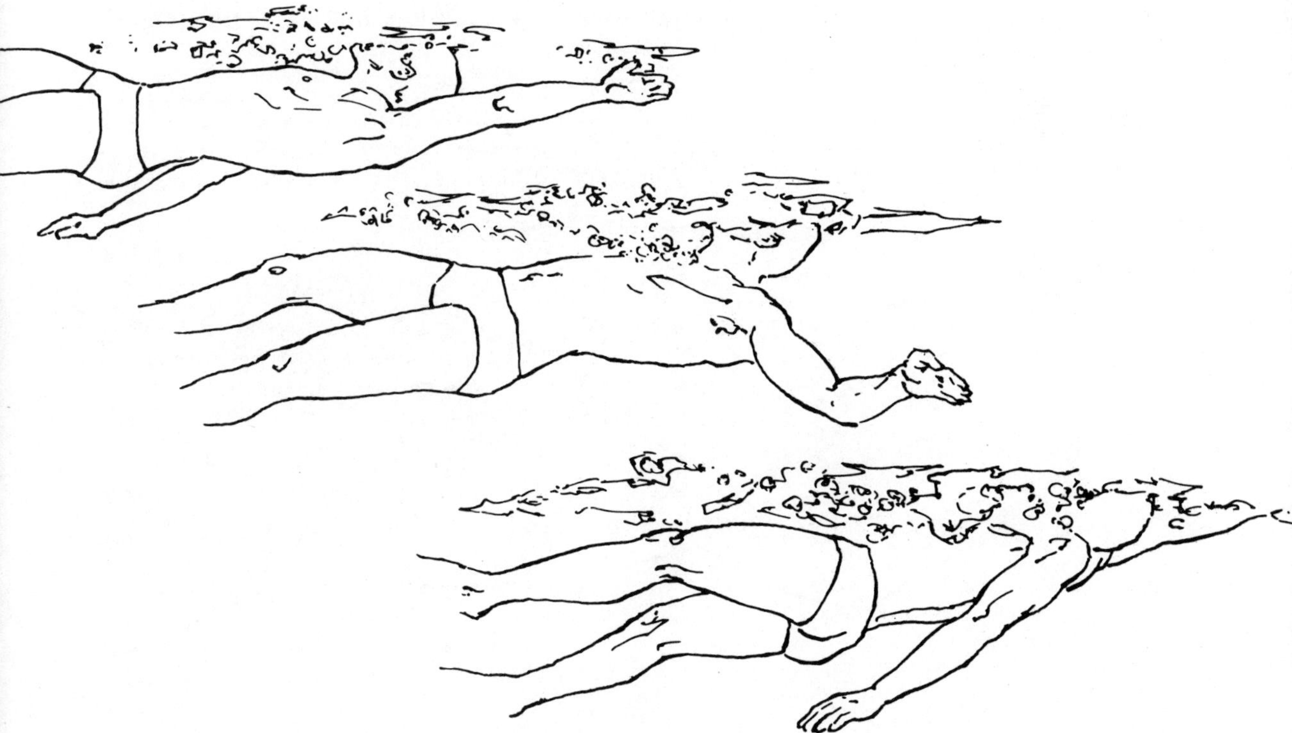

LOWER BODY

The backstroke kick is essentially just an upsidedown version of the crawl flutter kick. The chief difference is the timing of the power thrust. In the crawl most of the force is in the downbeat. With the backstroke it's the upbeat that is the power motion. And as with the other strokes, the kick is done primarily to stabilize your body and keep you riding properly in the water. Properly done it can, of course, give you added propulsion. To get both of these benefits you should take time to learn how to maximize the kick.

The backstroke kick is a shallow-water kick done ideally in a vertical space extending from 2 inches to 24 inches beneath the surface. Your primary source of power is in your hip and upper thigh. Let's suppose your right leg has just finished its downbeat. Your left leg should be completing the more powerful upbeat. As you reach the end of the kick the left leg should be straight, your toes pointed.

Then you begin the downbeat. Your left leg should still be straight as it kicks down, but your ankle should

be loose, allowing your foot to flex as you move your leg down. During this motion you can even allow your leg to stretch or hyperextend a little to get the most out of the downstroke. At this time your right leg is moving up, knee slightly bent, toes pointed. Your instep should feel the force of the water. On the upbeat your knee bends, raising your thigh toward the surface and cocking your foot down, toes pointed. Then your left leg should snap straight as though you were kicking an imaginary ball, sending a whiplike force through the water.

It's at this point that your right leg, completely straight, kicks down in a clean motion. This completes a complicated description of what is actually a very smooth and—once you do it correctly—a very simple sequence of motions. Once mastered, you can experiment until you find the kick beat that suits your individual style. Some swimmers do six beats for each left-right cycle of arm strokes. Others prefer a four-beat rhythm. Experiment until you find a rhythm that makes you comfortable.

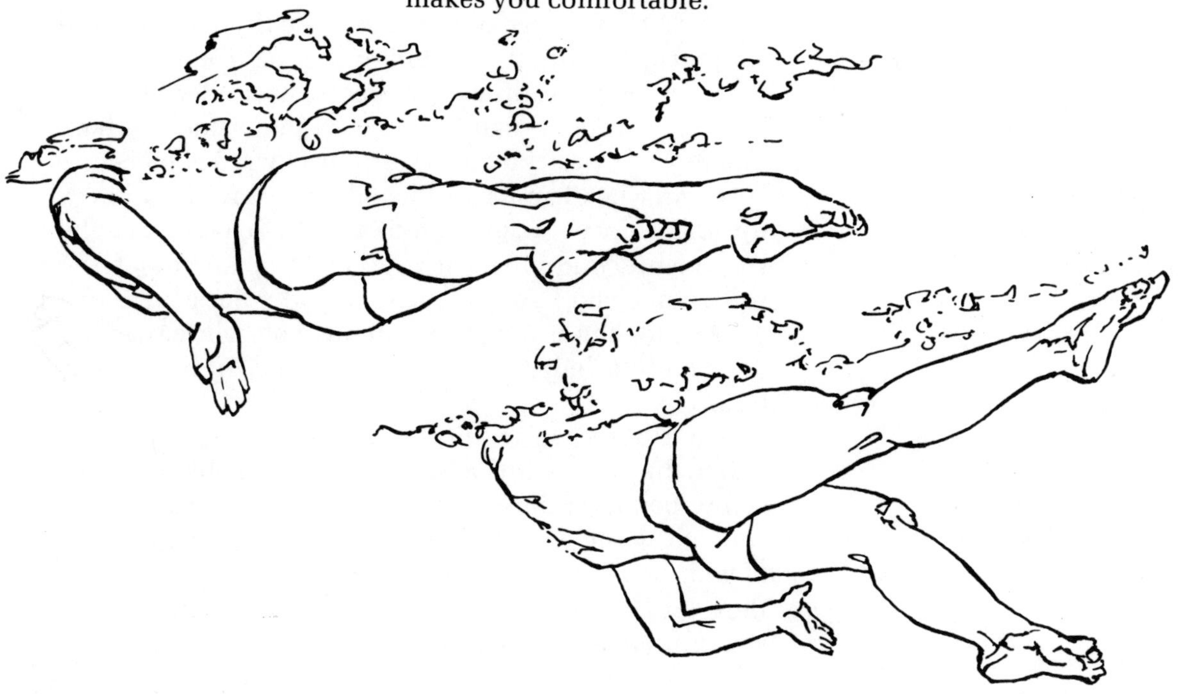

Points to Remember

- Keep your leg straight, ankle loose, on the downbeat.
- On the upbeat, bend your leg slightly at the knee. However, never break the surface.
- Don't kick more than 24 inches below the surface of the water. Don't break the surface on the upbeat.
- Minimize your hip roll as you kick. This will maintain stability and save energy.

THE TURN

The turn is a real moment of truth for the beginning backstroke swimmer for a couple of reasons. First, it is a little complicated. Second, there is the legitimate fear of hitting the wall before you get a chance to complete the turn. You will have to develop your own tricks—looking for a marking on the ceiling, for example, or, if you have a consistent style, simply counting your strokes.

You have a choice of two turns: the flip turn and the spin turn. The flip turn is highly acrobatic and slightly faster. As your leading hand nears the wall you begin pulling your other hand up toward the water's surface. The move is basically a twisting backward somersault. Drop your head and shoulders down, draw your knees up and into your chest, and roll backward. Let the somersault continue until your feet drop and touch the wall. Once you have touched, extend your arms above your head, hands together, and push off while twisting your body a half turn. This puts you firmly on your back.

The alternative to this is the spin turn. Here you touch the wall with your leading hand, letting your elbow bend. At the same time, raise your legs up and spin, allowing your other arm to swing in the direction of your body momentum. Swing your feet around until they touch the wall. Then push off, reassuming the streamlined backstroke position.

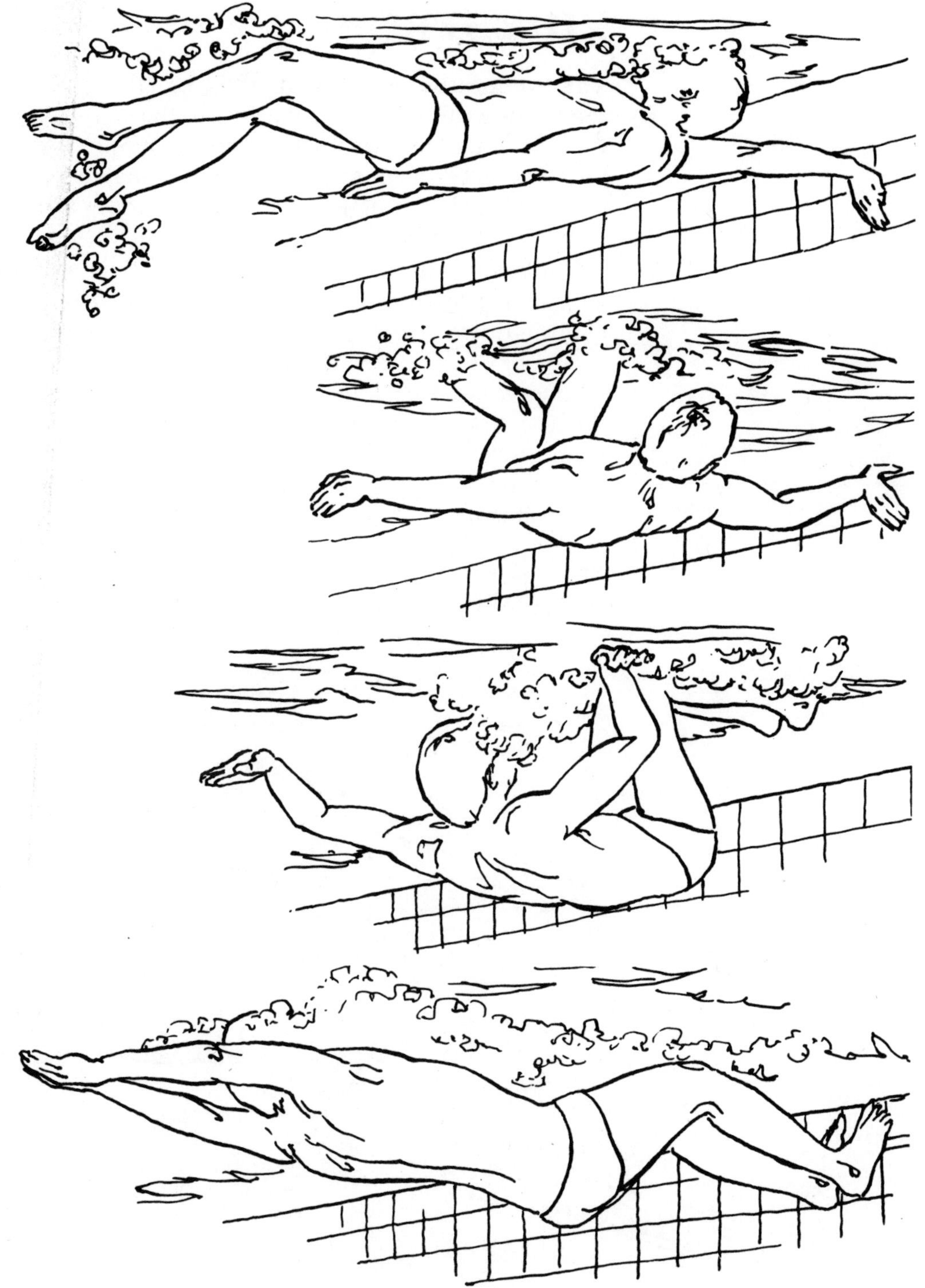

SIDESTROKE

There's nothing quite as soothing as gliding through the water with the easy synchrony of the sidestroke. Although this stroke was once used in competition it is today mainly recommended for long distances, as a carrying stroke for lifeguards, or just for relaxation. It's worth any swimmer's time to master it.

The sidestroke also serves as an excellent warm-up as you move into a full workout. And it's a good cooling-down stroke, just right for taking it easy in the water after an intense swimming session. It is, of course, a good back-up stroke in the middle of a distance swim, for example, if you find yourself tiring from your power strokes while still a good distance from shore. You can either stop and rest a bit by treading water or, by expending just a little more energy, switch over to the sidestroke and work your way in. Short of floating on your back with the tide, there's probably no easier way to move through the water.

UPPER BODY

Choose whichever side feels most comfortable to you for the sidestroke. What matters is how you ride in the water. Your neck should be turned up, lifting your head so the water level just barely brushes your lower cheek and your chin as you swim. To maintain proper body alignment, make an effort to keep your spine straight. This makes it possible for you to slip through the water in a streamlined fashion. As with all the other strokes, holding your water position—no unnecessary rolling, no jerky movements — increases your swimming efficiency.

To get into position for the stroke—assuming you're lying on your left side—extend your lower (left) arm fully forward. Your palm should be tilted downward and facing slightly to the front. Your high hand (in this example, the right) should rest on your upper hip, your arm lying along your side.

To begin the stroke, pull your left hand toward your chest, bending your elbow as you do. both your palm and the inner surface of your forearm will be used to

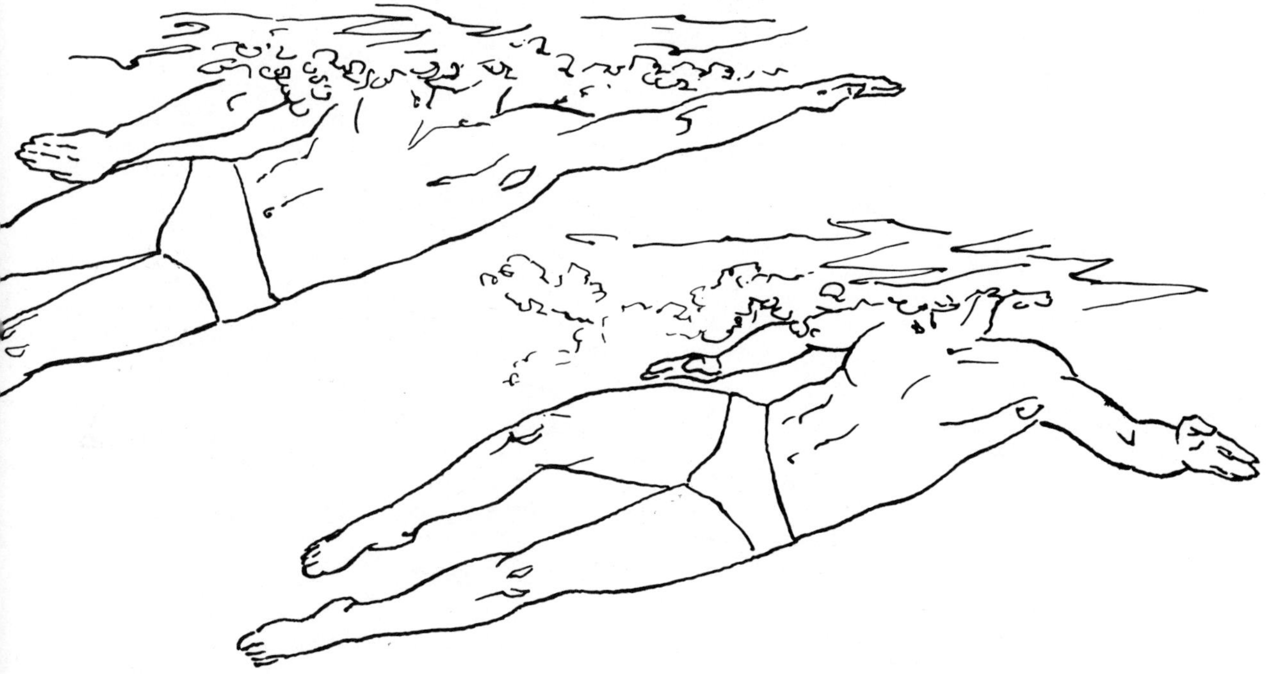

pull. As you move your hand and arm in past your shoulder, keep your elbow close to your body. Continue the motion as the pulling action becomes a rearward push.

Simultaneously, move your right arm and hand up toward your chest—elbow bent and palm facing down toward the bottom of the pool. To minimize drag, keep your arm and hand as close to your body as possible. At a point near your chin your hands will pass each other—your right hand moving forward, your left hand pulling back toward your feet.

Ultimately your lower (left) hand will finish the follow-through, ending the stroke near your thigh. A split second later this arm should shoot through its recovery phase, arm straightening and hand slicing through the water palm down for minimum resistance.

At the same time your upper (right) hand, which should now be up just beneath your shoulder line, should start pressing down toward your feet. When both arms are extended in opposite directions (lower arm forward, upper arm to the rear) you will be in your glide position.

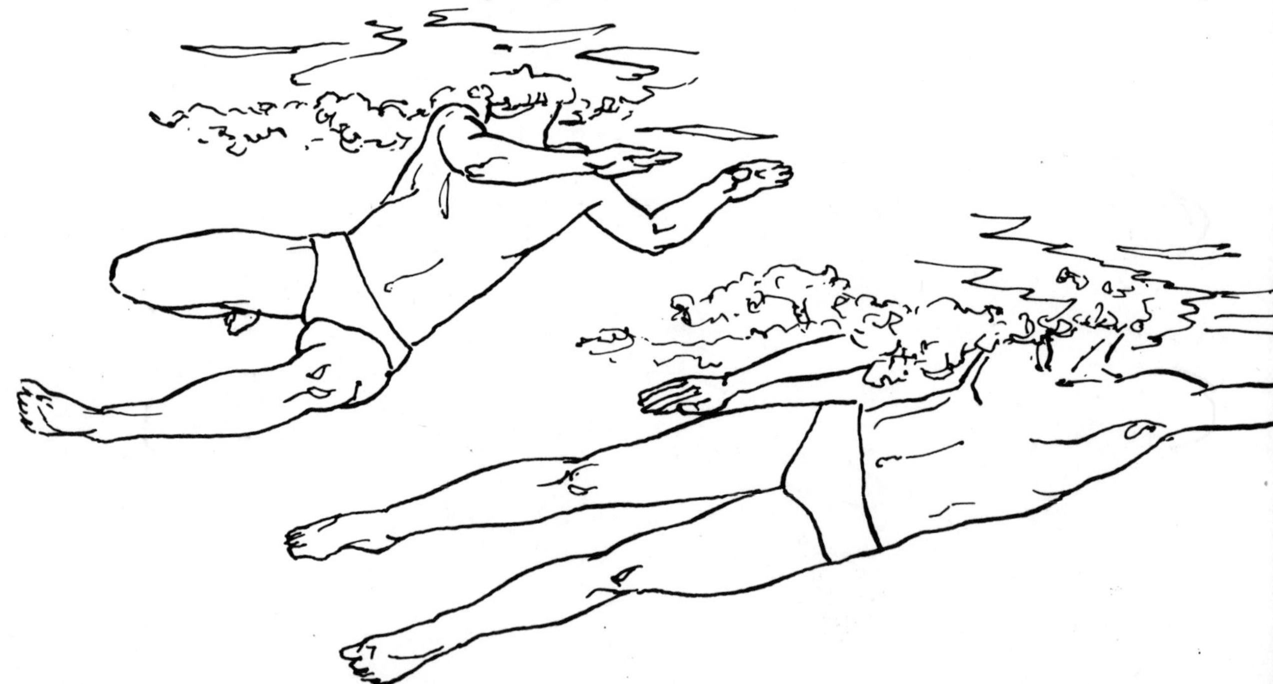

Points to Remember

- Lie on your side in a streamlined position.
- Keep your hands moving close to your body throughout all stages of the stroke.
- As your hands come together and pass, both elbows should be bent.
- Pull your lower arm in slightly toward the center of your body, not below it.
- The purpose of your lower arm pull is not only power. It is also to counteract the resistance of your dragging lower body. The upper arm, in combination with your kick, provides most of the thrust.
- Work on a smooth, even rhythm. Your hands should move in strong, even strokes.

LOWER BODY

The scissors kick is used for the sidestroke. The kick begins with you lying on your side. Bring your knees up to a point just below your waist. Your legs should be together, your toes pointed, your heels behind your buttocks. Keeping the legs bent, extend your top leg forward and your lower leg backward. Your top leg should be bent slightly more than your lower leg.

Now, with one sharp continuous motion, straighten your lower leg and partially straighten your bottom leg, snapping them together like the blades of a closing scissors. When you finish this motion your legs should be close to each other, in line with your upper body, with toes pointed. The inverted scissors kick is a variation on this. The top leg moves forward and the lower leg moves rearward. They are then scissored together.

Points to Remember

• For correct leg positioning draw your legs up so that your heels are under your buttocks. If your legs are too far forward, or back, you'll force a lop-sided kick. This will cause your body to swerve.
• In spreading your legs in preparation for the kick, use a relaxed and easy motion.
• Concentrate the power of your kick at the point where you bring your legs together.
• Straighten your leading leg before snapping it in.
• Your back leg should remain slightly bent until the very end of the kick, when it straightens and meets the leading leg.
• Keep your ankles flexible. Both feet will naturally point when you snap your legs together.
• Maintain a smooth, steady, cock-and-snap rhythm.

PUTTING THE STROKE TOGETHER

To view a well-coordinated sidestroke swimmer from above is to see what looks like someone alternately bunching his body into what appears to be a semi-fetal crouch and then stretching out into a long reaching glide. Specifically what happens with the kick and stroke is that when your legs are stretched out and then snapped together, your upper arm should also be finishing its pull and the lower arm should be reaching out ahead of you to begin a pull. Alternately, as your legs are cocking in readiness for the kick, your hands should be passing each other somewhere around your chin.

BREASTSTROKE

Of the major strokes available to a recreational swimmer the breaststroke is perhaps the most frequently used. There are a number of reasons for this. Not only does it offer you the luxury of seeing where you're going, it gives you a way of getting there that doesn't wear you out in the process. It is also tremendously practical. It's ideal for distance swimming, especially in rough and turbulent waters. It's a safe, protective stroke to use in debris-laden water, and it's a stroke used frequently in lifesaving.

Because of the stability and flotation gained through the breaststroke, it is only slightly more strenuous than treading water. It is probably the least tiring stroke to learn, for the movements in the water are basically natural body motions.

UPPER BODY

Proper body position is basic to an efficient stroke. The most important thing to remember in maintaining ideal water posture is to present as flat a profile as possible. Do not let the heavier, lower half of your body sink too deep as you move. Unlike the crawl, backstroke, and sidestroke, the breaststroke requires your arms to work together, simultaneously, throughout the stroke. You have to develop an even, symmetrical motion.

Let's start with your body in the glide position. Your arms are extended straight out in front of you. Your hands should be close to each other, palms facing down and slightly out to the sides, 6 inches below the water's surface. You begin the stroke by moving your arms, still extended, out to the side 6 inches below the surface. Rotate your hands so that your palms are facing firmly against the water. Move with a symmeterical sweep.

Bend your elbows slightly as you begin to feel the pressure of the water on your hands. Allow your forearms and hands to sweep both out and down. The more you move through the stroke, the sharper the bend in the elbow becomes. Throughout the stroke, concentrate on maintaining what is termed the "high elbow" position. This means keeping your elbows up toward the surface of the water and the backs of your upper arms roughly parallel to the surface. During the

stroking, your hands and forearms should dig down into the water but your upper arms should move on roughly the same plane throughout the stroke.

You should continue sweeping through the stroke until you have pulled your hands back to a point even with your shoulder line. Once you reach that point, draw your hands into the center of your chest and, with palms facing each other, extend your arms into the basic glide position.

Hand and forearm position is especially critical throughout this stroke. As you reach the glide position with your arms extended, the palms of your hands should face out and slightly down, your thumbs touching so that the backs of your hands form a V. As you move into the stroke you should be continually changing the angle of hand/water contact so that throughout most of the pull your hands will be facing rearwards and slightly in toward your body. Viewed from the front, the upper arms of a breaststroker basically move out to line up with the shoulders while the forearms and hands appear to move out, down, and back up to the body.

BREATHING

Taking a breath is considerably easier with the breaststroke than it is with the crawl. You take a breath with each full stroke. The technique for doing so is relatively easy to master. Very simply, you should lift your head out of the water high enough to inhale through your mouth, but no higher. If you raise your head too high, you will force the lower half of your body down into the water. This will throw your body off line. Keep your shoulders steady as you raise your head. Use your neck muscles to lift your head just enough for your mouth to clear the water's surface, and inhale deeply.

You should hold your breath as long as possible through the stroke before exhaling. The ideal time to exhale is just as you begin the pull. Then, during the latter stages of the pull, inhale deeply. When your head is in the water, before and during exhaling, face forward and down so that you are looking through the water at an angle of approximately 45 degrees.

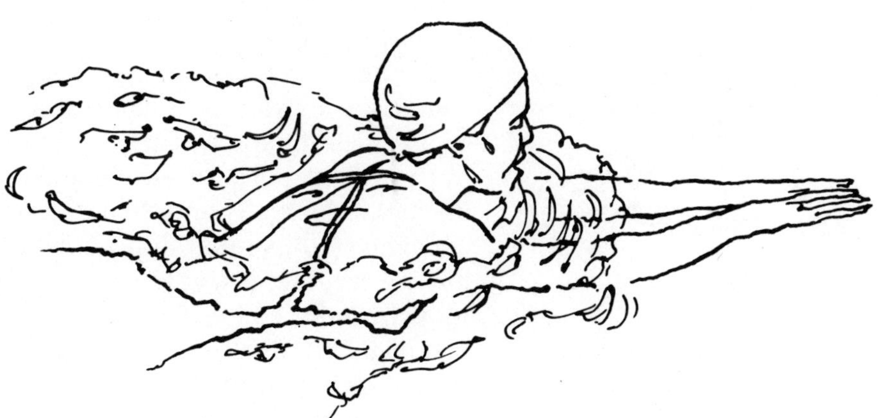

KICKS

Throughout the breaststroke you move your legs in a pattern that is an upside-down and reversed version of the motions you make with your arms. Let's suppose you are moving into your glide, ready to start the kick. At one time this kick was called the frog kick. Coaches encouraged their swimmers to mimic the contorted kick of that amphibian. It has since been modified to a less difficult and considerably more efficient flick kick.

During the beginning of the glide your legs should be extended and ankles relaxed, your feet pointing straight behind you. As you begin to kick, flex your knees, dropping them down, and draw your heels as close to your buttocks as you can. Your knees should be spread 18 to 24 inches apart. Your feet, the soles facing nearly skyward, should be 12 to 18 inches apart. Hold this position just long enough to cock your legs for the kick. At this point your feet should be at right angles to your lower legs.

Snap your legs straight back and together with a hard thrust—the power emanating from your pelvic area. In the last phase of this movement you should again flex your ankles so that your toes are pointed rearward. As you kick back and extend and straighten your feet, you should feel the force of the water on your feet. Extending the feet gives an added push to your leg movements. Glide briefly and then repeat the cycle.

If you're uncomfortable with this kick, or if you're having trouble coordinating it with your upper-body motion, take some time to work out alone with a kickboard. A final thing to keep in mind concerning your kick is to keep your heels beneath the water's surface throughout your entire motion. Any kicking that takes your feet out of the water wastes energy and power.

BRINGING IT ALL TOGETHER

Because the breaststroke requires what can be termed a pulsating power source, rather than the continual kicking and pulling of most other strokes, it requires slightly more concentration in coordinating kicking, stroking, and breathing.

Breathing is, of course, related directly to your armstrokes. And your armstrokes are related directly to your kick — that is, you are pulling with your arms when your legs are in their extended and recovery phases, and you are recovering with your arms when your legs are in the kick phase. Your arm and leg movements must be coordinated this way so you avoid "dead" power spots and maintain your momentum.

Here's a typical kick-stroke cycle. As you begin your pull, your legs are straight. You exhale as you pass the midpoint of your arm pull stroke, and as you finish the pull, you raise your face and mouth out of the water and inhale deeply. At that point you should be cocking your legs and moving your arms together and forward as you move into the glide. A split-second later you finish your inhalation and duck your face back into the water. Kicking at this instant sends you sliding forward through the glide.

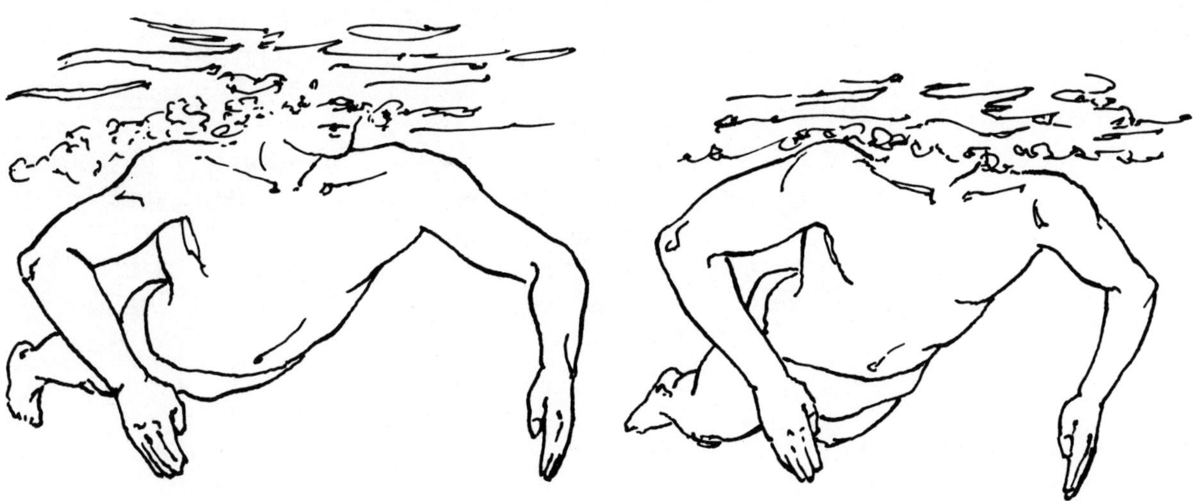

BUTTERFLY

The butterfly, an outgrowth of the breaststroke, was developed in the 1930's. It was officially sanctioned for Olympic competition in the mid-1950s.

That it took some 25 years to become accepted is understandable. Compared to the more conventional strokes—the backstroke and crawl, for example—it is a truly bizarre way to move through the water. And it is tremendously exhausting. Swim experts do not recommend it for beginning swimmers, and in fact, only the strongest experienced swimmers ordinarily utilize the butterfly as a basic stroke.

Among spectators, however, the butterfly has become very popular. It's showy and it's fast. It is, next to the crawl, the fastest water sprint-stroke.

UPPER BODY

More than any other stroke, the butterfly makes grueling demands on the upper body. And although it often appears that there is a lot of up and down motion with this stroke, there is actually much less than meets the eye, if and when the stroke is carried out properly. In order to reduce the strain on your arms, back, and shoulders, the up and down motion must be minimized. Through every phase of the stroke you must keep your body on as flat a plane as possible.

The stroke takes some getting used to and should be built up to over a period of time. Each in-water stroke cycle begins with you face down in the water and your arms extended straight out in front of you, approximately shoulder-width apart. Your hands should be facing palm out and tilted slightly down as you cut into the water.

Keeping your arms straight, begin to sweep your arms out to the sides. At the beginning of the sweep

you'll feel your hands "catch" in the water. And at this point you should start pulling more deeply down through the water with your hands. As you press your hands and forearms down, your elbows will, of course, bend. Make a point of keeping your elbows high in relation to your hands and as close to the surface of the water as possible throughout the stroke.

Continue pulling your hands, palms facing backwards, through the water. As you'll soon notice, this down and back stroking action creates a tendency for your head and shoulders to rise up out of the water.

Continue your stroke slightly in and back toward your hips, extending your arms. Just before the end of the stroke, give one last hard push with your hands and forearms to prepare for the recovery phase.

To begin the recovery, lead your arms out of the water by raising your elbows high. Moving your hands forward close to your body, extend your arms. Dig firmly into the water with your hands, and repeat the in-water action.

Points to Remember

- As your hands enter the water beginning the stroke, your palms should be facing out and slightly down.
- Keep your elbows on a plane higher than your wrists throughout the stroke.
- Once your hands pass beneath your shoulders, start pulling them slightly in towards your sides. Increase the bend in your elbows.
- During the final stages of the pull, keep your elbows up. Your hands, palms facing rearward, should be perpendicular to the bottom of the pool.
- To begin the recovery, lead your arms up and out of the water with your elbows.
- As you throw your arms forward, keep your hands close to the surface of the water.
- Practice making the recovery as fast as possible. Arm speed is critical.

BREATHING

You inhale during the final phase of the in-water arm stroke (after your arms have passed the halfway point of the pull).

The breathing cycle actually begins as your hands enter the water and you commence the downstroke. Raise your head as your elbows begin to bend during this downstroke. Exhale as you raise your face from the water. Exhale forcefully. And, during the latter phase of the in-water stroke, just before the beginning of your recovery motion, inhale deeply. (This should take place during a kick downbeat.) Then, quickly drop your face back into the water. Strive to inhale only on alternate full stroke cycles.

Practice inhaling quickly, your lower lip just clear of the water. Also, concentrate on using only your neck, not your shoulder muscles, to raise your head. This minimizes the shifting of your body angle in the water and makes it easier to maintain your pace.

KICK

During the early years of the stroke's development the frog kick was used exclusively. Now, however, most swimmers prefer the much more powerful dolphin kick. This kick begins with your body as a straight line, legs extended and toes pointed. For the upbeat you must thrust your hips, thus moving your whole lower body up towards the surface of the water. On the downbeat bend your knees slightly and cock your bent legs up. Then drop your knees slightly towards the bottom of the pool, and allow your legs to bend a bit more. When your legs are in this position, straighten them in a fast, whip-like action, exerting power from your hips and thighs.

Although your toes should be pointed throughout the kick, your ankles should remain flexible, giving you a little additional whipping action. When you finish this downbeat your legs will be straight (possibly slightly hyper-extended) and your hips slightly raised up in the water. For the upbeat, sweep back toward the surface, keeping your legs straight through the initial half of the motion. Finish the upbeat by bending and cocking your knees so that you can immediately follow with the downbeat.

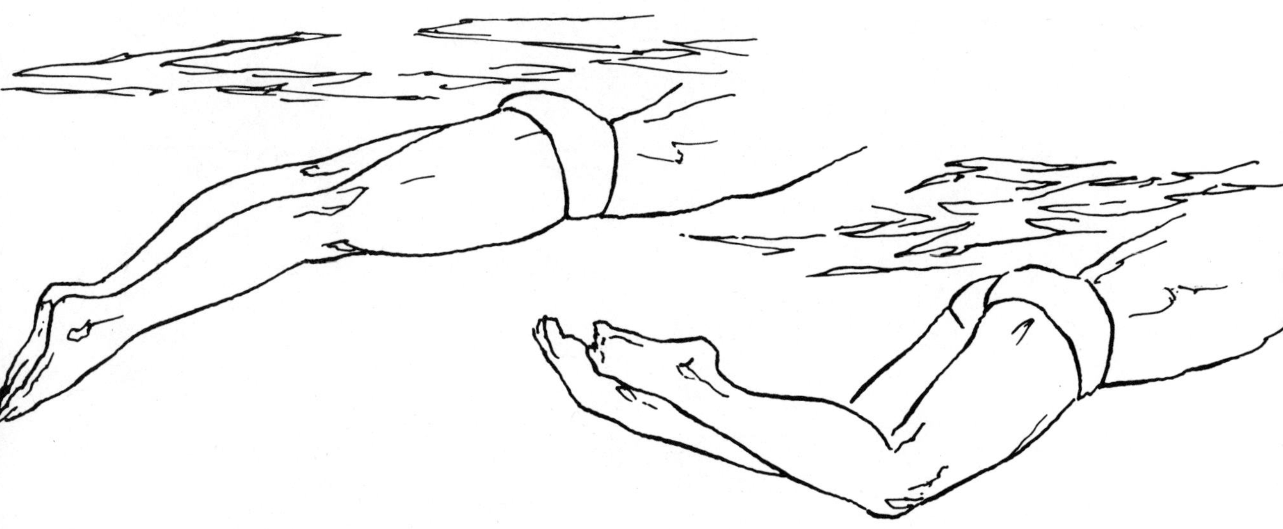

Points to Remember

- Try to keep your legs side by side throughout the kick.
- Bend your knees no more than 45 degrees to gain thrust for the downbeat. One of the most common kicking errors is to allow the legs to bend too much.
- Never let your feet break the surface.
- As your heels move up, lower your thighs.
- Work on building up the speed of your feet.
- Throw your whole body into each kick. This kick requires more hip and leg force than do other kicks.
- Visualize your lower body and legs as a flexible shaft. Try to duplicate a whipping action.
- There is no pause between the downbeat and the upbeat.

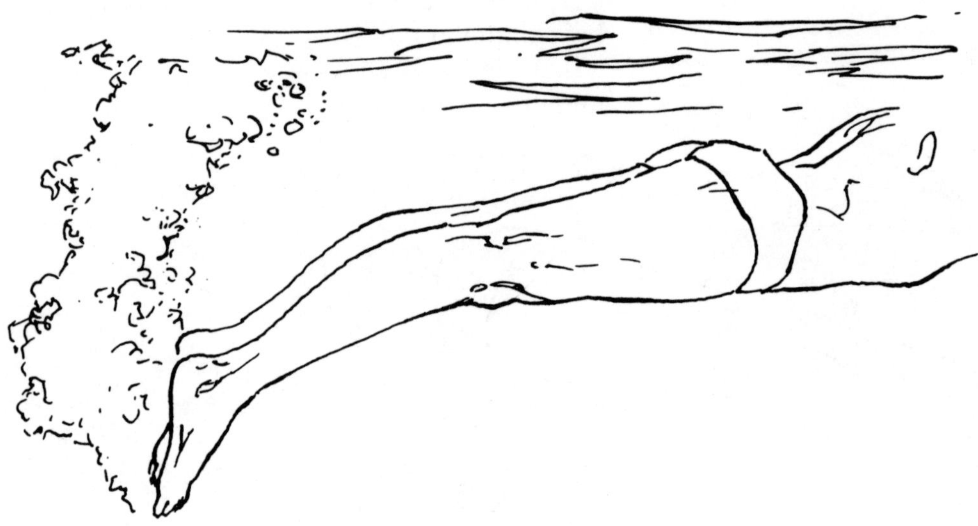

PUTTING IT ALL TOGETHER

Perhaps the most important thing to remember about the butterfly is that the stroke/kick ratio is rigid. For every in-water-recovery arm cycle, you must do two complete upbeat-downbeat kicks. The reason for this is that you need that constant momentum to keep your body moving on a streamlined plane. Your arms can't do it alone. Even after you're comfortable with the stroke and the kick, it sometimes takes a while to bring them together into a smoothly coordinated series of motions.

Your legs should be cocked and beginning a downbeat just as your hands are digging into the water to initiate the pulling phase of the stroke. The second downbeat should begin when your arms are a little more than halfway through the pull and are starting to swing back up to the surface of the water.

You need the first kick because during your arm recovery your power is at a low ebb; that is, your body is moving at its slowest. Only additional thrust can main-

tain the momentum. The second kick adds power to the final stage of your in-water stroke and balances off the destabilizing effect the arm stroke has on your body position.

Take your time as you practice the two-kick/one-stroke ratio and become comfortable with its rhythm. Too often swimmers forget and wear themselves out by kicking indiscriminately throughout the stroke.

As you gain control over the stroke motions, work on the finer style points. For example, since you'll be lifting your head to breathe only on every other cycle, remember to keep your face turned down and slightly forward throughout the non-breathing stroke. This makes your body more streamlined. Finally — a small point — one of your kicks, usually the first, should be the stronger of the two in each pair. It's a habit worth developing. It gives consistency to your overall motion.

THE TURN

Turning is the simplest part of the butterfly stroke. The only really tricky part is in the timing. You should be an arm's length from the wall just as you finish your recovery. In this way, your hands will touch the wall simultaneously with the completion of a stroke cycle. As you near the wall, adjust your strokes — shorter or longer—to touch at this point in your reach.

As your arms touch the wall, bend them slightly. Then, in a single motion, release one hand, tuck in your legs, and swivel your body, swinging your feet against the wall. If you plan to turn to the right, release your right hand and bring your right shoulder back and around. Push off with your trailing arm (in this instance the left). Swing this arm around to meet your leading arm in a streamlined position. Push off strongly with your legs and send your body into a glide. As your glide slows down to swimming speed, start your butterfly with a kick downbeat and a pull with your arms.

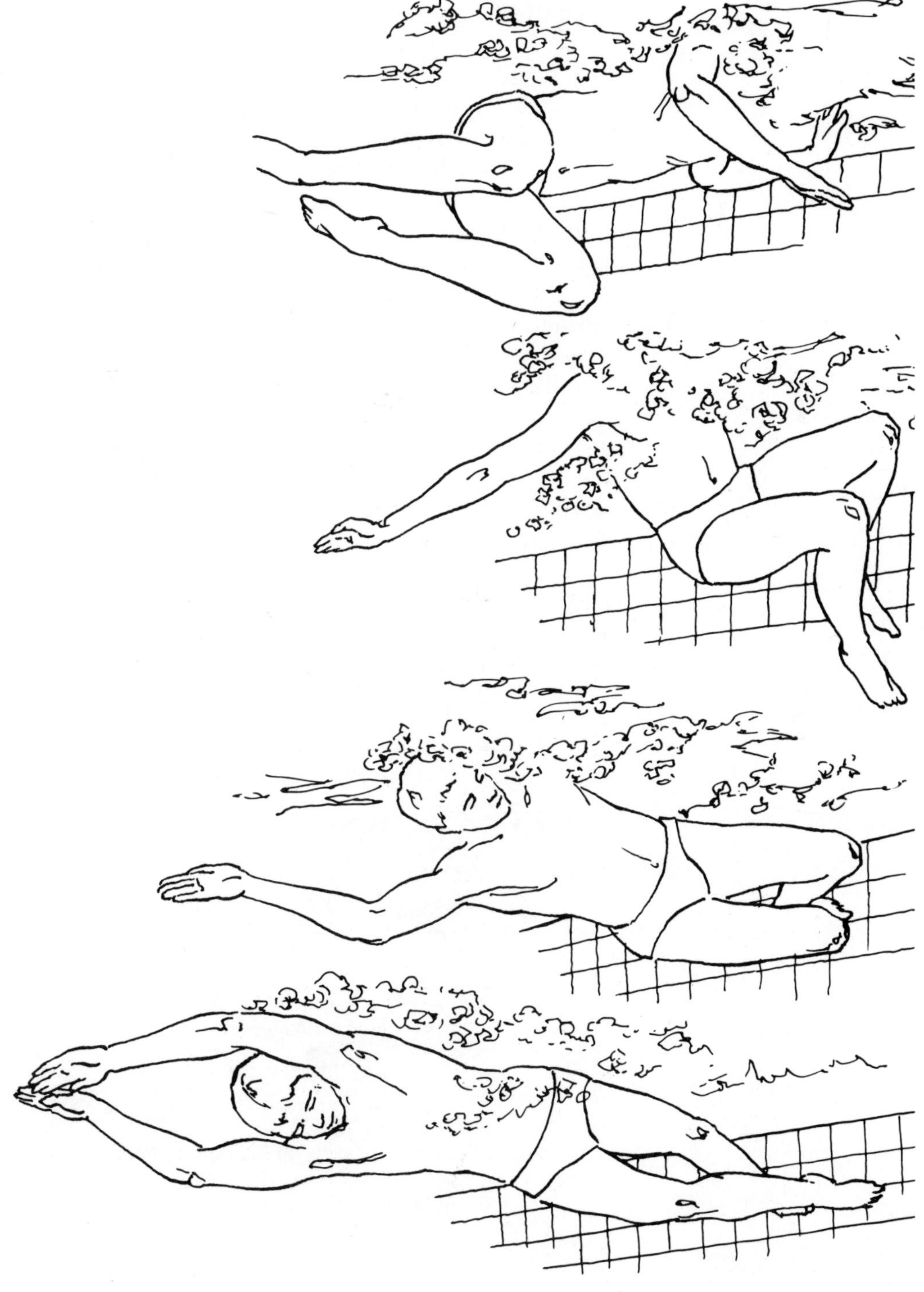

DIVING

If you feel comfortable in the water, you should work on a few dives. Not the intricate and dangerous board or platform dives done in competition — you need a personal coach for those — but some basic ways to get into the water quickly and comfortably.

If you've never dived before, find a quiet part of the pool where the water is at least three feet deep. Sit on the ladder or on the edge with your feet curled over the gutter. To get in position, tilt your head down, chin on chest, and extend both arms out in front. Thumbs should be touching and your palms should be facing down. Your biceps should be up to your ears. Now, keeping your eyes *open,* focus on a point in the water about three feet away, take a breath, and pushing off with your feet, arrow yourself into the water, hands first.

When you're comfortable with that, try a standing dive. Stand at the pool's edge with one foot curled over the edge and the other foot slightly behind. Position your arms as before, focus on that point and, after bend-

ing your knees, push off and out and down with one easy motion.

The racing dive, although considerably more interesting, is only slightly more complicated. Stand with both feet at the pool edge, your toes curled over the edge. Bend your knees slightly and bend over at the waist with your arms extended straight in front of you. To start, swing your arms back, and then swing them forward again, simultaneously pushing off with your legs and throwing yourself out over the water. You should travel out and up slightly so that you hit the water at a slight angle, hands first.

To try to dive off a *low* board, first do a regular standing dive from its tip to familiarize yourself with the sensation of diving from that height. To do it with a bounce, hold your arms straight out in front, then swing them back, bending your knees. When your arms swing forward again, bend your knees a second time and push up and off, putting your hands together over your head in the streamlined position. Follow the natural arc, straightening your body and legs as you move through the air. Hit the water hands first.

Moving Out

When you start swimming training you will have both physical and mental obstacles to overcome. The first physical obstacle is soreness. Muscles that haven't been used heavily before will naturally get stiff and sore. Fortunately this overall soreness of the breaking-in period will pass quickly once you get into the rhythm of your workout schedule.

More specific pains may linger. One type is what is known as a side stitch, a sudden sharp pain in your lower abdomen. According to Dr. Gabe Mirkin, this is very often a "gas pain" in your colon, or lower intestine. What happens is that your intestinal tract contracts rapidly as you exercise, pushing gas toward the rectum. If a hard stool blocks the way, you have pain—a side stitch. Two other possible causes for pain he suggests are eating too close to exercise time, and food allergies to milk or wheat products. When there's a lot of food in your stomach, blood also collects there to help your digestion. As a result, less blood is flowing to your intestinal muscles, and you get a stitch there. Also, some people don't have the right enzymes for digesting milk or wheat products and may get cramps in the abdomen that feel somewhat like side stitches.

CONTROLLING STITCHES AND CRAMPS

Dr. Mirkin offers various dietary suggestions for avoiding side stitches:

- Eat more fruits and vegetables and fewer starches (bread, potatoes, and spaghetti).
- Avoid eating three to five hours before heavy exercising.
- Avoid milk or wheat products up to 48 hours before

exercise time if you suspect you have difficulty digesting them.

It sometimes also helps if you time your bowel movements before an exercise session to avoid gas pain. If in spite of these precautions you do get a side stitch, push your fingers into the site of the pain and exhale slowly, Dr. Mirkin says. The pain will eventually disappear and you can continue swimming. Swim at a slightly slower pace to avoid having the problem again.

Cramps can suddenly and viciously tighten a muscle into a painful knot. Straining or injuring a muscle can set off a cramp, and so can the deficiency of certain dietary components such as salt, or minerals like potassium or magnesium.

According to Dr. Mirkin, shortage of potassium is probably the most common and one of the most overlooked causes of muscle cramps. We need potassium to keep firing the nerves that control muscle cells. People who have a potassium shortage may suffer from low blood sugar, indigestion, and muscular weakness. Eating more fruits and vegetables will help replace the potassium you use up in your system and, according to Dr. Mirkin, will decrease the chance of cramps.

Do not be daunted by the trouble your feet and legs give you while learning to swim, for it is only then you will have to eat the sour of the fruit. It will be all ripe, mellow, and sweet after you have learned it.

-JOHN LEAHY
The Art of Swimming in the Eton Style, 1875

Princeton University swim coach Rob Orr has found that, generally speaking, the better the condition of his swimmers, the less likely they are to have trouble with pains from side stitches and cramps. Of the two problems, side stitches tend to be a little more common. Orr has found two procedures seem to help control side stitches. One is to breathe on the same side as the stitch. For some reason this seems to help it clear up more quickly, if the swimmer keeps moving. The other is to apply rhythmic finger pressure to the location of the stitch. Press for 10 seconds and release pressure for 10 seconds. This on/off method works well for some, says Orr.

RANKLY, MY DEAR . . .

The second obstacle to swimming as a daily fitness habit is your state of mind. There are probably times when you feel really sluggish and dragged out. You know in your heart that exercise is good for you, and that you feel better after you've done it, and you know you should keep it up—but some days you just don't give a damn. It seems like too much of an ordeal to suit up, much less slip into the pool and do your regular number of laps.

There is no sure cure for these times when your brain and body feel stale, but you can minimize some of the natural reluctance you might feel about exercising by making it a habit, same time, same place. The habit will carry you a little, so you'll be working almost on automatic pilot as you prepare for a swim session. Once you get in the water, don't think of your total laps. That way you don't immediately get discouraged—"My God, ten laps! I'll never make it." Set yourself short-term goals—"If I feel O.K. after four laps I'll try a couple more"—and work accordingly. You may find four laps is all you'll want to do, but more likely than not, once you're warmed up and get in the rhythm of your workout, you'll find yourself finishing out the whole session.

It is interesting for me to work in the water and not simply against static weight. The resistance provided by the water allows for smooth movement and mobility and I think this is in itself a terribly valuable thing.

-EDWARD VILLELLA
The Water Beauty Book

KEEPING IT FRESH

Now, one of the problems of swimming, or for that matter any steady repetitious exercise, is that it can be boring. One of the simplest ways to cope with this is to find someone to swim with. Time passes a lot more quickly and you and the other swimmer can make a competition out of the exercise session to keep it interesting.

Since this isn't always possible, you sometimes have to rely on your own ingenuity to get through a session. One mind trick some people use is playing their favorite songs back in their heads as they swim. Just settle on a rhythm

Endure and persist. This pain will turn to your good in the end.

-OVID
c. 10 A.D.

that suits your swim tempo and stroke and kick to your own mental tune. Marathon swimmer Diana Nyad says that she simply counts stroke cycles to herself on her long swims to occupy her mind. Or if you're weak in one particular aspect of your swimming style—your kick, your breathing, your recovery—spend your swim time concentrating on that. That serves a double purpose; you both improve your swim style and keep your mind occupied.

MAKING PROGRESS

As in any sport, as you gain proficiency you learn ways of increasing your efficiency. For example, your breathing technique can make a great difference, especially with the crawl stroke. One mistake many novice swimmers make is to exhale by letting the air trickle out of the mouth in a thin string of bubbles. Olympic athlete Don Schollander recommends holding your breath and then releasing it in a single explosive blast just when you feel you can hold it in no longer. This helps your body make more use of the oxygen you've absorbed. There is a trick to inhaling too. Schollander says that some people make the mistake of opening the mouth too wide and end up swallowing water as well as air. The trick, says Schollander, is to open just one side of your mouth, the side farther from the water, and suck in air. There is a small air pocket formed there by the wake of your head moving through the water. By breathing through one side of your mouth, you take advantage of this small air pocket and can draw in air without taking in water.

BREAKING YOUR RECORDS

To keep your interest from flagging, it helps to have some type of goal. Distance is a simple one. As you get stronger you will most likely want the challenge of a greater distance. Even that may not be enough for some people. If you want to stir up your competitive juices you can also plot some of your practice sessions against the clock. Some coaches and dead-serious amateurs use a poolside pace clock, basically an oversized stop watch. You can probably do just as well with any wall clock that happens to be near the pool. But if you really want precise measurements and there is no pace clock available, for about $70 you can get a waterproof digital watch that has a built-in stop watch. They're available in most electronics and department stores under various brand names (usually the same companies that make pocket calculators).

LAYING WITH PACE

Swimming coaches realize that their athletes' minds as well as their bodies need stimulation, and for that reason, they use a variety of training techniques. The ones you most likely will use are: steady pace; slow/fast; interval training; fartleks; and a group event called the dauerlauf.

Steady pace. The most common way you'll be swimming is with a steady dependable rhythm, back and forth the length of the pool. This is a good steady stressor on your muscles, heart, and lungs, and it helps increase your endurance in a gentle way. For example, you might set yourself a goal of 500 yards and take a quick peek at a clock to see if your pace is holding up. The only problem with this is that a daily routine of nothing but steady-paced swimming can get a little monotonous. If that becomes your problem you have other choices.

Slow/fast. One method developed for and often used by high-powered swimmers is called, by swimming coach "Doc" Counsilman, "out slow–back faster." It is done just about the way it sounds. Divide your total practice swim distance into two equal halves. Swim the first half at a relaxed or moderate pace to help limber yourself up a little. Then, once you've passed the halfway point, pick up the pace and finish out the rest of your swim at that higher rate of speed. You can go by your own sense of mental time, or, if you want a more precise measurement, use whatever timepiece you have available.

Interval training. A technique used by athletes in various endurance sports, from swimming to running, is called interval training. It's a formal kind of fast/slow workout in which you do short bursts of speed laps followed by slow laps. The method gets its name from the fact that you do the fast and slow parts for a fixed interval of time and distance. The length of the speed intervals depends on your physique and stamina.

One method is to alternate one lap of high-energy swimming with three laps of relaxed swimming. Thus in terms of distance, this interval training is about 25 percent high effort and 75 percent easy swimming.

The advantage of this method is that it can build up your lung power in a short amount of time without undue strain. According to swim expert "Doc" Counsilman, you get more physical benefit by swimming the same distance at a fixed pace. However, this is a grueling way to train and you should not plan to do it every day. Most fitness experts recommend just one interval-style workout per week regardless of the sport.

Fartleks. If you hang around with runners you'll hear them talking about something called a "fartlek," which is Swedish for "speed play." This is a kind of free-spirit slow/fast training technique developed by marathon runners to alleviate the monotony of running at the same pace all the time and also to increase cardiovascular strength.

Very simply, by this method you swim fast when you feel like it, and once you feel tired, you downshift to a relaxed, slower swimming pace. Once you feel a little more rested you can then step up the pace and explode into a frenzy of intense swimming for a short spurt.

There are no ironclad rules for fartlek training other

than the ones naturally imposed by your endurance. You can swim those quick bursts of speed as often or as infrequently as you feel like it for about 30 seconds or so. If you want to make fartleks a little more interesting, you can always pair off with a swim partner for what is essentially a series of mini-races. For example, when you are part of the way into one of your laps you could stop, declare that it's race time and, on the count of three, have an instant sprint race for the far end of the pool.

Dauerlaufs. A more organized kind of strenuous training play is something called the dauerlauf, a continuous relay race that needs a small group—usually six—of willing swimmers. Two teams of three line up side by side, and on a signal the first members of each team take off and swim one lap, out and back, against each other. When his or her teammate comes back, the second swimmer of each team takes off for two laps of rapid swimming. As a result a properly paced dauerlauf can go on for an hour or more with everyone putting in some time of high-intensity fast swimming without feeling overexerted.

EASING IN, EASING OUT

Experiment with some of the different training methods here until you find one that suits your style. As a general rule, if you do decide to do some all-out swimming—a fast session of intervals, for example—make sure you follow a hard day's swimming with an easy day to give your muscles time to relax and recover. Don't try to force your body to work hard two days in a row. Spread out your intense workout days using fartleks and no more than one interval session per week.

Anytime you begin a swim workout, give yourself about 10 minutes, if you can spare it, to loosen up. Swim a slow lap or two, do some practice kicking at the side of the pool, or, even better if you can manage it, do the flexing exercises mentioned on pages 69–80 before you get in the pool. Princeton University swimming coach Rob Orr routinely has his swimmers do 10 to 15 minutes of loosening up before practicing in earnest and at the end of a training day has his swimmers "cool down" with about 100 yards of easy swimming.

RECOGNIZING PLATEAUS

How do you know when it's time to step up training? There is no hard and fast rule. It's something you'll have to discover for yourself by trial and error. It takes a little body awareness and some experimentation, but there are signs you can watch for. For example, you may find you are no longer breathless and feeling whipped the way you did when you began a stepped-up regimen, and so you are probably ready for an increase. You may find that you are getting in a rut with your present routine and, physically and psychologically, no longer feel challenged. If on your hard-training days you find you're not working yourself to at least 60 percent of your maximum heart rate (usually about 220 minus your age), then maybe you are ready for a stepped-up program. For example, someone who is 35 according to this formula should have a maximum heart rate of 185, and during his hard days, if he is pushing himself properly, his pulse should reach about 111.

What swimming coach Orr suggests is that you set yourself a modest goal, say a couple hundred more yards a day three weeks later, and start to work for it. You may find that you've underestimated or overestimated your body's abilities. It doesn't matter. You can make adjustments accordingly. The important thing is to have a goal and to be sensitive to how your body is able to fulfill it.

KEEPING IT UP

One last thing to remember is staying in shape. It's an unfortunate fact of life that it doesn't take very long to lose that terrific level of peak fitness it's taken months, even years, to acquire. According to Dr. Gabe Mirkin, this tendency of the body to slide back when it's not working out is called reversibility. Unfortunately it happens quickly with aerobic, endurance exercises, like swimming and running, that work the most muscles the hardest.

If you stop exercising completely, you will start noticing the effects of the layoff in as short a time as two weeks. You will get winded doing what used to be easy laps of the pool. Your muscles have already lost some of their ability to use oxygen. As you get further out of shape, your muscles will get sore once you start exercising again, a sign of weaker muscle tissue. In all, it doesn't take very long to go from being at your physical peak to being out of condition–roughly three to four weeks, according to Dr. Mirkin. The moral of these findings by fitness experts is that if you want to get fit and stay that way, you have to make exercising a lifetime habit.

"It's always the same," she said. "The end of the swimmer is sad."

-MARGARET CRAVEN
I Heard the Owl Call My Name

Competition

At each Olympic games, swimming turns out to be one of the most eagerly anticipated and watched sports. The reasons for its popularity are numerous: The most obvious are that all the events can be easily followed from one place; the action is fast and comes in bursts of energy; and the timing is split-second. Races have been won or lost by as little as a thousandth of a second. Another more complex reason is that the contestants of this sport are truly to be admired. Anyone who has ever swum from one end of a pool to the other knows that water is heavy stuff to plow through. To see swimmers in the 100-meter freestyle seem to fly through it and to realize the effort they are making and the discipline required can only win our admiration.

What is Olympic swimming? If you don't know much about the sport, it might seem confusing, especially at the beginning of the competitions when the poolside atmosphere is one of chaos as officials and swimmers scurry about and incomprehensible announcements blare over the loudspeakers. Essentially, the rules of Olympic swimming are not much different from those of other competitive swimming. The atmosphere, however, is very different—the most intense pressure and excitement known to any swimmer. To get the most out of watching the events, there are a few things that you should know.

First, an Olympic pool is always 50 meters long and is segmented into 8 lanes, each one just over 8 feet wide. The lanes are numbered from 1 to 8 beginning on the left, an ordering of considerable importance, as we shall see. The swimming strokes used are the ones we all know—the Australian, or front, crawl; the breaststroke; the butterfly; and the backstroke. Some of the 15 events

in Olympic swimming require the use of specific strokes, others a combination of the four, and still others are freestyle, meaning that the swimmer can use whatever stroke he or she prefers. Invariably the chosen stroke is the front crawl, the fastest way to get from one end of a pool to the other.

MAIN EVENTS

Freestyle events dominate Olympic competition, which has led to the criticism that there is too much similarity between events. There are seven of them: the 100-meter, 200-meter, 400-meter, 800-meter for women only, 1,500-meter for men only, 100-meter relay for women only, and 200-meter relay for men only. Relays are team events, four swimmers to a team. In the 100-meter relay, each team member swims 100 meters in sequence, so the total length of the race is actually 400 meters. The other events are the 100-meter and 200-meter breaststroke, the 100-meter and 200-meter butterfly, and the 100-meter and 200-meter backstroke. The competition also includes two medley events—the 400-meter individual medley and the 100-meter medley relay. In the former, a swimmer is required to use all the strokes, a different one for each 100-meter segment. In the medley relay, four team members swim 100 meters one after the other, each using a different stroke.

STROKES PLUS

Competitive swimming involves more than just swimming. Indeed, the details of the sport can be more important than the mechanics. As a spectator, your viewing and judgment can be more pleasurable and accurate if you know what to look for in a race. But before a race begins, look at the way the eight racers are lined up across the width of a pool. The positioning is indicative of the expected outcome of the race. Ordinarily, the swimmer with the fastest entry time is assigned to the lane just to the left of the center line, in other words lane number 4. The racer with the second-best time takes lane 5. Those with the third-best and fourth-best times are assigned to lanes 3 and 6, on either side of the ones taken by the first and second swimmers; the fifth-best and sixth-best are on either side of them, in lanes 2 and 7; and the seventh-best and eighth-best swim in the outside lanes, 1 and 8.

"Mark," his father would say, "how many lanes in a pool?"
"Six," the youngster would reply.
"And how many lanes win?"
"One, only one."

-ARNOLD SPITZ
and 9-year-old MARK SPITZ
as recorded in *Sports Illustrated*
March 9, 1970

The point of all this formality is that those swimmers with the best qualifying times are rewarded by assignment to the most advantageous lanes. During a race, the swimmers churn up waves that travel from the pool's center toward its outside. The swimmers in and nearest to the outside lanes—1, 8, 2, and 7—suffer the misfortune of a double dose of waves, those coming from the center and those rebounding off the walls. Though the waves are not great, they undoubtedly create an obstacle that can mean the difference between a win and a loss. Provided that lane assignment and competitor expertise are matched, the overall effect during a race will be that of a spearhead of swimmers, the fastest forming the spear's point and the slower ones its sides.

CHECKPOINTS

During the race itself, the three all-important details are the start, the turns, and the finish, as crucial to victory as speed and form. The shorter the race, the more important the start. Just as the starter raises his gun, you will notice that the racers lean forward on the balls of their feet so that they look as if they are going to fall into the pool. By the rules, they must be stationary when the gun goes off. The trick is to be moving toward the water with such timing that the starter can't see that there is any movement. The body so poised, it can spring into the water at the sound of the gun and be that much ahead of the others. This is very important in any race but more so in the sprints, such as a 100-meter event, in which there is just not that much distance to catch up to someone who has taken the lead through a good start.

The closest verdict in the Olympic Games was in the Munich 400-meter individual medley final on August 30, 1972, when Gunnar Larsson (Sweden) won by 2/1,000ths of a second in 4 minutes 31.981 seconds over Tim McKee (U.S.)—a margin of less than 1/8 inch, or the length grown by a fingernail in 3 weeks.

—Guinness Book of World Records

The starting guise doesn't always work; false starts are common. When it happens, the swimmers are alerted by a rope lowered into the water about one-third of the way up the pool, and they have to start over. In the Olympics, two false starts are permitted without penalty. A third disqualifies the swimmer who jumped the gun.

Turns are just as important as the start. Racers are made or broken by their expertise in these two areas. Competitors must touch the end of the pool when they turn, no matter the event. This does not have to be done with the hands, although the hands are ordinarily used in every event except the freestyle. In the freestyle the swimmer merely somersaults and pushes off the wall with his feet. In the backstroke, the butterfly, and the breaststroke, swimmers use their hands to spin their bodies around before they use their feet to power themselves away from the wall. A swimmer can be judged by how he comes into a turn. If he seems to coast up to the end walls, you know that something is off, probably his timing. A good swimmer should not break his rhythm when he gets to the ends of the pool but should incorporate his turn into the rhythm.

SMALL FRACTIONS

The third crucial part of a race that you as a spectator can watch with great care is the finish. Watch which swimmers coast to the finish. Those that do probably won't place well. Even more than turning, the finish requires timing. Swimmers say that they finish a race either "in phase" or "out of phase." "In phase" means that when a racer's arm is extended for the last stroke, he just touches the wall and automatically stops the clock recording the time in his lane. If his timing if off, he will find himself with half a stroke to go to touch the clock, and in all probability that will mean a loss.

The last crucial part of Olympic competition is form, and the keeping of rules pertaining to form is strict and unforgiving. In the midst of the excitement of watching a race, it's hard to believe that each of the competitors has spent months and months perfecting his or her form. In the breaststroke, for example, the head must be kept above water. If any water runs over the top of the head, the swimmer is disqualified. In the backstroke races, if a racer begins turning so that he is in a vertical position before reaching the end of the pool he is disqualified. Though rigorous, the rules on form are enforced to benefit the racer. Sloppy form not only creates a sloppy race, but also slows the competition. The rules demand a discipline that refines racing to its fastest state.

OFFICIATING

Much of the confusion just before an Olympic swimming event is due to the array of other people besides swimmers milling about the edge of the pool. These are the officials. A referee administers every race, his main role being to oversee the other officials, to settle disputes, and to get the race into motion by telling the competitors to step onto the starting blocks. The race is actually begun by the starter. When he commands, "Take your marks," the racers will move to the front of the blocks and wait for the gun to go off. Once the race is under way, other officials assume various duties. Halfway down either side of the pool, stroking judges pass judgment on whether or not each competitor's strokes conform to the rules. At the ends of the pool, other judges watch the swimmers turn, also to make sure that no rules are broken. Another set of judges eyes the finish. There are also timekeepers standing behind the blocks to record the time for each lap of the swimmer in that lane. Fortunately for the spectator, each of these officials is stationed in the same position for each race and can thus be recognized.

Olympic swimming is a special sport. As for any Olympic event, only a few athletes are chosen from the many. In the case of swimmers, these few are particularly devoted people who have spent most of their years in a pool. Mark Spitz began training and swimming competitively when he was nine years old. Most of us have neither the ability nor the desire to discipline ourselves to this extent. However, just because the Olympics are out of reach does not mean that competitive swimming is impossible to pursue. Let's imagine a scene far away from the Olympics.

EAL WORLD

The bustle at the pool's edge quieted as the eight swimmers mounted the blocks. Only a few clusters of spectators in the bleachers went on with their chatter and laughing. Someone shouted for a beer; two dogs yapped in play at the far end of the pool. Most of the racers, all in their middle or late thirties, looked calm but held their bodies expectantly. Their only obvious sign of nervousness was a constant curling and uncurling of toes over the edges of the blocks. One of them turned back to the gathering crowd, picked out a familiar face, and said with a smile, "Just stay right there–I'll be back in less than a minute." Then he concentrated his stare on the water and gulped in deep breaths of air.

Now the starter raised his gun and squinted along the line of figures at the water's edge. The spectators froze, their colorful clothing contrasting with their sudden silence. The racers bent their knees, leaned slightly forward, and hung over the pool. When the gun went off, an uproar of voices echoed off the water and bounced from wall to wall of the shell that protected the pool. "C'mon, Jimmy, do it for the Metros!" "Pull, pull; don't slice that water!" "Hey, you're way ahead of the DC's! Let it all out!"

In 58.33 seconds, the clamor changed from yells of encouragement to congratulations to the winner of the 100-meter freestyle. The last racer finished only 15 seconds behind the first. After a minute of rest in the water, he was helped out of the pool with just as much spirit and smiles as had been given to the other racers.

The eight men shook hands and patted each other's shoulders. Within minutes they had blended into the crowd, which by this time was talking about the next event, the 200-meter individual medley for women from 45 to 49 years old, an event that promised an even greater frenzy of competition and shouting than had the one just held.

"The nice thing about the masters is that you don't get the butterflies. Some people might, but I don't. There's not much emphasis on winning. The rules are nice and liberal. They encourage people to participate. It's fun. People have a good time."

-STEVE CLARK
Olympic swimmer—
3-time gold medalist,
1964 Olympics

WHETHER YOU WIN OR LOSE . . .

You could be part of this scene, one not uncommon since 1970, when competitive swimming programs across the country began to build momentum and attract adults wanting some excitement to enliven the often lonely hours they spent swimming lap after lap in an effort to keep in decent physical shape. Until a decade ago, competitive swimming ordinarily ended with high school or college unless one happened to be among the chosen few who continued training for a shot at the Olympics. All the years of building the muscles, the cardiovascular system, the timing, and the mental attitude, only to have it all turn to flab, inefficiency, and resignation when the academic gates closed.

When Don Schollander broke the 200-meter freestyle world record at age 17 in 1963, competitive swimming was thought to be the privilege of youth, a belief that was reinforced a year later when the young Schollander came home from the Tokyo Olympics with four gold medals. Then in 1972, 22-year-old Mark Spitz flabbergasted the world with his seven gold medals at the Munich Olympics. By that time, the aging Schollander, 28, had been put out to pasture. Certainly competition for anyone over the age of 30 was out of the question.

Not so, said Ransom J. Arthur, dean of the University of Oregon Medical School, who had both swum for and coached the U.S. Navy team. He was not willing to see the aging process take swimmers out of competition. "I was aware that it was entirely possible to train vigorously at ages which were thought in the past to be too great. I also realized that competition can be a spur to continued training. Otherwise training can be rather boring. After all, most people need some kind of goal other than general fitness."

In the late 1960s, Arthur tried to start a competitive swimming program for adults, but no one was interested enough to donate a pool and sponsor meets. Undaunted, he wrote a magazine article on the health benefits of swimming. Its publication opened the eyes of John Stannuth, then president of the American Swimming Coaches' Association, who offered Arthur the use of his training pool in Amarillo, Texas, and agreed to share in the costs of putting together a swimming program.

MASTERS SWIMMING

It was thus in Amarillo that adult (usually referred to as "masters") competitive swimming was born in this country with the first national championships in 1970. Sixty swimmers entered. The following year, there were 150. Obviously encouraged, Arthur took his burgeoning fountain of youth to the Amateur Athletic Union and asked that huge umbrella organization dedicated to the encouragement and development of amateur sports to underwrite a national masters competitive swimming program. The AAU agreed.

The AAU masters program no longer caters to a few hundred health nuts as it did during the first few years. It is now a sophisticated operation whose 10,000 members swim against each other in hundreds of weekend meets across the country throughout the year. It also maintains a national ranking of swimmers. The two high points of each year are the AAU Long Course National Masters Swimming Championships in the fall and the Short Course Championships each spring. Hundreds of members participate in these three-day affairs that offer a complete range of events.

While the times turned in might not frighten Olympic

contestants or even collegiate champions, they are nonetheless more than respectable. Indeed, AAU masters swimmers hold American records in various events. The sport is growing so fast that records are being broken every year. The first AAU-sponsored championships in 1972 attracted 300 contestants. The 1978 Long Course Championships brought 500 swimmers to the Brown University pool in Providence, R.I. Eight months later, over 1,000 swimmers showed up for the 1979 Short Course Championships in Mission Viejo, California. The difference between short course and long course, incidentally, is in pool length. A short-course event is held in a pool 25 meters long and a long-course event in a pool 50 yards long. Swimmers who can turn well are apt to do better in a short-course event; those who have superior strokes have a better chance in long-course competition.

All AAU masters swimming competition is held in pools, with the exception of the annual 3-mile race, usually held at Trout Lake, Wisconsin. If you are fond of long-distance racing, then the AAU program may not be the best. Long-distance races are not as frequent at AAU meets, so if it's competition you want, the AAU is a principal organizer.

EVERYBODY IN

Competition in an atmosphere of spirited democracy more than mere record breaking is the essence of masters swimming competition. Anyone over 25 years old who wants to swim competitively can join the AAU masters program. No experience is necessary. Democracy comes in the system of competition by age groups rather than a free-for-all of young against old. Members of the youngest group range in age from 25 to 29. The next group (each segregated by sex) is from 30 to 34, the next from 35 to 39 and so on in five-year increments into the 80s. Yes, there are about a dozen masters swimmers in their 80s and several in their 90s! Although not all compete in the nationals, they do swim competitively. Nellie Brown is an 86-year-old who rarely misses an opportunity to churn away the lengths. She shows up at most of the championships and to the cheers of spectators races against herself for lack of any other competition in her age group. The times she turns in are just about double those of women half her age, statistics that have a nice logic to them. But 86 years old?

Gertrude Murdock, 72, is a recent masters swimmer. She has sparkling brown eyes and the figure of a 20-year-old. She swam in her first meet in February 1978, and then entered the National Short Course Championships in San Antonio, Texas, that spring. She won the 500 and 1,650 yard freestyle events and the 100 yard breaststroke. She swims 400 yards every other day.

–Swim-Master, VII, 9

AAU officials feel that as the masters program continues, there will be more older members. "The over-80s aren't in large numbers right now," says Ted Haartz, national chairman of the AAU Masters Swimming Program, "but I would assume that over a period of time as people stay in this program, they will remain fit and live longer. We have far more people in their 70s now than we did four or five years ago."

Improved health is one of the cornerstones of the masters program. Members are constantly reminded that the pain and suffering they feel in the water as they struggle to better their times will pay off in increased alertness and mental discipline, better muscle tone, and a stronger heart. Many masters also adhere to Dr. Arthur's belief that swimming deters the physical breakdown of aging. Sixty-year-old Fred Wemger is an advocate. "When I was 45, I'd climb up a flight of stairs and I'd be tired. Now I feel great and want to maintain and improve my swimming into my sixties. It feels good. I feel 30 years old."

And there's 52-year-old Win Wilson, who swims 2,500 meters every morning because "I wanted to get back into shape. I couldn't get into jogging, and swimming just seemed like a good way to do it. I have friends who say I'm an absolute idiot, a nut. But this is what I do. That's just the way it is."

FRIENDLY ADVERSARIES

The camaraderie of competitive swimming, its emotional excitement, and the satisfaction that comes from physical exertion and good physical condition are all

part of the masters program. But how do you get into it? Practically speaking, the best way is to get in touch with the AAU office in the nearest city and get the name of the regional director of the masters program. He will be able to tell you when and where meets are held and what pools are available. You can also get information from the YMCA or YMHA. The YMCA, incidentally, has its own masters swimming program, which involves some competition. To compete outside of the Y and to be nationally ranked, AAU membership is necessary. AAU members can, of course, swim in Y meets if they are members of that organization.

Most masters belong to local swimming clubs affliated with the AAU. But many of these organizations are merely a state of mind and a name. Most do not have their own pools, with the exception of those on the West Coast, where swimming is so popular. Thus training can usually be done only after searching out the nearest pool, usually at a Y or on a college campus. But when a meet is held, contestants belonging to the same club will join forces and pull for that club.

PERSONAL VICTORIES

Thirty to 40 percent of registered masters swimmers never swam competitively before they signed up. Yet now they compete with and against former Olympic swimmers and college champions, coaches, and people who might have been swimming most of their lives. "Will I make a fool of myself?" is the question on the minds of many newcomers to the sport. The answer is that that is not the point of the masters swimming program. Don't think about anyone else; think about yourself and realize that the competitive aspect of swimming is only a spur to help put you in better shape.

"I encourage new swimmers to the program not to be either concerned or awed by what they see other people doing," says Ted Haartz. "You've got to keep where you are *today* in perspective. If you see somebody churning

"I first heard about masters swimming during the cold months of 1976 and decided to get in the water and rid myself of fat knees and too-rounded contours. Also, there were the ever-present frustrations of being a mother, wife, cook, chauffeur, etc. that needed an outlet. Two years later I participated in the first week-long masters clinic at Western Illinois University. I had no idea what I was doing in the brief time span between the sound of the gun and the finish. Let me tell you, I've had an eye-opening, mind-boggling experience."

–VEL PERRY
Swim Master, VII, 7

up the water next to you, you can't say, 'I don't belong here with him.' That's just the wrong attitude. I don't like to see people comparing themselves to other swimmers, because they don't know how long they've been at it, they don't know how much time they devote to it, and they don't know what kind of natural ability they have."

He continues, "There are four things you can say about swimming. Technique is important, conditioning is important, mental attitude for discipline is important, and ability is important. You can do something about the first three, but there isn't a damn thing you can do to make yourself a Mark Spitz. He had *it*, and a lot if it. There are a lot of us that don't have in our whole bodies what certain athletes have in their little fingers. We just have to do with what we have, and the masters program appreciates that."

Dr. Arthur, the guru of swimming for health, supports Haartz by asking the obvious question: "Look, how far behind can you get in a 50-yard race? Swimming is sort of anonymous when the water is flying. It's not like being lapped on a track with the whole stadium watching. If that happens in a 10,000-meter run, you really look like a charley. It doesn't happen in swimming; the masters program is just not set up to embarrass people." That champagne and beer relays are a part of many meets is witness to the good-natured side of the competitiveness. In these synthetic events, racers must down a glassful after each lap.

Even for the uninhibited there is far more to competitive swimming than signing a membership form and finding out when the next meet will be held. Training, the most rigorous and long-drawn-out part of any competition, is essential. When you become a masters swimmer, don't expect a coach to walk up and lead you by the hand into a training program. This might be true if you happen to live in an area where competitive swimming has reached enough popularity to enable members of the local club to build a pool and hire not only a swimming coach but also someone to teach other forms of aquatic exercise like diving, water polo, and synchronized swimming (ballet). Otherwise, training is very much an individual labor of love, done on one's own time in a pool of one's own finding.

COMPETITIVE CONDITION

How do you train? With a great deal of care, says Ransom Arthur. "The main advice I can give is to start very slowly and steadily increase your distance each week with the knowledge that it will be many, many months before you are in reasonable shape. I've taken swimmers from scratch and had them in pretty good shape after three years."

What Arthur means by starting slowly is just that. He suggests that a 50-year-old who is just beginning to train swim no more than three minutes a day and stop just as soon as he or she tires. Any feelings of faintness or chest pains should be heeded. Heart attacks while training are certainly not unknown and can lead to death by drowning if one is so foolhardy as to swim alone. Once in shape, a basic program should be followed of swimming at least three times a week for 45 minutes each time. Less than that is tantamount to no training at all.

Even if my chest is hurting and my legs are hurting, if you beat the clock, and beat your best time, it feels great.

-T. W. JOHNSON
73-year-old Masters Swimmer

Though adherence to this program will put one in shape and keep the muscles and breathing apparatus tuned for some competition, it will not be sufficient for the suddent bursts of energy or the endurance necessary to win three events in one meet, an accomplishment some masters swimmers strive for. Training programs are as individual as swimmers, and each successful competitor proudly talks up his training methods to colleagues and rivals. Tips are often publicized in *Swim-Master*, the monthly newsletter for AAU masters swimmers.

TRAINING TABLES

A few years ago the DC Masters, a very strong and enthusiastic team in the Washington, D.C., area, shared its daily training program with other AAU swimmers through an article in *Swim-Master*. The DC swimmers ranged from 27 to 50 years old and the training was designed to put them in top shape for the spring Short Course Nationals. They divided the training into three stages—early-season (November); mid-season (January); and late-season (April and early May) just before the Nationals. Training sessions held every day began with a warmup period: swimming 100 yards; kicking 100 yards (using a board to support arms and upper body); and pulling 100 yards (using just the arms), repeated three times. The actual training then followed and included competitive swimming, kicking, and pulling against the clock for a total daily distance of 3,925 yards. In mid-season, team members increased their distance to just over 5,000 yards, and training included sprints and a greater variety of events. Then, about six weeks before the Nationals, the team relaxed its distance to 3,825 yards a day.

A program such as this is every bit as serious as it sounds. It takes time and enormous discipline. Many swimmers who want to compete just cannot take any more time than to swim 1,500 yards a day, quite a difference from the 4,000 to 5,000 the DC masters were putting in. One swimmer wrote to *Swim-Master* that he complemented his daily 1,500-yard workout by lifting weights. Others do isometric exercises or run.

Training is grueling work no matter how it's done. After the initial excitement of feeling your body begin to firm up, your endurance increase, and your discipline improve, the hours of painful work pass into the gray world of drudgery even if done with a team. No matter if your teammates are swimming a few feet away, you are by yourself, immersed in the water and staring down at the tiles on the pool's bottom.

PERSONAL GOALS

It's a rare person who can continue such a regimen without relying on competition as a stimulus, one of the leading purposes of the AAU program. But even if meets are held as often as three weekends every month, not an unusual frequency, a swimmer cannot rely on the highs they provide to keep his body in shape. Between meets, training should never stop. Fortunately, the mind can trick the body into continuing to push itself; it tells the body that the satisfaction of all this boring work comes in competing against *itself*, always striving to better its winning time for a given distance. To a one, competitive swimmers have forced themselves to take refuge in lonely races against themselves.

"Most of the time we swim alone," says Ted Haartz, who held the AAU record in the 100- and 200-meter breaststroke in the 50-to-54-year-old-class in 1978. "And when I say ourselves, I mean that very personally. In the masters program, one should be competing against himself as well as against others in the National Championships. You don't have to get first place to come up with a time better than you've ever done before, and *that* certainly says something about your ambition and dedication."

WaterProofing

The water is an alien world. No matter how skilled you may be at propelling yourself through it, no matter how comfortable you may feel in it, no matter how passionately you may love it, you will never *belong* to it. We are simply not aquatic animals. Our external bodies, our internal organs, our minds, and our spirits—all are irrevocably locked to the land.

It is wise to remember this. For if the appeal of water lies in its absolute otherness, then there, too, lies its danger. Instinct, if nothing else, helps us survive on the earth. In the water, though, instinct is useless, or worse than useless. A swimmer suddenly in trouble will find himself fighting against an automatic need to open his mouth, to flail his arms and legs, to tense his every muscle. In other words, his instinct is compelling him to drown.

Approximately 7,000 Americans die each year in swimming accidents. Some are old hands, some are beginners, some are incapable of a single stroke. Some drown in oceans, some drown in lakes or creeks or rivers, some drown in kidney-shaped backyard pools. Some disappear solitary, in deep water. Some sink, surrounded by other people, in water that barely reaches their waists. But despite the disparity of circumstance, most of these deaths share one common characteristic: They don't have to happen.

By definition, drowning is suffocation. Water seals off mouth and nostrils, oxygen is kept from passing to the lungs, air is forced out of the lungs, and the body—its specific gravity now greater than that of the liquid around it—loses its buoyancy and begins to submerge. At

some point in this process, depending upon individual strength and endurance, death becomes inevitable.

Obviously, then, the best way to avoid drowning is to avoid those conditions most conducive to it. With few exceptions, a drowning is always the result of panic, exhaustion, an unexpected physical injury, lack of preparation, or just plain carelessness. By anticipating the most common hazards, by taking the necessary precautions, and—most important—by maintaining constant alertness, you can protect yourself from almost all swimming mishaps. You can, in fact, become virtually waterproof.

RAPTURES OF THE DEEP

The greatest danger facing a sports diver is not a jaws-gaping shark, or a bad-tempered moray eel, or a giant squid, or even a malevolent specter guarding a sunken treasure ship. It is, rather, what's technically (and lyrically) known as "raptures of the deep." The diver, transfixed and confounded by the unearthly beauty of his surroundings, loses all sense of time and direction. Not uncommonly, he will no longer be able to differentiate between up and down, top and bottom, and will—unless helped by his companions—drift in languid circles until his air runs out.

The surface of the water is just as beguiling and deceptive as its depths. More than one ocean swimmer, for example, has started back to what he thought was the shore only to discover that he is actually heading out to sea.

Many, too many, drownings can be blamed on this kind of disorientation (and also on the resultant panic). Which is why all swimmers—and this includes Olympic champions as well as people taking their very first dip—should always obey the following injunctions:

Never swim alone. This doesn't mean merely that there be other people in the water at the same time you are. (They're likely to be too involved with themselves to notice that you're in trouble; or, even if they do notice, they may mistake your desperate attempts to stay afloat for just some boisterous horseplay.) Nor, important though he or she is, will a lifeguard always be enough. A lifeguard may not be able to keep track of everyone, or may even be too busy saving someone else's life to reach you in time. No, what's needed is a swimming partner, a responsible friend who's aware of you at all times. There's no way to overemphasize the importance of the partner system. Resist, against all temptation, ever entering any body of water alone.

Drugs and alcohol. Drugs and alcohol typically impair physical reflexes, vision, and judgment. Worse, they dull the body's natural edge for self-preservation. Going into the water after using them is not only stupid but nigh-on suicidal. Besides, swimming itself is a natural high; using chemical boosts just robs you of the exhilaration of reality.

Never swim in the dark. Anyone who's ever walked along the shore at night knows how beguiling the water can be. Do not, however, be lured by its siren song. It's hard enough during the daytime to keep yourself oriented while in the water; at night it becomes, for all practical purposes, impossible. And don't be fooled by a bright moon. Moonlight distorts distance perception. What seems to be a safe 10 feet from the beach could turn out to be an anything-but-safe 10 yards. Reserve your after-sundown swimming for well-lighted pools.

Never swim in troubled waters. No one—at least, no one in his right mind—need be warned against swimming outdoors during a storm. It may be necessary, however, to devote a few words here to the subject of cloudbursts. At the first sign of rain, get out of the water. Fast. You'll probably be tempted to stay in. There's something spiritually satisfying about swimming in a gentle summer shower. But even the gentlest rain can generate atmospheric disturbances. Which means electricity—and you're out there floating in a substance that is a natural conductor of electricity.

Never leap before you look. On a hot bright day few things are as irresistible as plunging, headlong or rump-first, into the water. Resist it. Perhaps as many as one-third of all drownings are a direct result of the blind leap. Don't allow enthusiasm to wash away your common sense. To do otherwise is to chance knocking yourself unconscious on a hidden boulder or rock shelf, or entangling yourself in weeds at the bottom, or trapping yourself in a riptide invisible from the surface. Don't dive from any projection until you've first actually been in the water and have gauged the distance from surface to bottom.

The most common drownings are unspectacular affairs, happening in apparently "harmless" situations. Indeed most happen within 15 meters (50 feet) of safety.

–Drownproofing

Never eat and run (into the water). Just in case you weren't paying attention to your mother when you were young, here's some good advice: Do not go swimming immediately after eating. Many swimmers anxious to get into the action as quickly as possible gobble down their food and then rush straight into the water. Bad move. Again, it's absolutely essential to prevent enthusiasm from overcoming caution. Vigorous exercise—and swimming is very vigorous exercise indeed—seriously interferes with the process of digestion. This in turn may lead to nausea, cramps, or even—in cases involving older people—heart attacks.

First, eat. Next, relax. The water's not going anywhere. Besides, you don't have to stay dry until your meal is completely digested (which, incidentally, would allow you maybe three minutes of swimming before it was time for your next meal) but only until the initial digestive stages have begun. For most people, this means a mere 30 to 60 minutes.

Come in from the cold. Early season ocean and freshwater drownings are commonplace. The problem here is that the swimmer, body badly out of condition following months of winter inactivity, is not prepared to

> "Learn to swim," said Professor Odlum, "for neither Providence nor fate is always to be tempted by dereliction or neglect of precaution."
>
> *–The Life and Adventures of Prof. Robert Emmet Odlum,* 1885

deal with the exhausting effects of cold water. Typically, in any aquatic environment of less than 65°F, breathing becomes inhibited, blood circulation slows down, and an enormous amount of energy is expended in trying to keep arms and legs from being numbed. Under such conditions, fatigue can set in rapidly, so rapidly you receive no early-warning signs. If you're too far out, you may not be able to gather enough strength to return to land. And regardless of the temperature, always be sure to immerse yourself gradually into the water.

Never forget to come in, period. At first glance, this would seem too obvious to bother mentioning, but it's surprising how many people stay in the water well past the limits of their endurance. Once again, this shows how our human instincts mislead us when we are in an inhuman environment. When hiking on dry land, even the least experienced of us recognize the symptoms of exhaustion and will, instinctively, rest until our bodies inform us that we can safely move on again. While swimming, however, we're likely to misread or, for that matter, altogether miss the warning signs of physical fatigue. This is particularly true in warm water. Except when a swimmer is using a maximum of energy in a minimum amount of time (when racing, for instance), the symptoms of debilitation are so deceptively pleasant—arms and legs cushioned by languor, brain bemused and gently contemplative, a general state of lazy contentment—that many of us tend to ignore their actual meaning. Instinct will tell us we're feeling exceptionally good; foreknowledge advises us that we're courting serious trouble. Don't be fooled. Whenever you find yourself *too* relaxed in the water, it's time to get back to the shore as quickly as possible.

CHECKING OUT THE SITES

It stands to reason that safe swimming is most probable at safe swimming sites. Generally, swimming pools (both indoor and outdoor) are the least risky; "swimming holes" (that is, abandoned quarries, secluded stretches of creeks and streams, etc.) are the most risky; and lakes, ponds, rivers, bays, and oceans, in roughly that order, are between the two extremes from most to least dangerous.

Keep in mind that this is only the broadest of ratings. A placid lake, for instance, that has not been properly roped off for bathers may be more dangerous than the surf-pounded edge of an ocean. A river with a swift but visible current may be less hazardous than a shallow pond with an unexpected sinkhole. Even a swimming pool can become the scene of a fatal accident. In order to as certain whether or not only particular site is safe enough to swim in, it is first necessary to explore that site thoroughly.

Safe bottom. In any natural body of water, a good bottom features a gentle and very gradual descent from the shallows to the deeper areas. (In man-made pools and tanks, this slope is from the shallow-end to the deep-end sides.) The bottom must also be clear of silt, hidden obstructions like logs and boulders, dangerous debris like shards of glass or scraps of rusting metal, and treacherous sinkholes and stepoffs.

Safe shore. The sand (at oceanside beaches) or gravel (at riverbanks or lakefronts) should be smooth and well raked. On pool decks, the surfacing should be semi-smooth concrete or unglazed tile. And whether the swimming site is natural or man-made, the area surrounding it should always be free of potentially hazardous litter.

Safe water. In pools, both ends should be clearly marked, by inset tile or painted letters identifying the maximum and minimum depths. In rougher waters, such as rivers and oceans, those areas known to be safe for swimming should be marked off by buoys, lifelines, and booms. Even in comparatively tranquil lakes and streams, areas for various classifications of bathers (novices, intermediates, experts) should be defined by buoyed lines or by precisely lettered and prominently displayed waterside signs.

Safe supervision. All water sites—and this includes backyard pools as well as the ocean—should be carefully supervised. Supervision can mean paid lifeguards, volunteer lifeguards, or concerned adults with some lifeguard training who are keeping a wary eye on their kids. The emphasis is, of course, on rescue, but some attention should also be paid to enforcing the basic safety regulations (no diving from any surface other than a springboard or diving platform, no inordinate amount of horseplay, no wrestling at the edge of the water, and so on). Also, all necessary equipment should not only be at immediate hand but be in top working order.

TAYING AFLOAT

Almost every person, swimmer and nonswimmer alike, has one constant ally at all times in the water: the body's own natural buoyancy. Assuming the lungs are capable of holding a full capacity of oxygen, 99.9 percent of women and 99 percent of men (who tend to have a greater specific gravity than women) can float. The tiny percentage who cannot float are classified as sinkers.

Why, then, with such a built-in aquatic ability, do so many people nevertheless drown?

> It is not so easy a thing to sink as you imagined.
>
> -BENJAMIN FRANKLIN
> "Art of Swimming," 1768

Well, for one thing, we don't float equally well. Some panic too quickly; some weaken too quickly; and, as bone and muscle have greater specific gravities than fat (which is honeycombed with pockets of air), the plumper of us automatically have a certain physical advantage.

For another, no one can float indefinitely. If you're left stranded in the water long enough, neither Mark Spitz's skill nor your overweight girth would be enough to keep your head above the waves. Finally, the two most common (that is, the two most *instinctive*) flotation positions—the back-horizontal and the treading-water floats—are also, unfortunately, the most impractical. Few women and even fewer men can float completely relaxed on their backs. Legs, chiefly bone and muscle, are the first parts of the human body to sink; therefore, a great deal of energetic paddling of hands and feet is necessary for counterbalance. And of course, by its very nature, treading water requires a considerable expenditure of energy. Either way, the process of exhaustion is hastened. Eventually, the floater begins to pant and breathe in water. Without relief, drowning will result.

It might seem to be an insoluble problem, since what we need is a flotation technique that provides maximum staying power in return for minimum physical exertion. But in fact a technique already exists.

THE BREATHING CYCLE

In 1942, shortly after the beginning of World War II, Fred Lanoue, an associate professor of physical education at the Georgia Institute of Technology, read a set of statistics revealing that more American servicemen were dying as a result of drowning accidents than as a result of combat.

Determined to end this fearsome—and unnecessary—casualty rate, Professor Lanoue developed, in an astonishingly brief period of time, a new method of flotation that any person, regardless of actual swimming experience, can easily learn—and can guarantee its users the very best chance of survival in the water.

Lanoue based his method on scientific principles and common-sense observations. First, he noted that a floater's potential ability to remain alive is almost completely dependent upon his ability to remain as relaxed and as immobile as possible. Second, he discovered that most floaters expend most of their energy trying to keep their heads above the waterline. But he knew that the floater actually has to breathe only a few times each minute in order to maintain sufficient oxygen flow. Therefore, he reasoned, what was needed was a position in which relaxation—not accessibility to air—played the key role. Following some trial and error,

Lanoue devised just that: a position, actually a series of positions, that permits the floater to remain absolutely still for long intervals and that also provides a means of breathing without excessive exertion.

The technique, which Lanoue dubbed simply the "breathing cycle," is divided into five distinct steps.

1. Assume a vertical-rest position: In the face-down position, take a deep breath, and then allow your body to sink vertically until only your neck and upper shoulders remain above water. Properly executed, the vertical rest will support your body in a totally relaxed position. Any water that accidentally enters your mouth can simply be coughed out again.

2. Now assume the ready position in order to come up for air. Slowly cross your arms in front of your forehead, palms angled outward and forearms held together; raise one knee to the chest, and extend the other foot behind to stride position.

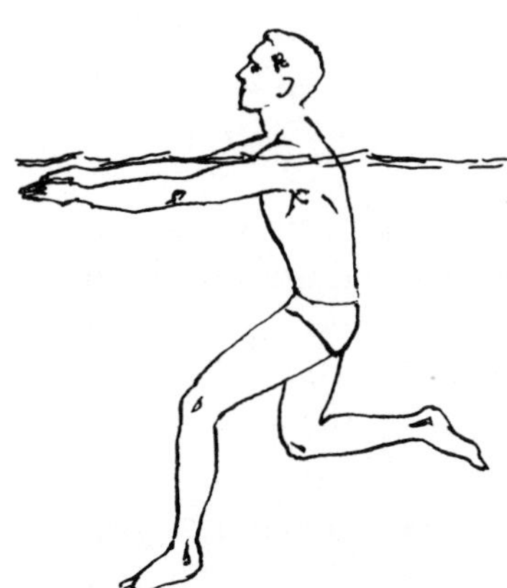

3. Exhale, raising your head as you sweep both arms out and down; at the same time, "step down" with both feet on the water. With your head above the water, inhale deeply again and. . .

4. Fold back into the water. Lower your head, chin to chest; relax your arms and legs.

5. Resume the vertical rest. Hold this position until it is necessary to come up for air, then begin again.

It's important to note that all movements are meant to be performed as gently as possible. Also, depending on your confidence and ability, leg and arm movements can be even more minimal than suggested here. The cycle is repeated as often as you need to take normal breaths.

THE TRAVEL STROKE

Lanoue was not entirely satisfied with his breathing-cycle technique. Although it solved the floater's main dilemma—i.e., how to breathe normally without burning up essential stamina—the minimal movement that was its virtue also kept the floater from reaching land.

He therefore went one stage further and developed the "travel stroke." Like the breathing cycle, which is always performed in conjunction with it, the travel stroke can be separated into steps:

1. At the completion of the inhale stage of the breathing cycle, do not resume the vertical-rest position. Instead:

2. Tip your head forward, bring your hands together in front of your forehead, and position your legs for a "scissors kick," i.e., front leg pointing downward and rear leg bent at the knee.

3. Extend your arms, hands still together, and then kick the rear leg back and down. This begins an underwater glide.

4. At the end of the initial glide, sweep your arms sideways and back until your hands are touching your thighs. This gives you a second glide. During this glide, breathe out air through your nose.

5. At the end of the second glide—which can last from 5 to 20 seconds—bring both knees up to your chest, arch your back, and. . .

6. Return to the vertical-rest position. When ready, perform the breathing cycle. The cycle and the stroke are alternated in sequence.

It is a peculiar fact that non-swimmers, upon being precipitated into the water, will do everything that is possible to drown themselves.

-GEORGE CORSAN
At Home in the Water, 1910

The travel stroke's advantages are readily apparent. Like the breathing cycle, it requires little energy and maintains relaxation. It can, again like the cycle, be performed equally well by swimmers, nonswimmers, and injured or handicapped persons. And, though it may seem a rather casual way to travel, the stroke can actually propel a trained user about 1 mile per hour. Best of all, just about anyone can use this stroke for several continuous hours without feeling great strain.

EXERCISES

Remarkably, a poor swimmer or nonswimmer will not only easily learn the fundamentals of the breathing cycle and the travel stroke but will also, nine times out of ten, learn it more easily than the fair-to-excellent swimmer. This is because novices have no ingrained habits to overcome. Although simple, the cycle and stroke represent a radical departure from traditional swimming methods. You may have difficulty overcoming your basic strokes.

Because of this, Lanoue and his disciples set up a series of training exercises especially designed to make the transition to the new flotation methods as gradual and painless as possible. None of these exercises is ever to be done without full supervision by someone already expert in them.

Treading water. You will, naturally, already know how to tread water. The point of this exercise is to demonstrate how the less you "fight" the water, the more you control it.

First, tread water in your usual way. Chances are, you will concentrate on keeping your head as high above the water as you can, consequently becoming very fatigued very quickly. Next, repeat the exercise–but this time you must use a minimum amount of leg action. This will familiarize you with the essential Lanoue principles of relaxation and natural buoyancy. Continue, with rest breaks, for 15 to 30 minutes.

Free-form floating. Lanoue's purpose here is two-fold: to show the swimmer his native ability to float without effort and to emphasize the importance of correctly timed breathing. First you inhale fully and stop treading water. Unless you're a "sinker" (p. 204), you will submerge briefly and then rise back to the top. Repeat the exercise until you can float back to the surface without making any instinctive paddling moves with hands or feet. Next, *exhale* fully and stop treading water. In this manner, you quickly learn that without air in your lungs you sink more rapidly and do not rise back up without some self-propelling movements. Repeat the exercise alternately with and without taking breaths–for approximately 15 minutes. At the end of this period, you will be used both to keeping your body relaxed and to always taking a breath before submersion.

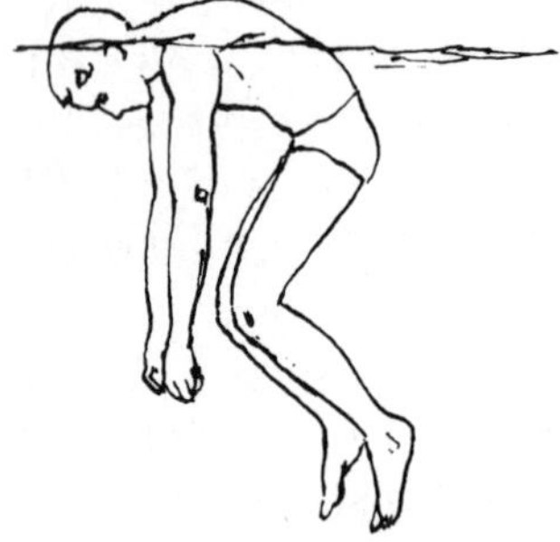

The mushroom float. One of the easiest ways to float, the mushroom position aids swimmers to relax their bodies completely while mostly underwater. Take a breath, place your face in the water, and clasp your knees to your chest. Remain in this float for as long as possible, concentrating all the while on feeling the cold air on your exposed back (the same method you'll use to orient yourself when performing the full breathing cycle).

The jellyfish float. This is a variation of the mushroom float and, more important, is an immediate antidote to a sudden attack of stomach cramps (see p. 206). Stand in chest-high water, spread your feet wide apart, take a deep breath, slide both hands down your thighs, and grasp your ankles firmly. If you avoid falling either backward or forward, your body will immediately rise to the surface.

Horizontal back float. As previously mentioned, most people mistakenly believe the best floating position is on the back. This exercise will help correct that belief. Float on your back in any way you can. In all likelihood you will have to use both hands and feet to remain horizontal. Next, stop all movement. Again in all likelihood the weight of your sinking legs will cause your body to become vertical. Repeat the exercise, this time taking a breath just before reaching the vertical position. Then repeat the exercise, this time placing your chin nearly on your chest and letting your arms and legs dangle. Continue repeating the exercise for at least 10 minutes. By the end of this time, you will have learned the proper way to keep your body relaxed, the proper way to hold your head (breathing is always easier from a face-down position, because the neck muscles have only to lift the head until the mouth is out of the water), and the proper vertical-rest position that initiates the breathing cycle.

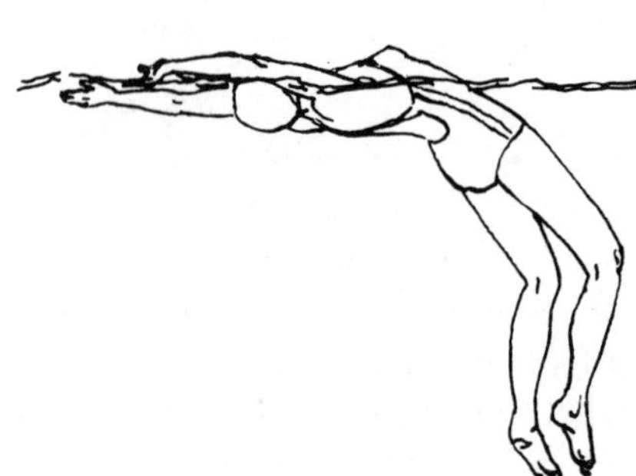

Breathing cycle. If you've performed the exercises correctly, you can begin learning the cycle. From now on, it becomes a matter of personal ability. Whether your role is that of instructor or of pupil, you should concentrate on breath control and relaxation of the limbs. Constant repetition of the five cycle steps will correct most of the common faults. Keep a particularly close eye on:

Failure to cross the arms in front of the forehead (step 2). This halves the length of the arm sweep, thus halving the time available to inhale.

Not completely exhaling by the time the head breaks the surface (step 3). This will prevent total inhalation from occurring.

A too-vigorous leg or arm thrust (step 3). Not only will this leave insufficient time to take air into the lungs but it will also cause you to sink back deeper in the water than is necessary. The deeper the descent, the harder it is to reassume the rest position. This increases the possibility of fatigue setting in.

Paddling with the hands to allow more time to breathe (step 3). You must learn to perform only one arm sweep per breath of air.

Delaying resubmersion by treading water (step 4). Cycle beginners will invariably experience an unpleasant tightness in the chest. (This is the result of either inhaling too much air or holding it in longer than necessary.) The tendency is to tread water until you feel you've gotten your breath back. This practice must be discouraged from the first, or you will never gain the confidence needed to become adept at the breathing cycle.

The ability to swim confers a comparative immunity from drowning on its possessor.

-CHARLES STEEDMAN
Manual of Swimming, 1867

As for relaxation techniques, you will probably accept the minimal-movement principle naturally as you continue your practice sessions. If you remain tense, however, there are several advanced methods of training that may be employed. Many instructors, for example, will tie a student's arms or legs (or sometimes both at once) in order to demonstrate most dramatically how little effort is required to remain afloat. These exercises contain an element of risk, however, and should be undertaken only by the most expert teachers.

DIFFERENT FOLKS, DIFFERENT STROKES

Disorientation, exhaustion, panic, the wrong move prompted by instinct, even lack of swimming ability—all can be forestalled by caution, planning, and the flotation methods. Now, however, it's time to discuss special crises and situations that require special remedies.

SINKERS

Most people are natural floaters. A few people are just as naturally sinkers. The irony is that often swimmers who lack buoyancy are also the best swimmers. Their rigorous training has so developed their bodies that little fat remains to lower their specific gravity. This condition is also shared by uncommonly thin men and women. If you suspect you're a sinker, try this simple test: Stand in chin-high water, fill your lungs with air, and let your body relax. If you submerge but fail to return to the surface, read the following section with particular care.

Because the sinker lacks flotation power, he cannot use the standard breathing cycle and travel stroke. Instead, he should learn two variations, also developed by Professor Lanoue, that will help him stay on top of the situation.

1. Assume the basic vertical-rest position.

2. Cross your forearms in front of your forehead. Adjust your legs so that the front-foot sole and the rear-foot top "hold" on the water.

3. Gently kick your legs (rather than simply straightening them) and at the same time sweep your arms sideways. The combined leg and arm action should give even the most drastic of sinkers enough time to take a full breath. Inhale.

4. As you tuck your head toward your chin, kick out again to keep from sinking too far below the water.

5. Reassume the vertical-rest position.

If even this variation fails to allow you to float without undue effort, you must use the travel stroke permanently. Here, too, the technique has been modified.

1. Assume a semi-vertical rest: nose and mouth above water; arms held out to the side.

2. You're now positioned for the glide. This is basically the same as the standard step, except that, unlike a floater, a sinker-swimmer is completely submerged beneath the water.

3. Execute the glide. Again, the step is similar, but the kick is stronger.

4. At the end of the glide, sweep your arms backward and *kick again*.

5. At the end of the second glide, start to move back to vertical rest, then kick yet again.

6. This brings your head out of the water, arms held out to the sides. Take a full breath, and begin the series again.

Although a sinker will not have the rest period allowed a floater, performing the modified travel stroke will maintain relaxation and postpone overtiring. There's one other important difference in this method: During the glide, you must not exhale any air—otherwise, you will continue to sink deeper into the water.

OVER-FLOATERS

A sinker's exact opposite is the over-floater, the person (usually but not always a woman) who has so much buoyancy that she or he has difficulty assuming the vertical rest. In order to combat this, over-floaters must expel air with exceptional force in step 3 of the breathing cycle. During the travel-stroke glide, they must also breathe out with great vigor.

CRAMPS

Cramps are perhaps the most feared of all swimming hazards—and unlike man-eating sharks, they are quite common. There are two basic types.

Leg and/or arm cramp. The danger here is not that sudden cramping in the hand, foot, or calf of the leg will incapacitate you—although extremely painful, it rarely has this type of power—but rather that the cramp will create panic. If you're suddenly assaulted by a muscle spasm, immediately—repeat, immediately—inhale deeply and tuck yourself into the vertical-rest position of the breathing cycle.

Once so positioned, grasp the cramped area firmly with one or both hands (depending upon your skill and the location of the cramp). Firm steady pressure will release the cramp, but you should continue kneading the muscle in order to restore circulation. If you fail to do this, the cramp will return. Also, change your stroke to avoid using the same muscles. One muscle spasm does not have to drive you out of the water; however, if a cramp recurs, particularly if it recurs in exactly the same area, you can assume you've had enough swimming for one day.

Stomach cramp. Considerably more serious is spastic cramping of the stomach or abdomen muscles. The reaction to this kind of cramping is as swift as it is apparently unavoidable. The swimmer is hit by such pain that he exhales, his knees are instinctively (there's that word again) drawn to his chest, his head is drawn down and forward, and he rapidly begins to submerge. Assuming you can fight yourself free from this doomed position, you must force your head back out of the water, take a huge breath of air, and quickly assume the jellyfish float.

Once in the position of extreme pain described above, a swimmer can sink like the fabled stone. In fact, people stricken with this severe cramping have been known to drown in the shallow ends of artificial swimming pools. The best defense against a severe stomach cramp is another swimmer. Alone, your survival odds are diminished. The only other measure you can take in self-protection is to be sure not to enter the water too soon after eating. The stomach cramp is sometimes—although, by no means, always—the result of lactic acid in the bloodstream, a condition resulting when too much blood is being used for the digestive process. Even this precaution, however, will not guarantee safety. The antidote is simple and bears repeating: Never swim alone.

O THE RESCUE

A distress call is impossible to ignore. If you spot a drowning fellow human, however, don't immediately jump into the water after him. Chances are this will only result in *two* drownings. According to the Red Cross, more swimming fatalities result from rescue attempts than from anything else. Only certified lifesavers have the know-how to make an in-water rescue. This doesn't mean that you stand by and watch while someone's folded neatly away in Davy Jones' locker, though. But it is critical that you remain calm and limit your own actions to those that you can control. And, seek out additional help instantly.

Anyone who is serious about the sport of swimming or, for that matter, anyone who owns or has steady access to a backyard pool or pond should enroll and complete the American Red Cross lifesaving course. It's a must. The benefits are many. You will receive a more thorough understanding of your relationship to the water environment, and gain a justified confidence in your own ability in the water. Most important, however, a life saving course trains and qualifies you to assess, react to, and resolve dangerous situations instantly. Information on where and when to take a course can be gotten from any local Red Cross chapter. Take the course.

About Pools

For thousands of years, the man-made swimming pool has been a symbol of extravagant hedonism. And not without reason, either. Emperor Augustus, for instance, ordered a pool the size of a lake built on his pleasure island of Capri and then, not yet satisfied, had it stocked with an assortment of game fish, live dolphins, and a beautiful if somewhat water-wrinkled harem of young girls and younger boys costumed as mermaids. Ludvig II, 19th-century king of Bavaria, flooded the entire lower half of one of his many castles, transforming it into a purple-tinted grotto pool complete with gondolas, singing gondoliers, and a luminous night sky rendered in painstaking detail on the walls and ceilings. In the early Hollywood-as-Babylon days of the film industry, even the most profligate movie stars were envious of Rudolph Valentino's black-marbled "pool of desire," lit each sunset by huge white candles molded to represent couples engaged in impressively various forms of love-making. And at San Simeon, William Randolph Hearst's fabulous estate, can yet be seen two stunning pools: one, outdoors, of white marble, and the other, inside a building constructed solely for it, of blue marble, both edged in gold tiling, surrounded by Grecian columns and Roman arches, and guarded by bizarre sculptures of legendary beasts.

Within the last few decades, however, thanks partly to the economic boom after World War II and partly to the more recent middle-class emigration to suburbia, the rich and the powerful no longer have exclusive claim to the swimming pool. In fact, considering all the privately owned pools (nearly 4.5 million at last estimate) and the countless pools maintained by city parks, school sys-

tems, health spas, country clubs, swim clubs, and inclusive YMCAs, just about anyone who wants to can now get into the swim of things.

S YOU LIKE IT

The result of such widespread accessibility is that swimming pools are no longer merely the sybarite's delight. Today, pools serve a variety of swimmers with a variety of interests.

Training. For beginners, the artificial pool is easily the best site for learning how to swim. Its shallow-to-deep proportions, secure guardrails and ladders, nonabrasive surfacing, immediately at-hand safety equipment, and all the other standard features of the properly designed pool make it an ideal place to gain skill and confidence in the water. (Former Olympic star Eva Bory, for instance, has had amazing success teaching children, some no more than two months old, basic swimming knowhow in conventional backyard pools.) For experts, too, the pool has its uses: It is the most practical spot to refine old strokes, explore new strokes, develop waterproofing techniques, and even acquire the techniques necessary for such highly specialized open-water sports as scuba diving and underwater fishing.

Exercises. The swimming pool, when correctly maintained and supervised, is considerably more tranquil than any body of water found in nature. The absence of waves, tidal currents, and underwater obstructions ensures a uniquely benign habitat for any form of shape-up, whether it be aquametrics, calisthenics, or lapping. There are, of course, some qualifications here—a crowded area, say, or a boisterous crowd can severely restrict you—but, in general, the pool may be regarded as a nearly perfect swim gym.

Competition. Although swimming meets are occasionally held in rivers and lakes, serious competing is always reserved for the pool. (In truth, it should be noted that the conventional type of pool is no longer considered adequate for racing and diving events, and special new features—bottoms that can be adjusted to different depths or sides contoured to reduce chop—are constantly being designed.) All the skills needed for race competition—arm whip, leg spring, entry and exit techniques, correct body position, coordination, timing, glide power, breath control, stroke rhythm—can be developed properly only in the consistent water conditions of an artificial pool.

Some people call a pool a backyard chiropractor.

-FRANK O'NEIL
Sports Conditioning

Playing. Thanks, again, to their singular placidity, pools are wonderfully suited for all sorts of aqua-frolicking. Water baseball, water basketball, water ping-pong . . . there's no end to the sports and games that can be played, either alone or in teams, in a reasonably sized swimming pool. And all the water games are not only great fun but a great way to develop confidence, coordination, and skill.

Luxury. Just because the modern pool has proved to be a useful tool doesn't mean that it has lost its function as luxurious toy. On the contrary, the swimming pool—especially the backyard recreational type—has lost none of its standing as the sybarite's delight. If you'd care to sample just how good the good life can be, spend a few weekend hours floating idly in the water on a Styrofoam easy chair, a drink in one languid hand and the Sunday papers in the other. That's luxury with a vengeance.

Safety. As should be readily apparent by now, the pool by its very nature is the safest of all swimming sites. Less than 10 percent of all swimming mishaps occur in pools. That's still too many, of course, but if you pay close attention to the safety discussion on the following pages, the possibility of your ending up as a statistic will be very slight.

EVERYPERSON'S POOL

There are, basically, two types of swimming pools: recreational and training. Although the first is designed mainly for fun and the second for serious workouts, they share several common features.

The bottom of a correctly built pool should gently decline from end (shallow) to end (deep). The bottom itself should be constructed either of smooth cement finish or of unglazed tile. (Glazed tile is too slippery; and although rough cement offers good footing, it can badly shred bare soles, thus promoting cuts, sores, and resultant infection.) Both ends of the pool should be clearly identified, by inset tile or painted letters, marking minimum and maximum depths.

People who own their own pool or who have the opportunity to swim in the nude should certainly take advantage of it.

-ILSE NOLTE-HEURITSCH
Aqua-Rythmics

The surrounding decks and runways should be surfaced with semismooth cement or with unglazed tile, too. Ladders from pool to deck should be mounted approximately every five meters. Any springboards erected on the deck should meet AAU standards of safety (among them: The board should not rise more than 2 inches from its butt to its tip, it should project well out above the water, and it should be covered with matting, preferably cocoa matting). For boards up to 1 meter in height, the water depth directly below must be at least 8 feet; for boards up to 3 meters in height, the depth must be at least 10 feet; and for any diving platform higher than that, the depth must be 15 or more feet. No two springboards should be positioned in such a way that they provide the same point of entry. A high board should never be built above a low board. And the portion of the pool featuring boards of any kind should be restricted solely to divers.

Because of the limited dimensions of recreational pools, no swimmer will ever be dangerously out of reach of a side or an end. Safety, then, is more a question of regulation than of rescue. Even so, avoid pools lacking either correct supervision or equipment (bamboo poles, shepherd's crooks, and ring buoys). Also pass up pools that permit such obviously dangerous horseplay as wrestling on the deck, throwing each other into the pool, diving from rafters or balconies, and so on. If you happen to be in a backyard pool, of course, it's a bit unreasonable to expect a lifeguard in attendance. Even so, the basic safety equipment should still be on hand and the basic safety rules should still be in effect.

If you're currently using a pool that does not meet these elementary qualifications, find yourself a better one—immediately.

POOLING AROUND

The most recent government estimates show that approximately one out of every three communities—small towns as well as large cities—now has some type of public pool facilities. Unfortunately, many of these pools, especially those found in densely populated areas, are less than adequate. The problem is not so much design as it is control. Typically, the community pool will only be able to handle reasonably small crowds. If as often happens—notably in the dog days of summer—too many people happen to show up at once, the pool's supervisory power is severely diminished. And no pool can ever be rated better than its ability to enforce the essential codes of safety and hygiene.

The first thing to check out, then, when pool hunting is whether or not the site has a maximum-capacity policy. The second thing to check out is whether or not the site honors its policy. If the answer to both questions is yes, next make sure that the portion of the pool reserved for recreation is safely separated from those areas used for serious swimming and for diving. Also, see if the pool has roped off a special section for the very young children. (You should investigate this even if you don't happen to have children; the precautions taken for youngsters are always a good indication of the overall reliability of that particular pool.) Finally, determine that the pool shares all those features already discussed. If you have any trouble finding a community bathing spot that fits all the necessary specifications, or if you merely want to save yourself some legwork, contact the local branch of the Red Cross and ask for advice.

Advantages. The community pool is cheap, convenient, and—assuming it's properly operated—pleasant. And as its main purpose (in theory, anyway) is to advance the public good, it should offer a generous variety of services (basic swimming courses, lifesaving training, childcare, etc.), activities, and equipment.

Disadvantages. There are, as already mentioned, two major disadvantages inherent in even the best-run community pool: sanitation and safety.

The problems in maintaining good hygienic standards are directly proportional to the number of people using the pool. Although the rules prohibiting swimmers from bringing food, drink, or unwashed bodies into the water are usually routinely upheld by the staff (no matter how overworked it may be), it's simply not possible to guarantee that everyone using the pool is free of disease. The result is that an overcrowded community pool is overcrowded with communicable diseases as well.

Then it occurred to him that by taking a dogleg to the southwest he could reach his house by water . . . He seemed to see, with a cartographer's eye, that string of swimming pools, that quasisubterranean stream that curved across the county.

-JOHN CHEEVER
"The Swimmer," 1967

Safety is also related, though not quite as directly as sanitation, to crowds. Explains one certified pool lifeguard: "A training pool is divided into separate lanes, which both controls traffic and provides us with strong visual contact with the swimmers. Also, in a training pool, everyone is pretty much doing the same types of things. In a recreational pool, though, even in a relatively uncrowded one, each person is doing something different. There's a lot more horseplay, too. It's pretty chaotic, too chaotic to be able to keep a close eye on everybody at once."

His solution?

"Well, one way to handle it would be to use the pool only during off-peak hours. Another way is to use the less-inclusive facilities offered by private groups like the YMCA. Probably the best way, though, is to take responsibility for your own health and safety each time you visit a community pool—and hope that everyone else there is willing to do the same."

BACKYARD POOLS

There are now nearly 2 million Americans who own in-ground swimming pools, and another 100,000 are expected to join the ranks by the end of the year. "Our product," recently crowed the National Swimming Pool Institute, "is no longer a fad but a way of life."

Despite its incredible boom, however, the privately owned pool is not—at least, not yet—available to everyone. Even if you have the money (the most modest in-ground pool costs several thousand dollars to install), you might not have the house. Even if you have the house, you might not have the proper amount of space. Even if you have the space, you might not have the permission of the zoning board. And even if you have permission, you might not have the correct type of soil conditions.

Keep in mind that these are merely the preliminary stages. Once you've determined the feasibility of a home

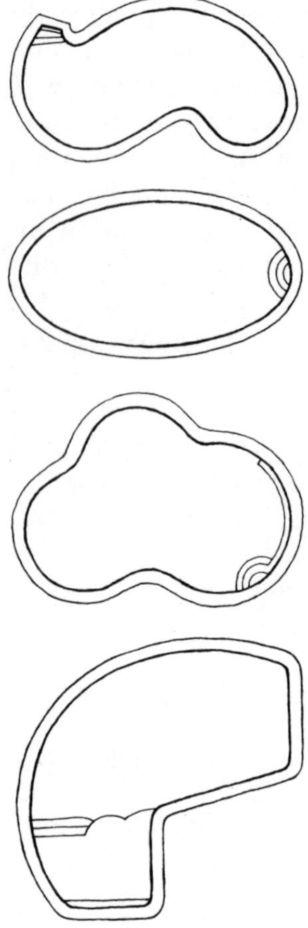

pool, you must then find a contractor, agree on a design both practical and attractive, and make literally hundreds of decisions regarding filtering processes, heating devices, surfacing, special equipment, disinfection products, building material . . .

Not that a pool you can call your own isn't worth all this work—for it most certainly is. But the work is detailed, and it should be specific to your needs. In a very real sense, each home pool is unique, and that prevents us from making many general statements here. In fact, about the only general thing we can say about the in-ground backyard pool is that its possibilities as a swimming environment are almost limitless.

Advantages. Read the last sentence again. Owning a pool gives you the kind of power that swimmers' dreams are made of. Inclement weather? No problem. Just invest in protective roofing and a good heating system. Indeed, if you have the funds, you can now purchase outdoor-pool insulation so effective that you could happily—and safely—paddle about in the middle of a hurricane. Want to hold your own meets? Still no problem. Any contractor worth his salt can build you a pool that would make the Olympic Committee's collective mouth water. Putting in backbreaking days at the office? Again, no problem. A little (though admittedly expensive) adjusting can transform any corner of your pool into a whirlpool bath. On and on it goes, and where it stops nobody knows. The amount of adaptations possible in a private pool are restricted only by the amount of imagination and amount of money available to the pool owner.

Disadvantages. If you dismiss such headaches as planning, installation, and maintenance as necessary evils, then the major disadvantage with home in-ground pools is kids. More than 200 children a year drown in backyard pools, and almost every death occurs because of inadequate or nonexistent adult supervision.

In order to protect your youngsters from injury or worse, take the following precautionary measures:

- Never, never leave a child alone in or near the pool.
- Place a fence and locked gate around the pool to prevent children from entering the pool area unattended or when you're not at home.
- Separate the shallow end from the deep end of the pool by a buoyed line (good) or a movable bulkhead (better).
- Do not permit any bottles, glasses, knives, razors, or any other sharp objects in or near the pool.
- Keep all lifesaving equipment and a *complete* first-aid kit readily available in the vicinity.
- Teach your children—and insist that any friends who use the pool teach *their* children—to respect the water.

ABOVE-THE-GROUND

Originally designed to be nothing more than small wading ponds for children, aboveground pools are used today on a considerably grander, more sophisticated scale. More than 3 million have been sold to date, ranging from the standard 12-foot-diameter tank to a 20-by-40-foot rectangle (used in many schools to teach swimming basics).

One of the reasons for their popularity is their size. The aboveground pool can easily be installed in an area that could never permit the conventional in-ground pool. Another reason is their portability. Aboveground pools have been mounted on flatbed trucks (so as to bring them into underprivileged areas), on front porches, inside living rooms, and even up in trees. But the main reason for their success is their inexpensiveness. Although there are some models that sell for as much as $22,000, the basic tank can be purchased complete for just about $500. It is this type—the one that offers the most radical alternative to the in-ground pool—that we will concentrate our attention on.

Advantages. Cost, mobility, and size have already been cited. Additional advantages include attractiveness (the newest tank models can be fitted with decks and foliage designed to disguise the shell), community acceptance (since the tanks are legally classified as "portable units," they neither violate any zoning laws nor are liable to property-tax assessment), and safe (tanks are now available with safety fences and access steps that can be swung out of reach of children).

Disadvantages. These are pretty much similar to the problems with in-ground pools, but there are also two additional problems.

The inexpensive tank's extremely small diameter makes any form of swimming, except for the most perfunctory, impossible. A couple of kicks and a couple of strokes will quickly propel you from one side of the pool to the other. Tanks are a perfectly reasonable way to cool off in the water. They also provide a reassuring environment to introduce small children to aquatics. Anything more elaborate, however, will require a considerably larger pool.

Furthermore, heating and filter systems are generally not available for the standard aboveground tank. (Some of the very newest models are so equipped, but the systems are quite expensive—almost as much as the tank itself—and are limited in capability.) There's not much you can do about the heat, except avoid the water if its temperature drops below 72°F. The lack of a filter system, though, can encourage the spread of infectious disease. It is therefore absolutely essential that everyone take a shower both before and after using the pool. (It would be helpful, too, to provide a footbath near the tank.) Also, some policing—preventing people with colds, other infections, or open cuts from entering the water—will be necessary.

SERIOUS SWIMMING

The serious swimmer is anyone—man, woman, or child—who wishes to use the sport as a means toward achieving a healthy body, an energetic mind, and a liberated spirit. And the quality of your swimming (and the quality, too, of all resultant benefits) will invariably depend upon the quality of your chosen swimming pool.

You can probably discard several potential sites immediately. ("Probably" because there are always, of course, exceptions to every rule.) Municipal pools, other than those located in sparsely populated areas, are generally too crowded—and too unsanitary—for practical consideration. Private-club pools, though more carefully supervised and better equipped, are often prohibitively expensive. Health-spa pools are usually too specialized (that is, reserved exclusively for therapeutic purposes). And backyard pools are, all too often, too small.

No, what's needed is an environment expressly created for serious swimming. Ideally, all you'd have to do would be to pick up the telephone, call the nearest AAU district office, and ask where the official meet competitions are held. (Pools employed in such meets must always be built according to the strictest standards.) As the time allowed for noncompetitive public attendance will most likely be limited, however, the AAU-sanctioned bathing spots are difficult to schedule for use on any regular basis.

The only solution is to take a deep breath and plunge into the Great Pool Hunt. But cheer up. It doesn't have to be a difficult search. For one thing, there are more than enough pools to go around. For another, all that's really required is a little luck, a lot of patience, and a fundamental knowledge of those factors that distinguish a good swimming pool from a poor one. If you just find the answers to the questions listed below each time you visit a new pool, you'll be able to begin your life as a serious swimmer almost immediately.

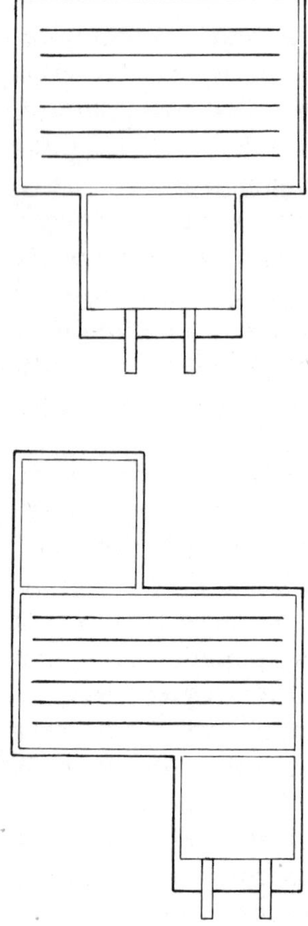

FUN AND FUNCTION

Thanks to the suppleness of new manufacturing materials, today's artificial swimming pool can be coaxed into virtually any desired shape. There are pools that twist, pools that turn, pools that loop and spiral and curlicue, even pools that form the initials of their owners' names. For you, however—which is to say, for the serious swimmer—the choices involved when selecting the proper pool are considerably less varied.

In truth, there's no variety whatsoever. Not, that is, in shape. The very best training pools are always rectangular in design. This is because the straight lines and right angles of its outline permit the maximum number of swimmers to use the pool at any one given time, allow each individual swimmer an exact measurement of pace and distance, permit the utilization of a wide range of strokes and kicks, and aid in the reduction of "chop" (more about this shortly).

More and more, nowadays, the classic rectangle has been modified into what is known as the "combined" pool. Essentially, this represents a complex of rectangular pools separated by thick concrete walls. The most often-used combined designs are the T-shape (consisting of two rectangle pools) and the Z-shape (three rectangle pools). The purpose behind these complexes is to divide the swimming area for different purposes—one pool may be used for training and racing only, while another is used solely for diving, and the third is reserved for children.

The combined pool is usually the most convenient type to use. Otherwise, you may be permitted in the water only at certain times; the other hours will be restricted to other types of swimmers and swimming. Often, the owner of a single-rectangle pool will install a movable bulkhead, so that the pool can be divided into two distinct areas, thus allowing both serious and recreational activities to take place simultaneously.

BASIC DIMENSIONS

Assuming that the pool in question has been designed for adult swimmers, with no provisions for either children or divers, the depth at the shallow end should be no less than 3½ feet and no more than 4 feet, and the depth at the deep end should be 7 to 8 feet.

The width will depend on whether or not the pool is ever used for AAU meets. If it is, then a minimum of six racing lanes must be provided. As each swimming lane is *always* 7 feet wide, the total width will be a minimum of 42 feet. If the pool isn't an AAU competition site, width becomes more variable. However, no good general pool will ever offer less than three lanes.

The largest swimming pool in the world is the salt-water Orthlieb Pool in Casablanca, Morocco. It is 480 meters (1,547 feet) long and 75 meters (246 feet) wide, an area of 8.9 acres.

–Guinness Book of World Records

As for length—well, most competitive athletes prefer the 50-meter pool (called within the sport the "fast" pool because it requires fewer turns when racing laps). Since this is an impractical length for most indoor swimming sites, however, and since good outdoor pools are hard to come by, the 25-yard pool is more than sufficient. Actually, even a shorter length will do (although you should keep in mind that too short a pool means you'll be doing almost as much turning as swimming).

One last point: Regardless of the actual dimensions, most states now require that pools provide 25 square feet of space for each swimmer.

LANES AND LINES

As already mentioned, each pool lane must be 7 feet wide. The lane lines on the bottom should be painted a dark color that contrasts with the general color of the pool. (Preferably, the walls and floor will be painted white, and the lines will be painted black.) Each line should be 12 or more inches wide, and should also be centered in the lane (in order to allow the swimmer to stay above the line, thus using it as a guide from one end of the pool to the other). Approximately 60 inches from each end should be placed a distinctive cross-lane; this serves as a warning to the swimmer that he's nearing the end wall (many swimming-pool accidents are the result of a swimmer too intent on his pace to avoid banging his head against a wall). The lane numbers should be indicated directly above each lane (numbered from left to right).

Except during competitive meets, there's no requirement that the lanes also be marked by surface lines. Even so, many pools do provide them. The lines should be tightly stretched (to eliminate sway), securely anchored, and distinctively marked (usually painted white in the middle, red on the ends). Usually, too, the lines will support a series of floats so close together that they form an almost continuous cylinder. Surface lines reduce chop, control traffic, and will also support a floundering swimmer.

GUTTERS

Gutters, also referred to as overflow systems, run along the sides and ends of the pool. Although there are various types of gutter, each specific system must have certain general specifications. Gutters should be approximately 6 inches in width and at least 6 inches in depth. Both back and bottom should curve smoothly to the front side (the side nearest the pool). The front inside of the gutter should rise vertically to the gutter lip, thus creating a flat internal trough that prevents spillback of water. The AAU insists that pool water should never be lower than the gutter-lip level; although this rule was designed for the benefit of competitive racers, it will be observed in any pool designed for serious swimming.

The gutter serves three basic functions. First, it keeps the water surface free of film and floating dirt. Next, it prevents too much water from spilling up onto the deck (a water-slicked deck has been the scene of many an accident). Finally, and possibly most important, the gutter eliminates the nemesis of all serious swimmers: chop.

Chop is swimming-coach slang for any and all turbulence in the water. It's at its worst, of course, during a race—six madly stroking swimmers will create an awful lot of waves—but it also results, quite naturally, whenever there's more than one person in a pool. A certain amount is unavoidable; too much, however, will make any real swimming impossible. The continual disturbance of the water (ripples from splashing novices, wakes from the more advanced lappers, tidal turbulence from people entering or leaving the pool) throws stroke rhythms out of sync, interferes with breath control, and generally plays havoc with technique. As this defeats the primary purpose of an artificial pool—which is to offer a constantly regulated environment of optimum swimming conditions—it only stands to reason that no pool allowing unnecessary chop is worthy of use.

Unless you're an engineer, examining the gutters will not help you gauge their efficiency (they're fairly complicated). Unless you have X-ray vision, watching the water will not help you determine the amount of chop (much of the disruption will be occurring beneath the surface). The only real way to make a judgment is to try out the pool. Swim a few steady laps. If you have any difficulty with your stroke, or if your time isn't as good as usual, or if you can actually feel turbulence pulling and pushing at you, then that particular pool is not for you.

By the way, several coaches have asked us to post this warning. Many of the pools now being built are installing a new overflow system called the surface skimmer. These are container-type gutters set in the top beam of the pool walls. They're popular with operators because they're inexpensive to build and require little maintenance. But although surface skimmers are perfectly legal, they're by no means perfect. The design does not significantly reduce chop, and the AAU suggests that pools using them should not be used for training programs or for racing competitions.

LIGHTS

The AAU-meet standards should be applied to all pools. On the decks, required illumination is a minimum of 100 foot-candles. Deck lighting must be shielded to avoid glare and reflections in the water. Required water-surface lighting is the minimum equivalent of 100 foot-candles, too. The placement of lights should be arranged so as to avoid shadows on the pool walls. Any windows above or to the sides of the pool are either to be securely shuttered or made of tinted glass.

HEALTH AND HYGIENE

Physical injury is not the only danger facing the swimmer. Many infectious diseases are all too easily spread in water. Conjunctivitis, ear, sinus, and eye infections, ringworm and other skin disorders, gastrointestinal illnesses, and the common cold are just a few of the problems you may take home.

Therefore, in addition to the periodic disinfection of the water itself the pool facilities must include adequate showers, toilets, dressing rooms, and drinking fountains. And all these facilities must be well cleaned, well lighted, well built, and—when necessary—well ventilated.

The pool's responsibility to good hygiene does not, however, end there. Sanitation rules must be sternly enforced. No one with an obvious or known infection is ever to be allowed in the pool. Everyone must take a shower before entering the pool area. No pets are ever allowed inside the bathhouse. No brushes, combs, towels, drinking cups, or soap bars are ever to be provided for common use. And overall maintenance of cleanliness—including the daily scrubdown of decks, showers, and so on—must always be in force.

WATER CHEMISTRY

This is a most important question. In order to answer it fully, you will first have to understand those vital elements that create the best possible pool water.

Eliminating bacteria. Although there are several disinfectants that will effectively control the growth of bacteria in water, most swimming-pool operators are required by law to use either chlorine or bromine. The former is cheaper, the latter is safer, but one of the two chemicals must be used if the pool water is to be deemed suitable for human use.

In its purest state, chlorine is a heavy, green, and highly deadly gas. In order to safely introduce it into the swimming water, it must first be liquefied in a machine (called a chlorinator) that also feeds and regulates it into the pool. The main objection to chlorine is that it can irritate the eyes. (Actually, this is the result of too little chlorine in the water. Through the mystery of chemistry, if there is too little chlorine it will combine with hydrogen to form chloramines, and it is this compound that stings and reddens eyes.) Continual care on the part of the operator is required to prevent this effect.

Studies involving utilization of pool areas have revealed that shallow water (under 5 feet) is where most people swim, regardless of their ability.

-Aquatics Handbook, 1968

Bromine in its pure state is a dark-brown liquid, practically as toxic as chlorine gas. It's fed into the pool by means of a brominator, a machine that passes bubbles of water through the liquid bromine and then adds the resulting solution to the water-filter line. Although bromine significantly reduces the likelihood of eye irritation, it tends to have an excessively unpleasant odor and to leave a brown stain on walls and bottom. It is also two to four times as expensive chlorine.

Eliminating algae. There are no less than 46 species of algae that form in swimming-pool water, and any of them can cause such problems as unplesant odors, cloudy water, foul-tasting water, and dangerously slippery decks, walls, or bottom. Algae control is very important to the comfort and safety of the swimmers. The most effective way to do this is via a process known as "super-chlorination"—that is, the raising of the chlorine level in a pool to its highest possible level. Pool operators don't like doing this, since it demands the closing of their facilities for 24 hours; neglecting a periodic super-chlorination, however, will eventually lose them their clientele. The rule of thumb here is not to patronize any pool that evidences excess amounts of algae.

Water balance. If you've been attending one pool regularly, you may have noticed the operator or one of his employees dipping a laboratory vial into the water every two or three days. This is the pH test—a vital function to the entire process of water quality control.

Briefly, pH is the measure of the degree of acidity and alkalinity in water. The scale ranges from pH 1.0 (indicating a very high acid condition) to pH 14.0 (indicating a very high alkaline condition). Either too much alkaline or too much acid will result in eye irritation, skin rashes, and foul odors. The balance, therefore, between these two conditions must always be carefully maintained.

Most authorities recommend that pool water be kept within the pH range of 7.2 to 8.0. In other words, the water you swim in should always be slightly alkaline. Besides neutralizing the effects of acid compounds, alkalinity raises the maximum safety level of chlorine, thus ensuring proper disinfection of bacterial and algae growths.

Pope John Paul doesn't have any hopes of competing in the Olympics, but apparently he's getting a little "rest and relaxation" by swimming. Workmen at the papal palace in the little town of Castel Gandolfo, Italy, have been digging a swimming pool in the palace gardens for the Pope.

-Swimming World

Both the testing and the controlling of pH are simple processes. They are also both required by law. No pool operator has any excuse for neglecting water balance. No pool that lacks correct water balance can be regarded as suitable for serious—or for any—swimming.

Water temperature. Most people are most comfortable in extremely warm water. Unfortunately, so are most forms of infectious bacteria. And, in addition to promoting bacterial growth, overly warm water lures swimmers into a dangerously relaxed state of lassitude. Conversely, water that is too *cold* may, as already described in our chapter on waterproofing, exhaust swimmers to the point of risk of drowning.

Pool water, then, must be maintained at a temperature ranging from 74° to 80°F. (The AAU requires a slightly colder temperature range—72° to 78°F.—for competitive racing events.) The only exception to this occurs when air temperature is above 90°F, which necessitates a water temperature no more than 72°F. As no all-year pool, either indoors or outdoors, can hope to maintain these standards without artificial devices, two separate machines—one for heating pool water, one for cooling pool water—are essential equipment at any bathing spot you're considering.

Water filters. There are too many effective filter systems to describe here. Suffice it to say, the only systems worth using are systems that do the job. If the pool water is cloudy, if the pool bottom is littered with debris, if the pool drains are clotted with hair and/or algae, then the filter system is not adequate, and you should find another pool.

Water charts. Some of the water conditions described above can be discovered through observation and a little trial swimming. For example, if the water seems too green and cloudy, there's algae growth present; if the water is green and clear, it is too alkaline; if the water is brown, it is too acid; if the water is cloudy in the morning and clear again at night, the filter system is overloaded; if after swimming in the water your eyes are irritated or your skin is red, there's too much chloramine present.

Other water conditions, however, are not so apparent. Fortunately, every state insists that pool operators keep a daily water record. The items recorded include the number of persons using the pool daily, the water and air temperature averages, all chemicals used for disinfection and pH balance, the dates when water samples for bacterial count are sent to health department services, and any unusual occurrences (motor breakdown, chlorinator malfunction, electricity loss, etc.) that affect water conditions. This record should be prominently displayed. If you can't find it, ask the operator to show it to you.

Fresh Water

There are two types of swimming environments for the freshwater swimmer. Rivers, accurately described by Blaise Pascal as "roads that travel," satisfy our need for exploration. And lakes, filled to the brim with lifeforms of every sort, satisfy our need to merge with nature. Each demands considerable skill and involves some undeniable risk. In return, though, each rewards with an experience you'd never be able to find on dry land.

Rivers are always moving, always changing, always challenging. In direct contrast, lakes are relatively stable, predictable, and mostly peaceful bodies of water—though that doesn't mean they should be dismissed by the adventurous swimmer. Lakes have one great asset unique to themselves: They exist as environmental laboratories, providing habitat and nurture for incalculable numbers of organisms living in symbiosis. To swim in an unspoiled lake is to become included in nature's system.

Although lakes are obviously less demanding of the swimmer than are rivers, statistically at least they are the most dangerous of all swimming sites. More people drown in lakes and ponds each year than in any other type of water. The statistics, however, are misleading. For one thing, most of the reported drownings are the result of boating, not swimming, accidents. For another, more people lose their lives in lakes because more people use lakes than any other water site.

While it is true that lakes—particularly secluded lakes—do present problems, if you are a reasonably good swimmer, if you are a careful swimmer, and if you have a reasonably good and careful swimming partner, the chances of mishap are very slim.

AKES

Except during gale or storm conditions, the lake is a gentle and benevolent medium for the swimmer. You do not have to be an expert before trying your hand (and foot) in its waters; indeed, it ranks just below the artificial pool as a great training site for the beginner. For all its tranquillity, however, the lake still presents several complexities for those who wish to experience it fully. And, as a *serious* lake swimmer, you will need a certain amount of skill, equipment, and foreknowledge if you are to enjoy lake swimming to its maximum.

First, you should be fully adept in the breaststroke, sidestroke, and backstroke. Although there are no strong currents in a lake, a brisk wind can stir up the water into a frothing, roiling frenzy. Not only strength but also endurance will be required to withstand such turbulence. You must therefore be able both to swim relatively long distances (at least 200 yards at a clip) and to remain immersed for a relatively long time (at least an hour in waters not lower than 65°F). In addition, you should be trained in all waterproofing techniques (especially the breathing cycle and the travel stroke).

Next, you're going to need some advance knowledge of the terrain. Each swimming site has its own peculiarities. The most peaceful-looking lake surface may conceal a virtual maze of hazards. Never enter a lake for the first time before checking out any potential dangers it may encompass—quicksand patches, for instance, or a bad-tempered population of snapping turtles—with people who know the lake.

WHERE LAND MEETS WATER

There is no one rule regarding how to locate the best lakeside entry spot. Each body of water, whether surrounded by highland woods or lowland marshes, has its own unique approach. Ideally, this approach will feature a gentle, gradual slope, an unobstructed view of the lake surface, and a firm-grounded footing. In reality,

though, these conditions may not always coincide. And even if they do, the corresponding water conditions may be poor. Because of all this variability, it's important that as much care as possible be exercised in approaching a lake. Whenever you, the lake swimmer, explore a new shoreline, you should use the same cautious savvy employed by any successful trailblazer.

The contours of the neighboring countryside will almost always correspond to the contours of the bordering water. Therefore, sloping land indicates a slope in the lake bottom. The more gradual the slope, the more gradual the drop into deeper waters. If land and water meet abruptly, the drop will be abrupt. Locating a broad and mildly declining patch of shore lying against a clear and undisturbed patch of water (discolored water indicates a muddy bottom; frothy, or aerated, water indicates submerged boulders and other obstacles) guarantees you a safe approach. If you are unable to find such a spot, you will have to make do with the closest thing to it. Be sure, in such an eventuality, that you've previously armed yourself with a long staff (a trimmed tree branch, four to six feet long, should serve). The staff will allow you not only to gauge the water depth but also to search out any treacherous spots along the water edge.

When approaching a marshy lake, you must *always* have such a staff. The soft, porous ground around lowlands water is invariably pockmarked by sinkholes, sandbars, bogs, and even quicksand, because the land acts like a giant sponge. Footing is a matter of prime importance. The staff is an essential tool here, often the only means you'll have to navigate your way through the mud. It's unlikely that you'll be able to find the same sloping shoreline offered by wooded lakes. Instead, you'll have to settle for any entry point that gives you access to the open water. One consolation, however, is that the marsh lake rarely (if ever) has any dangerously abrupt dropoffs. Once you've made your muddy way to the waterline, you can be reasonably certain that you're not about to plunge into a bottomless pit. In fact, you'll probably have to wade out for quite some distance before you're in deep enough for proper swimming.

There is an alternative to the mud. If the marsh lake is being fed by streams and creeks, find the largest one and enter it half a mile or so upriver. In this manner, you can swim with the current into the lake proper without having to contend with spongy terrain. No matter how thick and oozy the bog surrounding the main body of water, the land on either side of the stream will be firm and sloping.

BOTTOM LINES

The *shape* of a natural lake bottom is constant. That is, except for the ledges, dropoffs, and sandbars often found in the shallows, a lake can usually be described as a cup—declining on all sides toward the center, where the deepest water will always be found. The *substance* of a lake bottom, however, varies widely. It may be composed of sand, or gravel, or firm smooth earth, or volcanic rock. Despite the variations in makeup, there are only three lake-bottom conditions that concern the lake swimmer:

Weeds. Thick clumps of water weeds are often located in the shallows of the lake. Too tough and numerous to tear loose, these weeds can threaten a swimmer in only inches-deep water. If you become entangled, don't panic. Thrashing about will only wrap the plants tighter around your body. Just shake your arms and legs gently and steadily. If you are still unable to get clear, begin to swim slowly into deeper water. (The sidestroke is best.) Gradually, the weeds will unwrap of their own accord.

Sinkholes. Often covered by dead leaves or a thin coating of sand, sinkholes are small pitted areas that can entrap a swimmer's foot. If you use the staff when you first enter the water, poking it into the bottom just in front of you, you'll probably be able to avoid these pits. Sometimes, though, especially in marshy lakes, they are just too numerous to be avoided. Usually, you can remove yourself from one easily enough. Again, don't panic. Stand absolutely still in the water, and gently lift your leg. If your foot's lodged too tightly for easy removal, ease yourself down into the water until you can see the hole clearly. Chances are that a few scoops of your hand will widen the hole sufficiently to free yourself. If you're still stuck, call your swimming partner over. Together, you'll be able to dig yourself out of any difficulty.

Quicksand. This is sand held in suspension by water. It is usually found on the shores of marshy lakes, although it can also exist in highland waters. Despite the Saturday-matinee jungle-film lore, quicksand can be easily negotiated. In fact, mud or sand supports your weight better than water. If you should suddenly feel yourself caught in a patch of muck, do not try to free yourself while standing. This will only make you sink deeper below the surface. Slide forward, fill your lungs with air, spread your arms, frog-kick your legs, and breaststroke your way through to the water or firmer ground beyond. Even a moderate swimmer can, if need be, paddle his way through miles of bog, marsh, or quicksand.

Free utterly now, though
the freedom endure
but the space of a
perilous breath . . .
So plunges the downward
swimmer, embraced
of the water unfathomed
of man. . . .

-ALGERNON SWINBURNE
"The Lake of Gaube," 1899

Of course, you've got no business being trapped in the gunk in the first place. The staff will not only comfort you but keep you away from the gluey places. A good eye won't hurt, either. If you're in the middle of a long stretch of muddy shoreline, keep on the lookout for sandy spots littered with pebbles or twigs. This is a sure sign of good footing.

MOVING WATERS

There are no really strong currents in the water. There are, however, eddies, undertows, seiches, and whirlpools, and you should be prepared to contend with all of them.

Both the eddies and the undertows are located only at

the mouths of the streams and rivers that feed the lake. This makes them easy to avoid. Seiches are waves that—for reasons no one has yet been able to explain—exist in some mountain lakes. The waves swell up from the lake center and roll to the shore in a pattern that resembles the rhythm of the ocean. They are considerably smaller, though, and need not trouble anyone who's ever experienced surf conditions. Whirlpools—clockwise spirals of water that occasionally occur spontaneously as the result of increased water level and certain kinds of wind—are a bit more problematic. The best way to deal with them is to give them a wide berth. As vision is often impaired when swimming, this is not always possible. If you are caught in a whirlpool, remember that most of its power is on its surface. As the pool descends, its force decreases. Take a deep breath, dive under the water, and breaststroke for several yards outward from the whirlpool's center. You'll be free of it in a matter of seconds.

. . . A silvery current flows
With uncontrolled meanderings;
Nor have these eyes by greener hills
Been soothed, in all my wanderings.
And, through her depths, Saint Mary's Lake
Is visibly delighted;
For not a feature of those hills
Is in the mirror slighted.

—WILLIAM WORDSWORTH
"Yarrow Visited," 1814

Far more difficult are the turbulences created by a sudden gale. The resulting waves have been known to topple trees on the shore. The strategy used here is the exact opposite of the strategy used in the sea; that is, you must swim *into* the waves toward the windward shore. (If you swim with the wind, you'll only find yourself in progressively rougher water.) Cross the swells at a right angle, diving beneath the larger ones, until you've reached the lakeside from which the wind is blowing. The only exception to this tactic is when you're close enough to the leeward shore (i.e., the lakeside toward which the wind is blowing) to reach it safely within a few short strokes. Never remain in a lake during a storm. Furthermore, you should never swim the breadth of a lake on a windy day. Instead, swim along its length, following the shape of the shoreline as closely as you can.

One final note: Never dive, headfirst or rump-backwards, into untested water. Boulders and fallen trees have a habit of lying just beneath the surface.

Cirrus

Cumulonimbus

FOUL OR FAIR

Because of the suddenness of lake storms, and because, too, of the infamous unreliability of meteorologists, it's helpful to learn how to recognize the natural warning signs of a coming storm. Some examples:

Clouds. *Cumulus clouds* (white, fat, and dome-based) usually mean fair weather. If the cloud bottom becomes dark, it's a sign of possible rain; if the bottom becomes either pink or coppery, a storm's rising. *Cirrus* clouds (feathery wisps on top, puffy clouds moving in the opposite direction beneath) indicate bad weather within the next 24 hours. *Cumulonimbus* clouds (dark and huge) are thunderheads. Count the seconds after a flash of lightning appears underneath one until you hear thunder. Every five-second interval indicates a mile. Twenty-five seconds, and the storm is five miles away from you. More immediate rainstorms, brief though wet, are marked by shapeless clouds. The faster the clouds gather, the faster the storm will be over.

Wind. Prevailing breezes keep leaves and bushes rippling in an orderly manner. When the leaves begin to ruffle and show their undersides, the wind is changing. North and east winds bring cold and rain along with them. The summer northeaster can carry a storm that will last several days. South winds often indicate the arrival of rain within a day. Southeast winds often reach gale force. The winds presaging fair weather blow from the west, the southwest, and the northwest. (Remember, though, that a mild wind on land can be a violent wind over water.)

Sky. A deep-blue sky, even one populated with numerous clouds, is a good sign; a white-tinted sky, even a cloudless one, is a bad sign. A red sunrise and gray sunset signal storms; gray sunrise and red sunset signal fair weather. "Sundogs"—halos seen around either the sun or the moon—often warn of a coming thunderstorm. A misty sunrise can be interpreted as clear weather all day.

Other Signs. A fair day is marked by heavy morning dew, falling temperature, rising barometer, campfire smoke rising straight up, and spiders—yes, spiders—spinning webs. A storm day is marked by muggy atmosphere, extra-loud insect noises, rising temperature, and a falling barometer.

THE STING

The lake is a laboratory of nature. All kinds of life forms prosper within it. The vast majority of insects, reptiles, fish, and animals exist in perfect adaptation to the water. If you observe the most commonsense precautions—do not, for instance, try to pet a beaver or chuck a woodchuck under its chin—they won't bother you. There are a few species, though, that do represent a threat to swimmers. There's nothing personal in this; they're just conditioned to attack anything that frightens them.

The trick, then, is to avoid those places where they're most likely to be found. Water moccasins and corals, both semi-aquatic poisonous snakes, are quite familiar residents of lakes throughout the United States. They're no danger when actually swimming in the water, as they'll immediately veer away from any disturbance. It's when they're sunning or sleeping that they represent a hazard, since they'll be too sluggish to attempt to escape and will instead strike out at whatever they perceive to be a menace (that's you). In order to protect yourself from snakes, keep away from sunlit rocks and protruding sandbars.

. . .We leaned in the bedroom window
Of the Old Bavarian Gasthaus,
And the frogs in the pool beyond thrilled with exuberance,
Like a boiling pot the pond crackled with happiness,
Like a rattle a child spins round for joy, the night rattled
With the extravagance of the frogs. . . .

–D. H. LAWRENCE
"She Looks Back," 1917

Many four-legged critters also inhabit the lake environment. Otters and beavers are most typical, but you may even come across an occasional fox or mink swimming from one shore to the other. As long as such animals feel safe, they represent no danger to the human swimmer. Come too near them, though, and you may end up with a bad bite. If this should happen, you must wash the wound with soap and water, flush the bitten area, bandage it, and consult the nearest physician. Unless you've been able to capture the animal, you may as well steel yourself for the rigors of antirabies treatment.

The fierce snapping turtle is the monarch of the marshy lakes, and you'd be wise to steer clear of his kingdom. These turtles, easily recognized by their unusually long necks and tails, spend much of their time beneath rocks on the lake bottom. If you should have the misfortune to disturb one, you could be in for a painful fight. The full-grown snapper has a jaw as powerful as a steel trap, and has been known to bite off fingers and toes of incautious bathers and fishermen. If a turtle does remove a chunk from your hide, apply tourniquet and bandage, and seek medical help. You'd do much better, however, simply to leave the lake rocks unturned.

Last but unfortunately not least are the insects. Not only mosquitoes, but flies, chiggers, ticks, gnats, wasps, bees, and leeches teem throughout the lake locale. The majority are more an annoyance than a true hazard (although some insects can, of course, transmit disease), but you should nevertheless make some effort to avoid them. Stay away from high-grass banks (especially early in the morning and early in the evening), avoid swimming beneath anything that even remotely resembles an insect nest, and rub your body periodically with insect repellent.

OVER AND UNDER THE FALLS

Waterfalls are, in a word, wonderful. Although river waterfalls are far too dangerous to approach, the lake waterfall is pure joy—an aquatic playground that satisfies both the adventurer and the poet.

The smallest falls, those that spill smoothly over the face of a small hill unobstructed by rocks or tree trunks, can be enjoyed pretty much like a watery version of the sliding pond. After first making sure that top and bottom are clear of dangerous debris, climb the hill, enter the water perhaps fifty or so yards upstream, turn over on your back, point your feet toward the edge, and just go with the flow. It's quite a trip.

When dealing with the larger falls, the ones that bristle with boulders and trees, you will not be able to swim over the top. You may, though, still approach such a fall from the bottom. The best way to do this is to swim below the surface. As you near the spray, dive and continue stroking ahead as close to the lake bottom as you can reach. There will still be turbulence, but it shouldn't be much more bone-shaking than a brisk Jacuzzi bath. Once you've swum past the cascade itself, you'll emerge up into a placid yet eerily lit lagoon. Above you the dancing foamy water; in front of you, the wet-slick rocks; behind you, the translucent curtain of the falls. It's a very special place to be: mysterious, awesome, and impossibly beautiful.

RIVERS

The machinery that animates the rivers of the earth is a simple one: gravity. A river invariably begins in the highlands; more often than not, the source is merely a small pool or sinkhole in which rain, melted snow, and other naturally induced water collects. Once the banks of the source are no longer able to contain it, the water breaks free and begins its journey down the hilly slopes. The steady trickle eventually forms streamlets, the streamlets combine into streams, the streams collect into one river, and the river—gaining more and more momentum as it rushes onward, and gaining, too, more and more water in its headlong surge—broadens and deepens until it merges with the sea.

Each river is unique. Some, like the Nile and the Mississippi, are subject to flood seasons that may double their width and increase their rate of speed tenfold. Some, like the Amazon, change shape and size continuously. And most do not empty into the ocean but instead into lakes, into larger rivers, or even into subterranean pools miles beneath the earth's surface.

All rivers can be separated into two categories: fast and slow. Fast rivers are usually young rivers (i.e., less

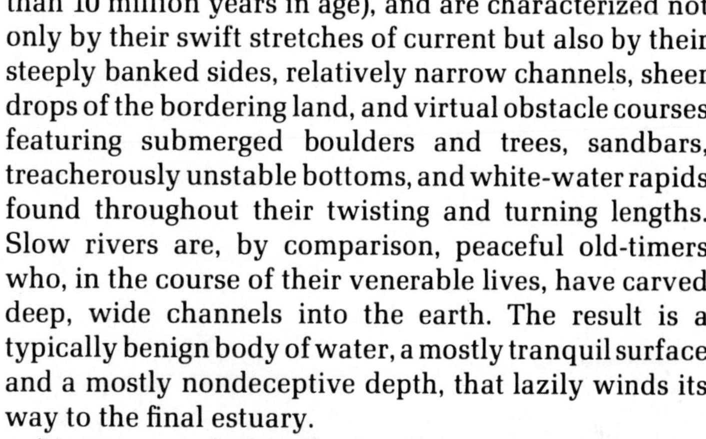

than 10 million years in age), and are characterized not only by their swift stretches of current but also by their steeply banked sides, relatively narrow channels, sheer drops of the bordering land, and virtual obstacle courses featuring submerged boulders and trees, sandbars, treacherously unstable bottoms, and white-water rapids found throughout their twisting and turning lengths. Slow rivers are, by comparison, peaceful old-timers who, in the course of their venerable lives, have carved deep, wide channels into the earth. The result is a typically benign body of water, a mostly tranquil surface and a mostly nondeceptive depth, that lazily winds its way to the final estuary.

(Keep in mind, though, that this, too, is generalized description. The Colorado River, an ancient by any geographic standards, has been channeling its path through rock for millions upon countless millions of years now—forming, in the process, the Grand Canyon—but it still boasts some of the fiercest white water on this continent.)

For the conventional swimmer, the distinction between old and young, slow and fast, rivers is not all that important. Either type will have more than enough quiet areas to swim safely.

TOURING

For the unconventional swimmer, the distinction is essential. The real adventure in river swimming lies not in paddling across its breadth but rather in touring some of its length. And for this it must be approached in the same manner that a traveler approaches the road: as a means on which to make a journey. With this one difference, however: The road is simply the means to an end; the river is both means *and* end. The good traveler must have some knowledge of his road, its shortcuts, oases, and pitfalls. The good swimmer, though, must—for the distance he remains in it—become as one with the water. Swimming in the river is not, for example, like canoeing in the river. There's little time to drift, even less time to enjoy the passing scenery along the banks, and no time whatsoever to relax. Instead, what's needed—what's *demanded*—is constant attention to the inconstant whims of the water.

He sat on the logs, smoking, drying in the sun, the sun warm on his back, the river shallow ahead entering the woods, curving into the woods, shallows, light glittering, big watersmooth rocks, cedars along the bank and white birches, the logs warm in the sun, smooth to sit on, without bark, gray to the touch; slowly the feeling of disappointment left him.

-ERNEST HEMINGWAY
"Big Two-Hearted River, Part II"
1938

Finally, you'll do well to remember that although proper preparation and skill will greatly diminish the dangers involved, river swimming is never a completely safe undertaking.

GETTING READY

Before you take stroke one in a river, you must already have acquired some vital swimming abilities.

For instance, you must be able to swim a long, continuous distance with a strong, steady stroke. Just how long a distance is a matter of some conjecture among the experts. All do agree, however, that the safe *minimum* be no less than the broadest part of the river expanse you're planning to travel through, plus—in order to allow for currents and winds—an additional equal of that distance. In other words, in order to swim in a section of river that is 200 yards across at its widest point, you should be able to swim comfortably nonstop a distance of at least 400 yards.

You must also be capable of remaining in over-your-head water, using a variety of stroke and flotation methods, for no less than 30 minutes.

You must be reasonably adept at the following swim styles: *the basic sidestroke* for its power and speed (useful in breaking free of strong currents or in swimming either across the currents to the shore or against the current back upriver to a safe haven); *the basic front crawl* for its streamlined speed; *the breaststroke* for its steady reliability and unimpaired vision; *the back crawl* for its nonrigorous demands on the body; any elemental flotation/propulsion technique, such as *the dog paddle, the human paddle*, or *the trudgen*; and both *the floating cycle* and *the traveling stroke* methods of waterproofing.

The fundamental strategy involved in crossing a river's width is to employ the sidestroke and—if necessary—the back crawl. The strategy when traveling down the length of a river is to use a combination of the front crawl (perfect to hitch rides on the currents for short periods) and the breaststroke (absolutely necessary in order to see what lies ahead), with brief interludes of a more relaxed paddle and sculling stroke. Because of these variations, you should be thoroughly rehearsed in smoothly changing from one stroke to the next before venturing into the river.

Your swimming partner—and you must have a swimming partner—should be as well versed in these techniques as you are. In addition, you should both have a working knowledge of lifesaving procedures, including mouth-to-mouth resuscitation.

Tom stirred up the other pirates and they all clattered away with a shout, and in a minute or two were stripped and chasing after and tumbling over each other in the shallow limpid water of the white sand bar. . . . They came back to camp wonderfully refreshed, glad-hearted and ravenous. . . .

-MARK TWAIN
The Adventures of Tom Sawyer, 1876

KEEPING WARM

There are two contrary phenomena that contribute to the temperature of a river. As the flow is continual, the water never remains in one spot long enough to be heated much by the sun. But, again because of the flow, the action of the water molecules, constantly in motion, produces internally generated warmth. This explains why the river temperature is so uniform (highland and lowland stretches will seldom differ by more than a few degrees) and also why the river is the coldest natural body of water during the warm weather and the warmest during the cold weather.

In practical terms, this means that rivers—unlike oceans and lakes—can be comfortable bathing sites for much of the year (mid-spring, say, to late autumn). Even so, there are always exceptions, and you must take great care that the river you're swimming is not too cold.

And just how cold is too cold? According to the American Medical Association, the "average" person (i.e., women weighing 110–135 pounds, men weighing 145–200 pounds) can swim strenuously for 10 minutes in less than 40°F water, 15–20 minutes in 40–50°F water, 20–40 minutes in 50–60°F water, and for one to several hours in 60°F-and-above water. Should anyone stay immersed until his or her body temperature drops below 95°, hypothermia may set in. This condition can lead to gangrene, coma, and eventual death.

The safest time to swim in the river, then, is from late spring to late summer when the river temperature will rarely drop beneath 65°F. If, however, you wish to chance a swim in colder waters, wear a loose-fitting woolen jersey. (Wool is absolutely the finest material for keeping warm when wet; if money *is* the object, however, Polyester Fiberfill II or Polar Guard make good—and inexpensive—substitutes.) Not only will the jersey trap body heat, but it will also provide additional buoyancy. Better yet, of course, is the aforementioned wet suit. When encased in one of these, you may plunge into the river at any time of year without fear of overexposure.

SUITING UP

You could dive buck-naked into the roaring river and reemerge, several miles downstream, with a whole skin. You could, that is, if you happen to have the skills of a champion athlete, the instincts of a fish, and the luck God has reputedly reserved for fools and drunkards. The rest of us, however, are going to need some equipment aids before attempting a river tour.

The Wet Suit. The best, and happily least expensive, kind of wet suit is made of neoprene with an inner lining of nylon to facilitate donning and removing the suit.

Critics claim the wet suit is cumbersome. This is true—but only for as long as it takes to get used to it. They also state that a wet suit deprives one of many of the sensory delights of swimming, and that using one on a river tour is like taking a shower while wearing a raincoat. This is a more serious charge. There's no doubt that the wet suit will prevent you from ever feeling completely merged with the water.

On the other hand, say the disciples, the wet suit provides three important services. First, it will cushion the inevitable collisions between your body and the various rocks and tree branches submerged in the water. Second, no matter how closely fitted the suit (and this is especially true for those made of neoprene), there will always be quite a bit of air trapped inside, thus increasing your buoyancy. And third, this air pocket will also act as a natural insulator, maintaining the body heat necessary for long submersions in the river.

As a beginning river swimmer, it will not be necessary for you to purchase a suit immediately. Its advantages will become more apparent when you're ready for more advanced touring, and at that point you'll probably want a wet suit without urging from anyone.

Flippers. River currents are often as unexpected as they are unexpectedly strong. No matter how carefully you've prepared, chances are you'll be forced to fight your way through several of them before journey's end. As this accumulative effort can be exhausting, a pair of good rubber flippers will preserve vital energy. Just about any reputable brand will do, though you should take care to buy the smooth-surfaced type. Rippled and webbed flippers, wonderful in the unbounded ocean, may snag against twigs and boulders in the cluttered river.

Masks and Goggles. In and near water, human eyesight is always at a disadvantage. When light is refracted from water, the image focused off the retina becomes blurred in outline and hazy in detail. Because a mask—or goggles with a secure headband—traps air between the eye and the viewplate, the light passes through the retina normally and the resultant image is clearly defined. Once in the water, you must depend on your eyes to locate trouble spots ahead; clear vision, only possible in the water with the aid of a mask, is a fundamental imperative for the river swimmer.

Gloves. In any water less than 60°F. gloves made of

either rubber or neoprene can be worn to prevent numbness or—in extreme cases—frostbite. In warmer waters, however, they're not only unnecessary but a bulky nuisance.

A Knife. Now don't start fantasizing about a death-defying swim, knife blade gripped between clenched teeth, through a watery jungle of dangerous beasts. The only creatures you're likely to meet in the drink will be too busy making their way up- or downriver to pay much attention to you. (The marginal exception here is water snakes—see page 236 for details.) Considerably more threatening will be the innate obstacles—clutching weeds, snatching tree branches, snarls of fishing line—you may encounter. The standard hunting knife, single-edged and safely sheathed, will cut, pry, and hack you out of such entanglements.

CHECKPOINTS

Almost any river is the right river. Your job is finding the right *stretch* of that river for swimming. The easiest way to go about this is to select the largest river in your vicinity and then call some local service—a swimming club is good, the Red Cross is better, but best of all is either a state or federal parks office—for consultation. Before you make your final decision as to the section you plan to swim in, thoroughly check out the following considerations:

Although age is the determining factor in the general speed of a river's course, you do not have to be an expert on geology before choosing one to swim in. After all, old rivers have many stretches of fast water, and young rivers have just as many stretches of slow water. Because each river is extremely varied in its nature, there's no accurate way to gauge overall speed (although it would be safe to say that a river's currents—with the one great exception of white-water rapids—rarely exceed 5 knots). However, the *relative* speed of any specific part of the river, young or old, can be gauged by advance knowledge of its dimensions and terrain.

You should find a length of river that features breadth (the wider the section of the river, the less swift the currents), considerable depth (the deeper the water, the less hidden the currents), and an overall area reasonably free of boulders, fallen tree trunks, and concrete or iron bridge supports (the fewer the obstructions, the less forceful the current).

If you're in a more daring mood, you could scout out a stretch on lower and more steeply sloping territory (the river will course faster as it nears sea level), bracketed on either side by an extremely curving shoreline (currents will always be strongest in the river bends), and intermittently troubled on its surface waters by series of wavelets (surface disturbances, like waves, will usually appear just as two separate currents combine in an increased rate of speed and strength).

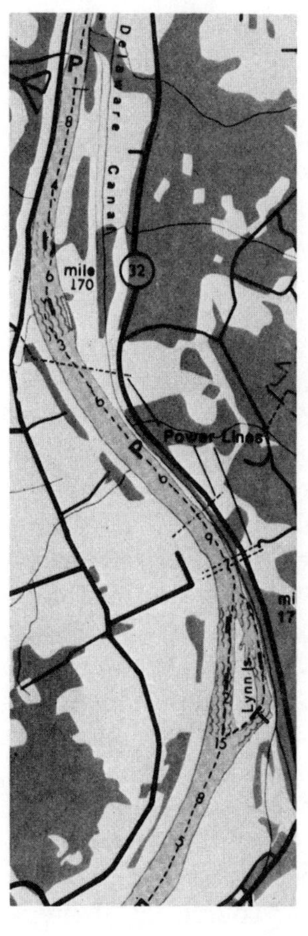

RAMPS AND STAIRS

If, however, you wish to sample as much variety as you can hope to find in one 2- to 3-mile length, you'll be looking for a stretch of river that contains all—or at least most—of the above-cited features. Fortunately, this isn't as difficult as it may sound. Imagine a long descending stairway, each progressive step a bit broader than the one above, each linked by a variously angled ramp. The "stairway effect" (to use the naturalist's term) is characteristic of a typical river pattern. The river begins as a small body of water (the top step), spills down a slope in the landscape (the top ramp), and flows out to the next plateau—widening and deepening its channel in the process—until it reaches another slope. This process is repeated over and over again, with ever-growing cumulative force, until the river reaches its final plateau and either pours into a larger river or lake or broadens into a seaside bay.

> Above . . . where the river curved left into rapids, they stopped at a pool at the foot of Che-Kwa-La, the falls on a stream that fell into the river. . . . They stood for a long time watching the troubled restless water of the falls coming to rest in the deep quiet pool, and neither spoke.
>
> —MARGARET CRAVEN
> *I Heard the Owl Call My Name*

Because the pattern is so consistent, step-ramp-step, you should have little problem locating a likely stretch. Simply pinpoint that spot where the water is within a mile or so of tumbling down to its next level—clearly identifiable by the narrowing shorelines, the darker-hued water, and the increasing surface disruption—and use it as the debarkation area for your tour. If the river runs true to form—and be certain of this in advance—you will enter into a brisk but never overpowering course, swim down an exhilaratingly rapid decline, and end up blissfully drifting about in a peaceful haven of shaded banks and dappled light.

A river tour such as this will make considerable demands on your skill, training, and nerve, but it will also offer a comfortably large margin of safety. The ideal river stretch may not be in your immediate vicinity, but it will, more than likely, be within an accessible distance. At any rate, the reward of traveling down the right river will always outweigh the effort involved in finding it.

URRENTS WITHIN CURRENTS

In the most elemental sense, the entire river is a current, one that severally rolls and races and wafts its way down the sloping earth to the ocean basin. Within that single unyielding flow, however, are contained a myriad of smaller currents. Even though most are not dangerous in themselves, they can still carry the unwary swimmer into serious difficulties. Beginning on page 247, we will discuss the best ways to navigate through, around, and under them. First, though, it's necessary that you learn how to recognize them.

The Mainstream. Also called the watercourse, the mainstream is the single consistent current, other than the river itself. A wide path of water running through the deepest channel in the riverbed, it is propelled by gravitational pull, downstream winds, and—as it nears its estuary—tidal forces. The mainstream is generally about 1 knot faster than the river course, is always

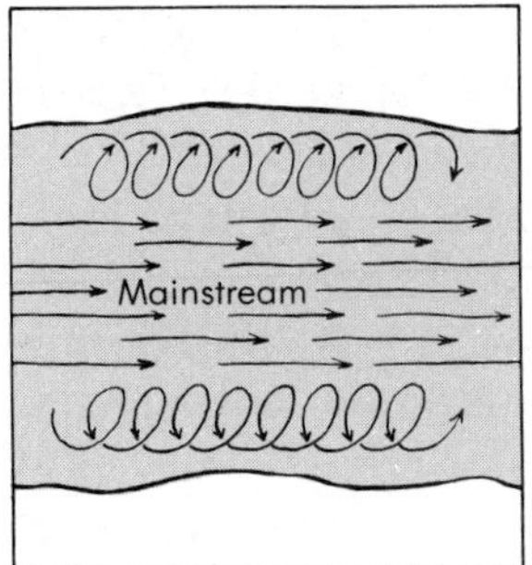

stronger on the surface than on the bottom, and is approximately parallel to the contours of the "dominant" shore (i.e., that riverbank curving toward the river). It is this last facet, by the way, that makes the mainstream current so easy to detect. In straight stretches, it invariably runs through the center of the river (where the water reaches its greatest depth). Along river bends, it runs on the outside of the dominant bank. And although the so-called S-curves—a series of bends appearing, one after the other, in quick succession—are too complicated to generalize about (because the sandbars that often form on either side of the S can deflect the mainstream into less predictable designs), the current's dark colors still make it highly visible.

As you'll be spending most of your river tour in the mainstream, it's essential that you know where to look for it. You must also be able to identify the other major river currents. Some are helpful, some are comparatively harmless, some are to be strictly avoided.

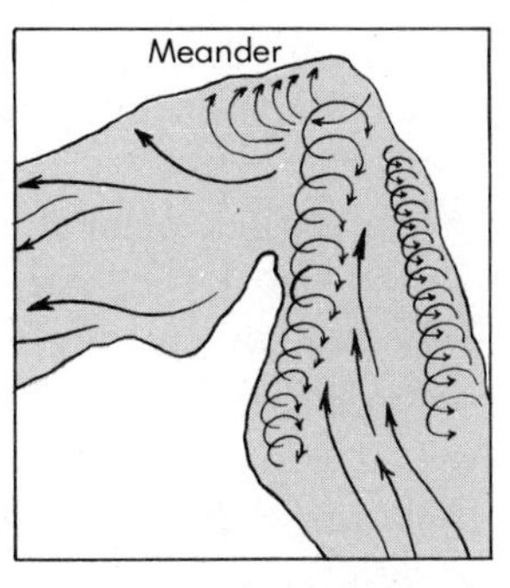

Meanders. As a river swings around a bend, centrifugal force creates a rotating backflow eddy known as a meander. In the highlands, the water velocity will not yet be rapid enough to create a strong meander; in the lowlands, though, this eddy can generate a very powerful undertow. In general, meanders are not easy to spot. The safest way to circumvent them is never to swim near the bank of a river bend. Stay instead on the outside of the curve.

The Shear Zone. This is also the result of centrifugal force. The shear zone is that space lying between a meander and the mainstream current. Since it's the water's reaction to two conflicting flows, the zone is marked by boils, upwellings, and wavelets. Don't let its bubbling appearance fool you; the shear zone is not difficult to pass through. Even better, dive beneath it and head for deeper waters and the mainstream current.

The V-Flow. When traveling through a river stretch obstructed by various visible objects—boulders, trees,

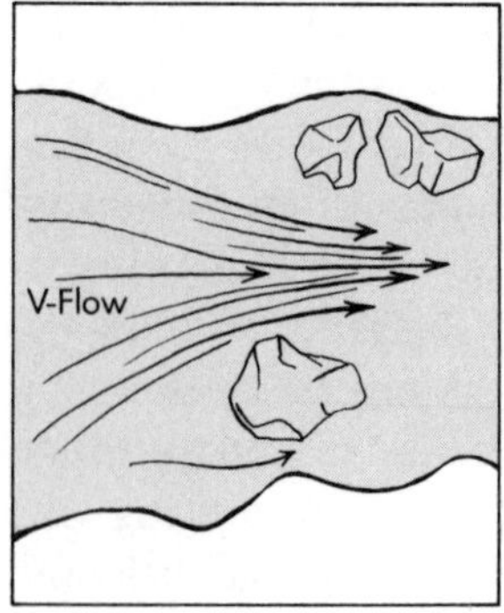

pylons, and bridge abutments—keep your eyes alerted for a dark-colored V-shaped patch of water. This indicates the detoured mainstream flowing safely between the obstructions. Head straight down one arm of the V, and the current will carry you out of harm's reach.

The Inverted V-Flow. If, however, you're swimming toward a white-colored inverted V (that is, with its apex pointing back upstream), change direction immediately. For one thing, the apex of the V is aimed straight at a hidden obstacle—probably a submerged rock—and to continue on the same course will lead, at best, to a severe bruising. For another, the area between the arms of the V is a very turbulent shear zone you'd do better to avoid.

White Foam. Rivers, naturally, do nothing *but* flow over submerged obstructions. The only real danger for the swimmer is when the river flow is too shallow to avoid scraping your body against the object. Keep a sharp lookout for any patch of water that is aerated (i.e., foamy). This is a sure sign of an obstruction resting too close for comfort to the surface. Unless you're snugly in the mainstream—which you can trust to carry you around the object—make a wide detour.

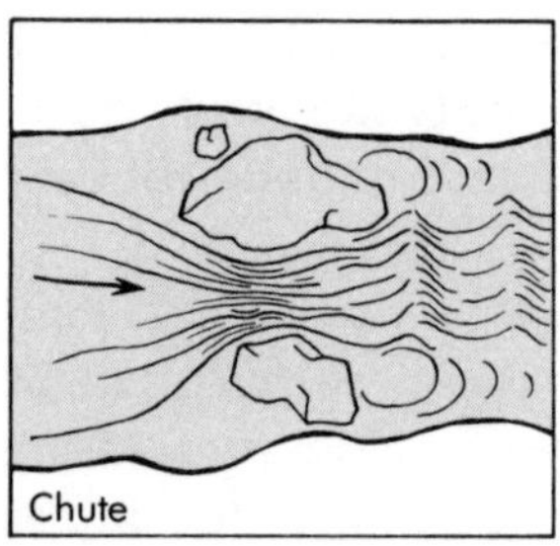

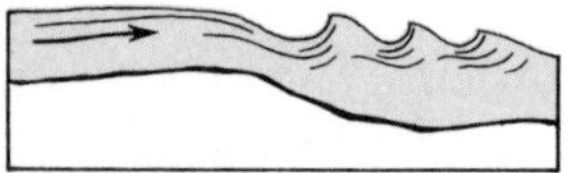

Chutes. These are brief, but fierce, surges of water passing directly beneath fallen tree trunks or—less often—between two closely spaced bridge abutments. If there's no white foam in the chute, there's no real cause for alarm. Just brace yourself for a fast trip.

Pillows, Rollers, Souse Holes, and Haystacks. Whenever the flow passes over a steeply sloped river bottom, a sudden dropoff is created. The pillow is the swell of water rising, the roller is the resulting wave rolling back upstream, the souse hole is the depression between the two, and the haystack is a permanent wave formation farther downstream. Swimming through the dropoff is an exhilarating experience. It's also fast and occasionally dangerous. Happily, you'll see the dropoff long before you are in the middle of it. If you've any doubts about your ability to negotiate it, just swim for the nearest shore, walk past the haystacks, reenter the water, and start swimming again.

Warning: All these various currents, eddies, and backflows—especially the dropoff ones—also exist in white-water rapids. Formed by a series of ledges beneath the surface, urged on by an incredibly ferocious current, rapids are no place for a swimmer. Of the six classes of white-water conditions defined by the AWA (American Whitewater Affiliation), only the first two are recommended as suitable for canoeists. You, however, are not in a canoe. You are not in any type of craft whatsoever. It's a good idea to remember this. Your body has not been painstakingly designed for buoyancy. Do not attempt to pass through any kind of rapids. It's true that swimmers have been known to try their skills in the white waters. (Of course, swimmers have also tried going over Niagara Falls.) The smart ones—which is to say, the ones still with us—travel in groups and are linked together with inner tubes, wear life jackets, and carry an assortment of first-aid devices. As a novice river swimmer, however, you should avoid them.

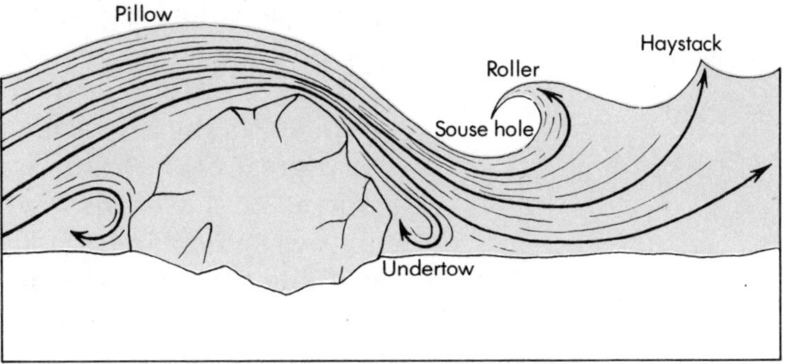

Oceans

More than 70 percent of the earth is covered by the oceans. We sun ourselves on their beaches, we play in their shallows, we've even begun to explore their depths. The dazzle of light upon the blue-green water, the roar of surf against the shore, the tang of salt in the onshore wind—the sight and sound and taste and smell of the ocean—stir the shared memories of our species. Life was born in the sea. Life is sustained by the sea. And each time we return to the sea, we return to our origins.

Considering its tides, currents, and eddies, its waves, its storms, its always-changing nature, and its often-dangerous inhabitants, the ocean—that is, the coastal edge of the ocean, called the tidal zone, in which we habitually bathe—is a surprisingly benign medium.

There are, of course, some problems, but then you're bound to find problems in any form of water you choose to swim in. Besides, some of the disadvantages of sea bathing can also be considered advantages. For example, the various pulls and tugs and general disruptions both above and below the ocean surface make the steady use of just one swimming style impossible. You must employ an entire bag of tricks, kicks, and strokes—and you must be ready to shift from one type to another as often as the ocean shifts rhythms. However, this will not only give you a great deal of practical training as an all-around swimmer but will also eventually develop in you an intuitive understanding of the vagaries of the water and an ability to adapt to them.

One might expect the sea to be among the most dangerous swimming sites. Statistically, however, it is one of the safest.

This apparent contradiction can be explained by one key word: vigilance. The ocean is so obviously a potential hazard to a swimmer that extraordinary safeguards have been developed for protection. Today, nearly every public beach has trained lifeguards (one for every 75 to 150 bathers), first-aid stations (often manned by paramedics), and a complete assortment of lifesaving equipment from lifelines to lifeboats. The result? Although there are drownings on bathing beaches—and remember, each year people drown in any and every type of water, including bathtubs—they are uncommon. In fact, next to the artificial pool, the ocean shoreline is the safest of all bathing locales.

SALT WATER

The average cubic mile of seawater contains 166 million tons of salt (most of which is created from chemicals released through the erosion of aboveground mountains and underwater rock). In the combined oceans of the world, there are 330 million cubic miles of water. Join these figures together, and there would be enough salt to spread 500 feet deep over every inch of ground on the earth's surface.

Salt creates many possible problems for the ocean swimmer. It can, for instance, inflame sensitive eye tissue enough to impair vision temporarily. It can also irritate other parts of the body, particularly the ears, nose, and throat. It can make the slightest cut throb like a deep wound, it can damage or completely destroy hair cells, and it can—if too much is swallowed—harm the kidneys and the liver.

But salt water has one great advantage that makes its disadvantages seem minor indeed. It is extraordinarily buoyant.

To me the sea is like a person—like a child that I've known a long time. It sounds crazy, I know, but when I swim in the sea I talk to it. I never feel alone when I'm out there.

—GERTRUDE EDERLE
30 years after becoming the first woman to swim the English Channel
New York Post, Sept. 5, 1956

This extra buoyancy is invaluable to the swimmer. All swimming strokes, regardless of type, are designed for two purposes. First, they propel the swimmer through the water. Second, they keep the swimmer afloat. Because of the natural buoyancy of seawater, less of the energy of the stroke is required to keep the swimmer afloat and more of it is available for propulsion purposes. Thus, ocean salinity can increase both the speed and the distance achieved with any of the standard swimming styles. It is not unusual for a swimmer barely able to complete four laps in an artificial pool to discover that he can travel perhaps as much as twice the distance, at perhaps as much as twice the speed, in a tranquil stretch of sea.

According to Archimedes's Law, an object will float in water only if the density of the object is less than the density of the water. That is, the object must weigh less than the same volume of water does. Place a cubic meter of iron into the water, and the iron sinks. This is because a cubic meter of iron is denser than a cubic meter of water, and so it displaces the water and passes through it. Place a human body in the water, and it will remain buoyant only if the water is denser than it is.

Now, human bone and muscle are denser than water, but nevertheless, most people will float—see page 204 for the exceptions—as long as they can keep their lungs filled with air, because water is much denser than air. As soon as a person loses the capacity to inhale completely (in other words, as soon as a person grows too exhausted to take and hold a deep breath), he or she will sink.

Seawater is denser than fresh water. Let's say that fresh water has a density recorded as 1.0. Seawater, then, with its vast amounts of dissolved mineral salts, would have an average density of 1.0275. This increased density means increased buoyancy, and thus it's easier for the swimmer to stay afloat in seawater.

AVES The early Egyptians described them as the heartbeats of the world. The ancient Greeks depicted them as half-savage horses, with spume-white manes and seaweed-green tails, harnessed to the chariots of the sea god, Neptune. The Cretan civilization worshiped them as sacred proof of its own imagined immortality. Old salts have spun horrific stories of their fury, poets have dedicated epics to their regal implacability, lovers have felt them as the very image of passion, and the Beach Boys have made a fortune singing about riding them in to the California shore.

In truth, however, the waves of the sea need no metaphor or top-40 tune to give them grandeur. They are their unadorned selves, magnificent.

They are also, to a novice ocean swimmer, more than a bit frightening. Even the mild-mannered undulating waves typical of a gently sloped beach can seem threatening if you're not used to swimming in the sea. As for the waves found on windy and steep beaches—rolling in from the far horizon, thunderously breaking against the sand, dissolving into wildly churning foam—they will often appear to be impassable.

> There is a way a wave rises above the ocean horizon, a triangular wedge against the sky. If you stand where the ocean breaks on a shallow beach, you see the raised water in a wave is translucent, shot with lights.
>
> -ANNIE DILLARD
> *Pilgrim at Tinker Creek*

But they aren't. Discounting those mountains of water created by earthquakes, hurricanes, and other acts of nature, surf waves are easily navigable. You can glide over them, dive below them, swim in their wake, or coast on their crest. Obviously you can't swim through a choppy sea with the same steady stroke that's possible in the quiet waters of an artificial pool. However, you *can* swim—and negotiating waves is fun. Before you begin, though, it will be helpful to keep in mind a few fundamental facts.

NOT WHAT THEY SEEM

For instance, waves are a most deceptive phenomenon. Their appearance is that of a section of water rolling steadily through the ocean. Actually, however, it is basically the wave *form* that moves forward; the water itself is only stirred up by the wave —which is, in turn, being driven by the wind—rotated in an elliptical path, and redeposited in nearly the same spot that it started from. It looks like a mass of ongoing water, but actually the water is only rotating around an almost completely stationary axis.

There are several ways you can visualize this. If you stretch a blanket or sheet on the floor, weigh down one side, and give the other side a sharp flip with your wrists, you create a ripple effect from end to end. Flip it repeatedly, and you create a series of ripples—or waves. The particles of material composing the blanket are not traveling along the surface, of course, but merely moving up and down as the wave passes. An even simpler way to understand this principle of motion is to drop an empty bottle or a cork into the water. As each wave approaches, the bottle will move up its leading slope, slide down the back slope, and end up floating in pretty much the same position as before. If the water itself were moving, as it does in a river, the bottle would move along with it.

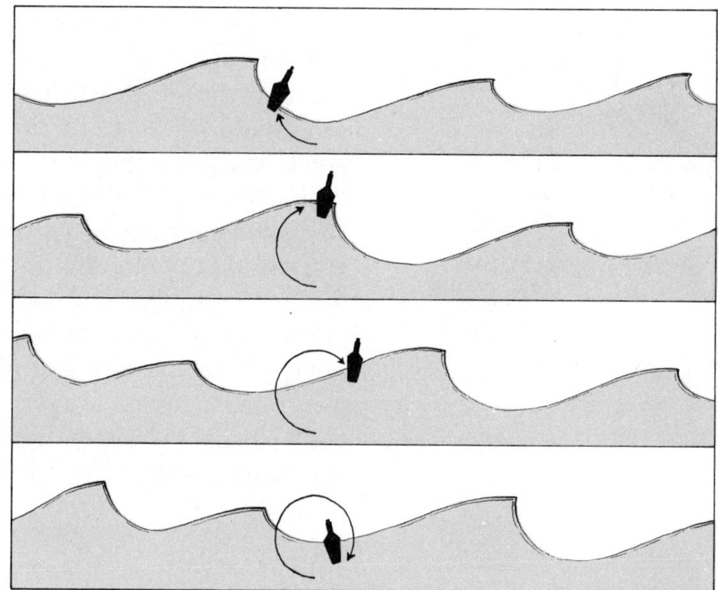

Bottle shows that while wave forms move, water moves at a lesser rate. As the wave moves from left to right, the bottle simply drifts in an imaginary circle. When the wave has passed, the bottle will have moved forward only a short distance.

Most inexperienced people bathing in the ocean tend to panic whenever a big surge of water starts moving their way. The fear is based on the belief that the wave will push them down beneath the surface. In order to avoid this, they'll break their stroke, or begin racing back to shore or—worst of all—flounder. The proper course of action—with one exception, which we'll get to in a moment—is to continue to paddle and kick. Like the bottle, your body will be briefly and gently lifted by the wave, then returned back to the same place.

Try it for yourself. Better yet, swim out far enough to assume the breathing cycle (p. 198) and float quietly for awhile. After several waves have rolled under you without mussing your hair, you'll never lose control at the sight of one again.

WAVE WATCHING

It was the Phoenicians, the first real sailors, who coined the axiom, "Always keep one eye on the waves of the sea. Every seventh one is dangerous." It's a myth, of course; but, even so, any myth that persists, as this one has, for more than three millennia must have a grain of truth in it somewhere.

And the grain here is to be found in the suggestion that we should *observe* the waves. It's excellent advice. A great deal of important information can be gathered simply by a few minutes' study of the wave patterns of any given beach on any given day. As an ocean swimmer, you should develop the habit of a preliminary survey of the water (no matter how familiar the beach) each and every time you're planning to take a dip. (Not that you're likely to need much encouragement. We are, as a race, as passionate wave watchers as we are stargazers.) Once you've learned how to prepare yourself by careful wave watching, you'll be able to swim well in even the choppiest seas.

WAVE ORIGINS

Before discussing what to look for, however, it might be a good idea to discuss just exactly what it is you're looking at.

What you're contemplating is, in fact, the end result of a process that has often begun thousands of miles away. Most waves are born as the by-product of wind driving against water. In the open ocean, waves usually begin as choppy wavelets that intermingle with each other in no predictable pattern. Such a confusion of waves is called a sea. Once the waves begin traveling out from under the winds that first formed them, their more regular and surging motion is called a swell. And when, finally, they break against the shore, they're collectively called surf. Before dissolving into foam and thunder, an individual wave may have been rolling across the water for many days at a speed that often averages 35 miles per hour. If you are reading this book while on a California beach, for example, that surf wave crashing against the sand at this precise moment may have started its journey a week before off the coast of New Zealand.

The waves echo behind me. Patience—Faith—Openness, is what the sea has to teach. Simplicity—Solitude—Intermittancy . . . But there are other beaches to explore. There are more shells to find. This is only the beginning. . .

-ANNE MORROW LINDBERGH
Gift from the Sea, 1955

Indeed, the origin of the surf is the first thing the careful wave watcher will look for. If the waves have a steep shape and a choppy rhythm well before they reach the breaker line, they are relatively young waves (the more irregular the pattern, the more recent their birth) created by local storms. If the waves are more consistent in their shoreward roll, then crest high all long their advance and break with a loud roar, they have done some hard traveling. Count the seconds between crests. If there's a reasonably stable interval of 10 to 18 seconds following each one, the waves' birthplace is several thousand miles beyond the horizon.

By determining the relative age of the waves, you will be able to know in advance the best swimming strokes to use, either those designed for power (in the young choppy surf) or those that allow a more leisurely pace (in the older and more regular waves).

STUDY THE SURF

Another important visual observation is the identification of breaker type. Experts—which is to say, both oceanographers and surfers—generally divide them into two separate categories. "Spillers" or "rollers" are marked by a steadily cascading line of feathered foam down their front slopes. These breakers typically roll in toward the beach for long distances before dissolving, and so they are much loved by surfing hot-doggers.

"Plungers" (the Australians call them "dumpers") are just the opposite: waves that begin to curl relatively close to the beach and then crash with a savage force. Although plungers can bruise you up quite a bit if you're unfortunate enough to get caught on the breaker line, they provide good swimming conditions. As they surge up so near the shore, it is easy to swim out past them into more placid waters.

Incidentally, if you're familiar with the configuration of the beach, you can pretty much predict which type of surf wave will be breaking against its shore. This is because the shape of the beach usually determines the shape of its breakers. Spillers are characteristic of a shoreline with a gently sloping bottom, and plungers of a bottom that rises abruptly to the beach. There's an interesting cause-and-effect cycle at work here: The waves first shape the beach, wearing down rocks into pebbles and grinding pebbles into sand; but then the wave-shaped beach perpetuates the shape of the waves.

SIZING WAVES

During your wave-watching vigil, you may notice that waves clustered together seem to be smaller than those rolling in majestic solitude. This is because waves will only grow to a height of approximately a seventh of the distance between crests (i.e., the "wave length"). Any higher, and they'd tumble into whitecapped foam. This means that it's only in the open sea, what mariners call fetch, that the waves will reach full size. Just how large will usually depend upon how hard the wind is blowing. (The general rule of thumb here is that a wave will never be higher in feet than half the wind's speed in miles per hour. In an 80-mile-an-hour hurricane, for example, the waves will rarely loom larger than 40 feet.) By the time the swell has come close enough to shore to begin transforming itself into surf, the wave size has greatly diminished. Its speed now slowed by the shallowing ocean floor, it begins to be crowded by other waves rolling in behind. Eventually its back slope overtakes its front slope, forcing it to curl up into a peak. When the peak leans too far forward, gravity topples the entire wave onto the beach.

THE BREAKER LINE

No two waves will ever break at precisely the same spot. Nevertheless, there is a general area that can be pinpointed as the breaker line. (Keep in mind, though, that depending on wind velocity and tide pull, the breaker line may change several times during the course of a 24-hour period.) Since so much ocean swimming involves ocean surf, it's a good idea to understand the mechanics of the process. If you wish to see it for yourself, find either a beach spur or a wharf that juts out at a right angle from the shoreline. Assuming that your observation point is long enough, you should then be able to get a seagull's-eye view of how the wave slows, crests, and tumbles.

WATER DEPTH

There are two final facts you can determine from a few moments of study: the size of the breaker and the depth of the water in which it breaks. The advantages here to

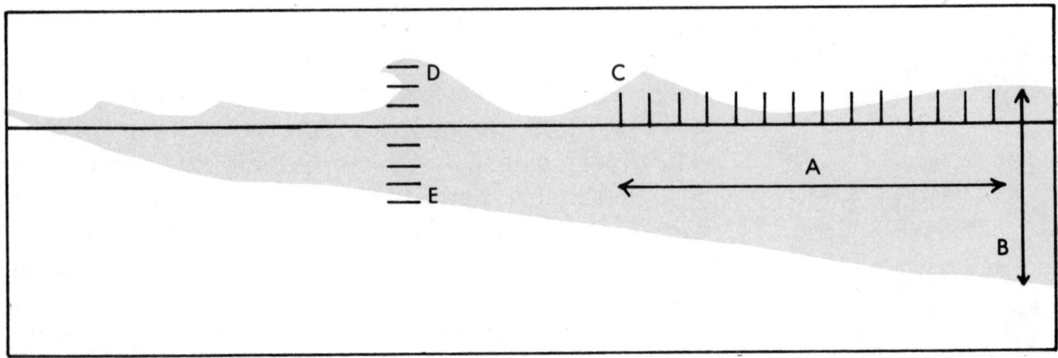

A wave breaks in shallow water. The drag of the bottom shortens the wave length (A) to twice the depth of the water (B) and forces it to peak (C). The wave breaks when its height (D) reaches a ratio of 3 to 4 with the water depth (E).

ocean swimmers are obvious. Not only can you accurately judge the size of the waves you'll be maneuvering about in, but you will also be able to determine the water depth.

All one has to do is walk down the beach slope toward the surf until the eye can align the crest of a breaker with the ocean's horizon. The vertical distance measured by the eye to the *lowest point* reached by the retreating water of the previous wave is equal to the height of the wave being measured. Now, a little rudimentary arithmetic is needed. A wave breaks when the ratio of its height to the water depth is approximately three to four. If the wave height can be ascertained to be 6 feet, let's say, then it will be breaking in 8 feet of water.

GETTING IN, GETTING OUT

If you spend a few minutes wave-watching each time you head out for the beach, you'll have no reason to be daunted by any kind of fairweather ocean condition. How you use the information garnered from your observations will pretty much depend upon your own skill and confidence as a swimmer. There are a few constants about sea bathing, though, that everyone—novice and expert alike—should attend to.

LEMENTARY OCEAN SWIMMING

To gain the most benefit from ocean swimming in terms of both sport and exercise, you should have at least a basic proficiency in several swimming strokes. It is recommended that you develop these various strokes—and also learn how to change strokes without breaking stride—in a swimming pool. The ocean is not the best place to learn, since its many variables prevent concentration on technique.

Human Stroke. Also sometimes called the advanced dog paddle, this is a simple but invaluable form of ocean swimming. The body position should be as flat as possible; the leg stroke should ideally be a flutter kick; the arm stroke should be the standard dog paddle (hands open, pressing down and back in the water). Because it allows you to keep your head above water while moving, the human stroke is particularly helpful when you are approaching the beach or a stationary object—a floating dock or buoy—in the sea.

Finning Backstroke. This is the most elementary of all backstrokes, the one commonly used in recreational swimming. The body position is flat on your back (head submerged to the ears); the leg stroke is the conventional frog kick; the arm stroke is performed by pressing arms and hands sideways along chest, hips, and thighs, then pushing them out in the same way the legs are pushed out during the frog kick. This is the most relaxing of all strokes and will allow you to rest while still making some progress through the water.

Sidestroke. Possibly the most natural swimming style for human beings, the sidestroke has already been described in great detail (page 00). It's particularly important to ocean swimmers because it is a strong yet relatively relaxed method of propulsion and, too, because it provides the opportunity to swim with one hand.

Trudgen Crawl. Technically referred to as "the alternating overarm stroke," the trudgen was the first crawl stroke ever developed. Your trunk and legs should be as flat as possible in the water, and your head never submerged above the chin. The arm stroke, which requires some hours of practice, is an overarm sidestroke performed on alternate sides (first right, then left); the leg stroke is a similarly alternating scissor kick. Although primitive and rather clumsy when compared to the crawl strokes used in freestyle competition, the trudgen gives you maximum power for minimal effort and also allows a clear field of vision.

Frog-Kick Breaststroke. Beginning on page 00 are complete instructions on the various techniques and training methods involved in the breaststroke. Not by any means an easy skill to master, the breaststroke is nevertheless essential for ocean swimming. Its power and speed will help you when you're swimming in strong currents, and it is also the best stroke to employ over long distances.

In addition to these five strokes, you should also be thoroughly baptized in all elements of the waterproof techniques, including the flats, the breathing cycle, and the travel stroke (pp. 199–200).

Ultimately, however, despite lifeguards and lifesaving equipment, we must take responsibility for ourselves. Before heading out from the shore, you should have the following abilities.

Be able to swim at least one-quarter of a mile–without any strain. This is true even for waders. Perhaps it is especially true for waders; tides and currents are sneaky, and before you know it, one may jar you off your feet and pull you out to deep water. Experienced swimmers can also be pulled in. The strength and endurance to stroke your way back to the shallows is a must.

Be able to surface dive to a depth of at least 10 feet. This will help you avoid huge waves and also help you recover friends who failed to avoid them.

The sea is the best place for swimming.

-EDWIN T. BREWSTER
Swimming, 1910

ENTERING THE WATER

Unless the waves are breaking an unusually long distance from the shore, you are going to have to move out beyond the breaker line in order to do any serious stroking. Don't be in too much of a rush. Once you've gotten a sense of the breaker pattern, time your entrance so that you're *between* breakers when you reach the line. If the wave length is too short for this, it's no great problem. Just face the oncoming wave–you should never turn your back to a breaker–and dive through its center as the wave is peaking. If the waves are clustered tightly together, it's sometimes better to simply sink beneath the surface until the entire series has passed over your head.

After you've passed the breaker line, you're ready to swim. Use any of the aforementioned strokes, or improvise your own. Keep in mind, however, that offshore breezes sometimes create an illusion that the waves are running against you and are carrying you into deeper water. Also keep in mind that the ocean is not so much a harsh mistress as it is a fickle one. Wave rhythms–and currents, too–are liable to change. To avoid disorientation–and to avoid miscalculation of distance, too–always swim parallel to the shoreline. Spot a stationary object on the beach and use it as a reference point. Periodically change your stroke to the human stroke or the trudgen crawl–either of which keeps your head above the surface of the water–so you can run a visual check on your reference point.

RETURNING TO THE BEACH

The stroke preferred by most ocean swimmers for the return to shore is the sidestroke. This is probably because it is powerful, it is relatively easy, and it allows one hand to remain free, which is helpful for use as a scull to maintain balance against high waves. Returning past the breaker line, like entering it, requires timing and a sense of the ocean's rhythms. Basically, you let the waves do much of the work. Swim toward the shore in the trough of a wave until you can feel a new one rolling in behind you. Then, treading water, turn back to meet it; take a deep breath; either dive through it or sink below it; and, once it's past, swim in *its* trough. Take your time Don't panic. And remain as relaxed as you can.

Hence in a season of
calm weather
Though inland far we be
Our souls have sight of
that immortal sea
Which brought us hither,
Can in a moment travel
thither
And see the children
sport upon the shore
And hear the mighty
waters rolling evermore.

-WILLIAM WORDSWORTH
"Intimations Immortality," 1807

BODYSURFING

There's an alternative way of returning shoreward, one that's as sportive as it is practical. This is bodysurfing, the use of your own body as a surfboard. Use the same technique described above until you reach the spot where the waves are breaking. Wait until the most likely surf rolls in—you're looking for a foam-feathered wave that's peaked and is now just beginning to curl—then assume the bodysurf position and glide all the way back to terra firma. All that's needed is a good sense of timing, a steady stroke, and a taste for fun.

• Once you've selected the wave, swim in front of it at a fast crawl. (Although a little clumsy at first, the trudgen will serve nicely.) Wait until you feel the wave lifting you up and then forward.

• Next, drop your head (to bring the weight of your body forward) and point your arms and hands out front.

• As the wave starts to topple, lift your head and pull your arms back along your sides. If you've caught the surf just as it's breaking, you may be able to ride it all the way in to shore without losing your balance. If you wish, you can also—for the sake of the sport—try bodysurfing in different positions:

• *The corkscrew.* Drop your right shoulder, raise your left hip, and you will revolve continually as you're riding in the wave.

• *The half corkscrew.* After half a revolution, straighten both shoulder and hip again, and you'll be bodysurfing on your back.

• *The water walk.* Bring your hands in front, hands locked together, palms down, and press the water, and you'll be able to raise your body and surf on your hands.

If at any point during the process you've miscalculated timing or position, you can simply pull out of the bodysurf by rolling forward and then diving beneath the wave and back up in its trough.

CURRENTS

Throughout the oceans of the earth run currents, great eddies of water driven by winds, temperature, and planetary rotation in never-ceasing circles. The "turbidity" currents, those undersea avalanches of silt-heavy water, are responsible for gouging out the huge canyons and mountain ranges that make up the aquascape of the ocean floor. (Its deepest chasm, the 35,800-foot-deep Mariana Trench, located in the western Pacific, could contain all of Mount Everest with a good 6,000 feet to spare. Its longest mountain range, the Mid-Atlantic Ridge, extends more than 10,000 miles.)

The Gulf Stream, named and first charted by Benjamin Franklin, is a 50-mile-wide, 1,500-foot-deep river that travels eastward across the North Atlantic at speeds ranging up to 5 miles an hour. The Labrador Current, sweeping billions of tons of water each minute from the Arctic Circle, transports hundreds of icebergs—some weighing more than 150,000 tons—into the transatlantic shipping lanes. And there are many other impressive ones, too—the Kuroshio Current, the West Wind Drift, the South Equatorial Eddy—all of them variously affecting the ocean.

The currents affecting the ocean swimmer, however, are not quite so grand, although their often surprising rate of speed, their power, and their variability can represent problems for the unsuspecting. You can avoid currents easily if you're alert, and if you do happen to become suddenly enmeshed in a current's coils, it will not prove difficult to get out of it.

There are two fundamental rules in dealing with currents of any kind:

Know what you're getting into before you get into it. If you're bathing at a populated beach site, there will be posted instructions regarding any particularly treacherous currents that may be running through the water. If the beach is a deserted stretch of land, it would be a good idea to make a call to local authorities and ask whether there are any strong currents you should be aware of.

Never swim against a current's pull. Sometimes, despite all precautions, you may still unknowingly enter a current's zone. This doesn't mean you're in trouble—as long as you remain calm. Too many people panic and try to fight back. It's strictly no contest. Even the most modest ocean current has a traveling speed of 3 to 5 knots. Even the most powerful swimmers cannot, as a rule, propel themselves faster than 2 knots. Rather than engage in a battle, you do better to accept the current's superior strength and swim across it until you're out of its side, or go with the flow until it has petered out.

There are all sorts of currents and eddies, but only a few really plague the ocean swimmer. They are longshore currents, riptides, sandbar runbacks, offsets, and—actually less a current than a by-product of one—undertow.

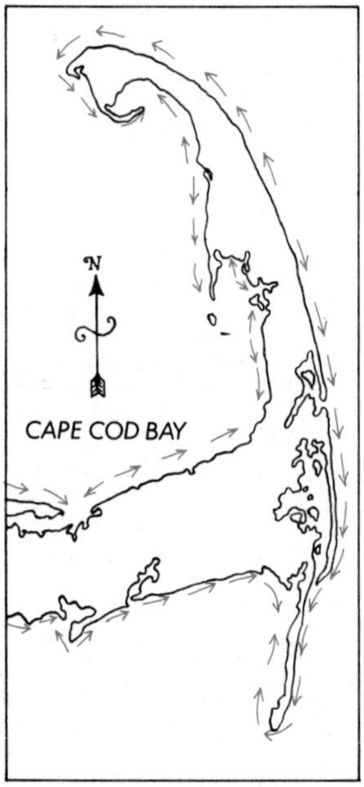

LONGSHORE CURRENTS

You may notice while wave watching that breakers often approach the beach at an oblique angle. Remember: Shallow water acts as a brake on the wave's rate of speed. If the shoreline bottom is not perfectly level—and few ever are—the slope of the wave bends to match the contours. The part of the breaker in shallow water slows, the part in deeper water continues to race ahead; and so when the breaker topples, it does so at an angle. This produces a flow of water that runs parallel to the coast and also explains its name: the longshore current.

A swift, strong, though usually narrow surface stream that's driven by the wind, the longshore current takes on

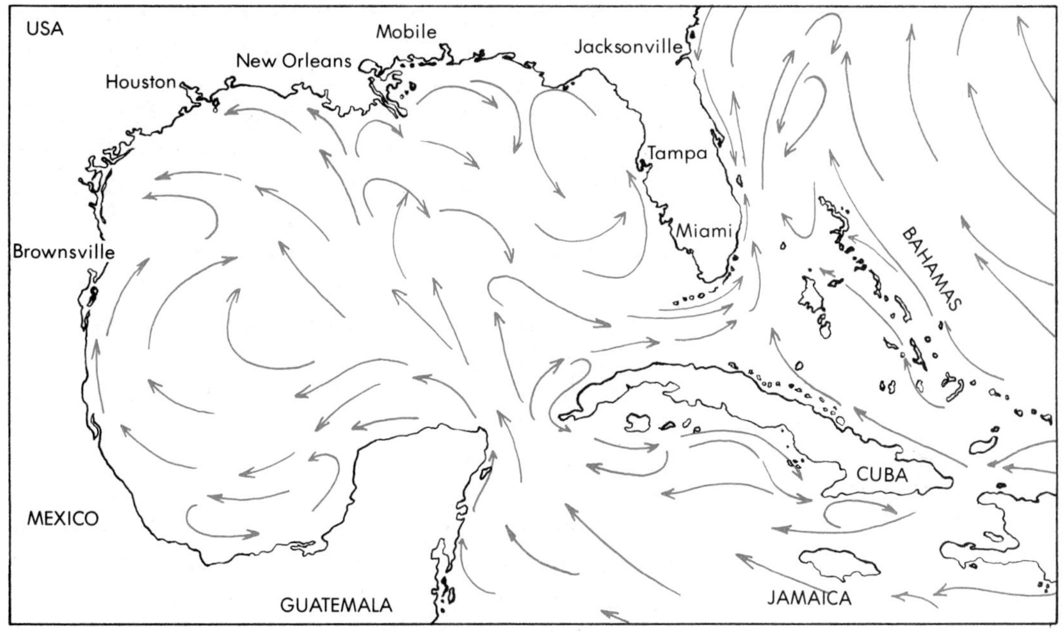

the same contours as the shoreline. Because there's no visible difference between it and the ocean water proper, and because, too, there's no way to predict its dormant or its active period, the chances are good that sooner or later you'll find yourself swimming in one.

When this happens, don't be alarmed. The current's power is undeniable, but it can be overcome. (Besides, there is no type of current that will ever pull you beneath the surface and hold you down.) You have two alternatives. To break free of the pull of the current, turn to shore and use either the sidestroke or the breaststroke to swim across it as rapidly as you can. If the longshore current is too vigorous for this, or if you're too exhausted to ford it, simply assume the human stroke or trudgen and let the current carry you along with it. As soon as it takes you around the end of a jetty or point of land, the wind that's been urging it forward will die down, the current will weaken, and you'll be able to safely cross it to the beach.

RIPTIDES

"Riptide" is a misnomer, as riptide currents are neither caused by tidal movement nor characterized by a "rippling" pattern. Instead, they are usually created by the runback of the breakers. A riptide occurs after every heavy set of waves at the same location on any given day. The reason for this is the channels the riptide scoops out of the ocean floor. Each channel acts as a kind of funnel through which each successive riptide passes. However, as the breakers are also shifting the bottom, these channels never last for more than 24 hours or so.

Though not very wide—no more than 10 to 15 yards across its broadest point—a riptide will flow along at a speed exceeding 4 knots. This means a very good swimmer who's trying to go against the current can be carried away from the beach at a speed of perhaps 2 knots an hour. The only solution is to swim across it—the breaststroke, because of its power, is the best suited for this—and once free of the current, back to shallow water.

Fortunately, riptides are easily located. Whenever there's heavy surf you'll see a stream of brown-stained water running back out to the ocean in a clearly marked path. (The brown color is from the sand the riptide is carrying along with it.) You should also be able to identify it by a small semicircular pool of foam just outside the breaker line; as the riptide runs through the surf, the breakers' foam is swept along with it. Finally, you can locate a riptide by watching the waves break along the shore. At certain consistent spots, they'll either break late or not at all. It's there that the riptide currents have dug their distinctive channels, and the greater depth of the channels prevents the surf from cresting. Thanks to their high visibility and their repetitive patterns of travel, riptides can be—and should be—effortlessly avoided. If, nonetheless, you are trapped in one's grip and you can't summon the swimming strength to cross it, immediately go into the breathing-cycle position. Accept your situation. Maintain a regular breathing pattern. The riptide will eventually subside. The most important thing now is to relax and save your strength for the swim back to shore. The more you struggle, the more you'll exhaust yourself. Your knowledge of stroke styles and waterproof methods will help you get safely back to the beach again.

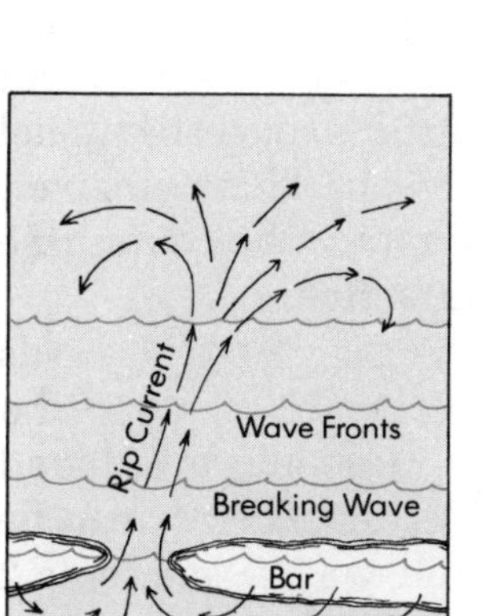

RIP CURRENTS

Similar in width and speed to the riptide, these currents are only present in beach areas that feature offshore sandbars. They occur when the wind changes direction and pushes the longshore current out through gaps (the result of natural formations or of storms) in the sandbars at those spots nearest the water's surface.

Although the rip current has a force equal to that of its cousin, the riptide, it is not nearly as troublesome. For one thing, it is almost impossible not to see the rip current in the water, marked as it is by a streamlet of discolored water arrowing back to the ocean and foaming through the sandbar gap. For another, the current instantly dissipates on the other side of the gap. This not only frees you from its grip but also allows you an opportunity to rest on the bar until you're ready to step to one end and head shoreward.

The only situation that may be at all difficult is when a person is pulled from a longshore current unexpectedly into a rip current. And even then, your biggest danger is yourself. If you both recognize and yield to the current's brief domination, you'll have nothing to worry about. The rip current will inevitably disperse.

OFFSETS

These are comparatively minor currents that run in a roughly diagonal path away from the shore. Although it's suspected that sudden changes in water temperature are responsible for the offsets, no one seems to be certain why they always travel in an oblique line. At any rate, offset currents are quite mild as far as speed is concerned—so mild, in fact, you might not realize you're in the middle of one until you've been pulled out a distance from the beach.

To release yourself from an offset, you must swim diagonally across it (any stroke will do). This means that you must first determine the angle of the current's flow. As offsets are seldom discolored, and as they are not fast enough to carry telltale signs of foam, it's suggested that you tread water and spit into the stream. This will give you a reference with which you can trace the course of the current. It's inelegant, but it's effective.

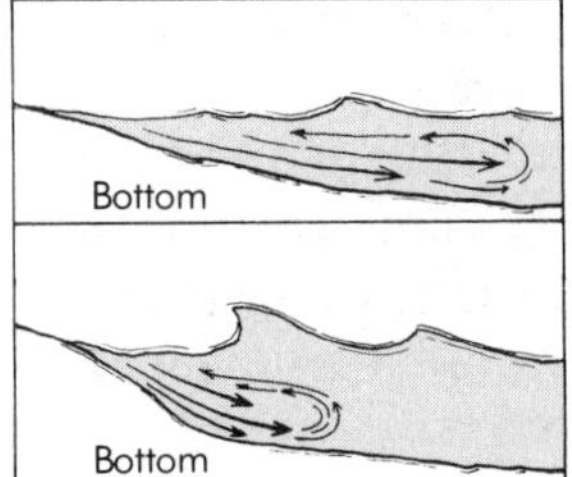

UNDERTOW

This is another example of mistitling. An undertow does not "tow" people under the water; instead it washes people into the water much in the way a suddenly yanked rug will cause people to lose their footing. Indeed, since it is the result of a strong surf running back into the ocean, undertow can scarcely be called a current at all. Even so, there are many myths about its ability to pull people beneath the water's surface and hold them there until they drown.

In one sense, any beachfront will have an undertow. As any dissolved breaker runs back to the sea, it causes a backwash effect. However, only on beaches that have a severe slant and an abruptly rising bottom will this backwash become strong enough to pull people after it. There's double reason for the unusual power of some undertows: The steep contours of the shore cause strong breakers, and the downhill slant back to the ocean accelerates the speed of the runoff.

But although a strong undertow can pull you into the water, it cannot hold you beneath the surface. This is just an old wives' tale, probably prompted by the fact that you do not have the same amount of buoyancy you usually have in salt water. After a large wave has broken, there is so much air in the water that it is less dense, and thus the swimmer finds it a bit more difficult to stay afloat. This effect lasts only as long as it takes the air to filter its way back up to the surface, which is just a few seconds, although to someone unexpectedly dumped into the drink it may seem more like a few minutes.

If you are pulled into the water by a strong undertow, the best thing to do is stretch yourself out at full length. This will keep you from being scraped along the often sharp-shelled bottom. Other than that, just relax. The whole thing will be over before you know it.

The only real danger presented by an undertow is to elderly folk and kids. The former may possibly end up with some bad bruises or even a broken bone. As for very small children, there are reported instances of them being seriously injured by a wave's backwash. Occasionally, there's even a fatality. When taking youngsters to the beach, always try to avoid areas that feature plunger-type breakers. Also, never allow any child who can't swim to play in even ankle-high surf unless there's adequate supervision.

TIDES

If the waves can be called the heartbeats of the ocean, then the tides can be called the ocean's breath.

Twice a day, in a time pattern so regular that it can usually be predicted for years ahead, the gravitational pull of the sun and moon moves the oceans of the world up onto and back away from the bordering land. Actually, the land is also moved, and the surrounding air as well. Each time the waters of the earth rise, so do the continents (a 10-foot-high tide equals about a 6-inch outward bulge of the continents), and the outer atmosphere fattens out several miles. Human beings are similarly affected. Composed as we are mostly of seawater, we gain and lose approximately a quarter of an ounce of body weight in rhythm with the tidal pull.

In comparison with the majestic breakers, the rising and falling tides seem a rather inconsequential phenomenon. But consider this: Waves only transport water molecules a few inches; tides transport the entire ocean. And although the ebb and flow of the tides is often so imperceptible that only the results—exposed sea floor or covered beachfront—are visible, there are areas in the world where tides reach staggering proportions. In the Bay of Fundy, located along the coast of New Brunswick, for instance, the daily high tide lifts the water some 40 feet and also sends a 4-foot-high wall of water barreling up the narrow arms of the bay (this is known as the Fundy Tidal Bore). Each time the tide rises in the bay, it carries with it enough water to quench the thirst of the entire population of the United States for three months—if it were fresh, of course.

MOON VERSUS SUN

For the most part, though, the tidal force is as inconspicuous as it is inevitable. Each day, as the moon swings about the earth, its field of gravity generates an outward bulging movement in all the oceans. The water rises on the side of the earth facing the moon in response to its pull. The water also expands outward on the side of the earth opposite the moon, as both planetary and lunar rotation takes over from, and creates a force similar to, the gravitational flow.

The ebbing tide is a countereffect on the part of the sun. Although so distant it has no more than half the tidal influence that the moon has, the sun still—depending on its position—alternately reinforces and offsets the moon's tow. When all three celestial bodies—earth, moon, and sun—are directly in line (as during either a full or new moon), both solar and lunar gravity combine in an enormous surge of power to produce the unusually high tides called spring tides. When all three bodies are at right angles to one another (as during either the moon's first or third quarter), the exact opposite situation occurs. The forces of gravity partially cancel each other out, resulting in the unusually low tides called neap tides.

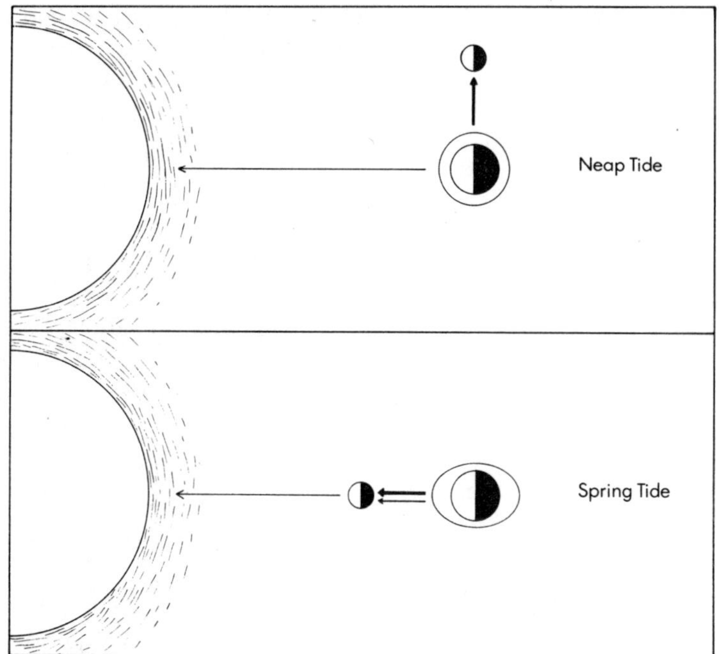

Tides are caused by the gravitational pull of the moon and sun. When the moon and sun are at right angles to the earth, their force produces a small rise and fall called neap tide. When the moon and sun are in line with the earth, their stronger pull produces a high, or "spring" tide.

SWIMMING WITH THE TIDE

The clockwork movement of the tides does not play a very large role in ocean swimming. There are a few points, however, worth considering.

Surf conditions are always the strongest during low and high tide. If you enjoy stroking your way over, through, and below the breakers, schedule your swimming time accordingly. If you want to avoid heavy waves, try to swim at an hour midway between low tide and high.

The ebb and flow of tide also seems to affect—no one's quite sure why—the strength and speed of longshore and riptide currents. The more the water recedes, the less powerful the current; the more the water expands, the more powerful the current. Tides do not, though, either create or disperse a current. Even if you swim at the precise hour when the tide is at its lowest point, there's no guarantee that the currents typical to that stretch of water will be absent. The most you can expect is that any longshore or riptide present will have perhaps only half its usual pull.

And as long as we're on the subject, if a riptide happens to push you offshore, it will be helpful to know what the tide conditions are. When the tide is going out, swim diagonally across it to a corner of the bay or shore. This is because the tidal pull, though considerably weaker than the force of the riptide, is still strong enough to demand some counteractive force on your part. Crossing it obliquely will diminish that force, and conserve your energy for the swim itself. When the tide is coming in, however, aim directly for the middle of the beach area, since the tide is in your favor.

Finally, the new or full moon's spring tides will often be filled with drifting debris. Litter—cans, bottles, and so on—is an unfortunate feature of populated beaches. When the water rises, this junk is swept into the surf. It can be hazardous, especially when the rubbish has sharp or jagged edges. Carried on the crests of breakers, litter can bruise or cut swimmers. Worse, some of the objects float beneath the water's surface, creating an even greater danger. There's not much you can do about this; just remember to exercise as much caution as possible whenever you're swimming in high tides.

ATER LIFE

There are three major areas of the seas in which life flourishes: the water surface, packed with trillions upon unimaginable trillions of microscopic animals and plants; the open ocean, kingdom of some 20,000 species of free-swimming fish (and some mammals, like the whales); and the shallow-bottomed beachfront, home to all sorts of marine creatures. It is the last that will be of interest to the ocean swimmer.

Essentially, the news is good. You have little to fear from the critters that crawl, scurry, and float around you. Oh, the occasional crab may nip your toes, or a nearsighted fish bumping into your leg may give you a jolt, but most coastline citizens will quite gladly leave you alone.

Now for the bad news. There happen to be some exceptions. We'll discuss some of them individually below. If you should be bitten, stung, or otherwise injured by any of them—except perhaps a minor jellyfish sting—you should seek medical attention as soon as possible.

SHARKS

Although there are 250 known species of sharks, only a few have proved at all dangerous to humans. These are the great whites, the bizarre hammerhead, the deep-sea makos, and the appropriately dubbed requiems. The majority of sharks cruise in temperate or tropical waters, but they are found in nearly all latitudes and have even been known to find their way into rivers and lakes. The shark appetite appears to be affected by water temperature. The warmer the water, the hungrier they get.

Despite several thousand years of stories—including a certain recent film—sharks almost never attack swimmers. Most injuries and fatalities result from shipwrecks in the high seas, when the sharks—driven into a feeding frenzy by the presence of blood in the water—indiscriminately attack anything that moves, including each other. The last large shark assult on man occurred in 1945 when the U.S.S. *Indianapolis* was torpedoed in the South Pacific. Since then, the number of shark-related deaths has dwindled steadily. Since 1960, in fact, an average of only one person a year has been killed in U.S. waters by sharks. That's not a very high rate; three people die each year in this country alone from bumblebee stings.

Even so, there are sharks off every beach in the world, and surf swimmers have been known to be bitten—sometimes severely—by them. Chances are you will never encounter, let alone see, a shark. Just in case, though, here are seven rules (originally drawn up by the

U.S. Air Force Survival Commission) to reduce the dangers from these undeniably horrific beasts:

- Don't swim or skin-dive without a companion. Sharks are nervous; the sight of two large forms floating about will generally send them running for safer waters.
- Don't swim at night, or in very murky water. Sharks are sensitive to light, and prefer darker stretches of the sea.
- Don't stay in the water when you have a bleeding wound. Nicknamed "swimming noses," sharks can smell blood nearly 1,000 yards away.
- If a shark moves in, he's probably just curious. Hit him on the snout. This will probably frighten him away. Don't strike him on any other portion of his body, though; his incredibly rough hide will cut your skin and make it bleed, and once the shark senses the blood, he's going to be a lot harder to get rid of.
- Don't carry any food, or any speared fish, into the water with you.
- Don't trail arms or legs from an air mattress or raft. Sharks are attracted to dangling objects in the water.
- Upon sighting a shark, do not, under any circumstances, begin to thrash about in the water. He'll only swim in for a closer look. Just swim away as smoothly as you can to either shore or a moored raft.

Let us not mention barracudas or tropical moray eels—they attack divers only on television.

-ROBERT STÉNUIT
The Deepest Days, 1966

BARRACUDAS

These cigar-shaped, razor-toothed fish, often four to six feet long, are common along the Florida coast and the shorelines of the West Indies. They are most dangerous when encountered in murky water; nearsighted, they have trouble recognizing their natural prey—which does not, you'll be happy to know, include humans—and will attack anything they sense nearby.

The most unnerving thing about barracudas is their native inquisitiveness. Attracted by moving objects—

like hands and legs—they may often circle a swimmer for an uncomfortably long time. If you find yourself being inspected by one, just swim to shore as quickly—but also as smoothly—as possible. The fish may follow for a moment or two, but will lose interest once you enter more shallow waters.

STINGRAYS

The barb-tailed stingray (or stingaree) is an unusually flat fish with a powerfully venomous sting at the tip of the tail. This sting can be driven through a man's foot, and—if the stingray is large enough—the venom can kill. Fortunately, the stingray (and its harmless look-alike cousin, the manta ray) is a shy creature that would never make an unprovoked attack on a swimmer. Unfortunately, the stingray likes to rest on the bottom of the surf, where it is well camouflaged. If stepped on, the ray will lash out with its tail in self-defense.

The rays are found in temperate waters, as in Florida, California, and the Caribbean. To avoid treading on them when walking through shallow water, shuffle your feet through the sand bottom. The disturbance will alert the ray and send it flapping away in fright.

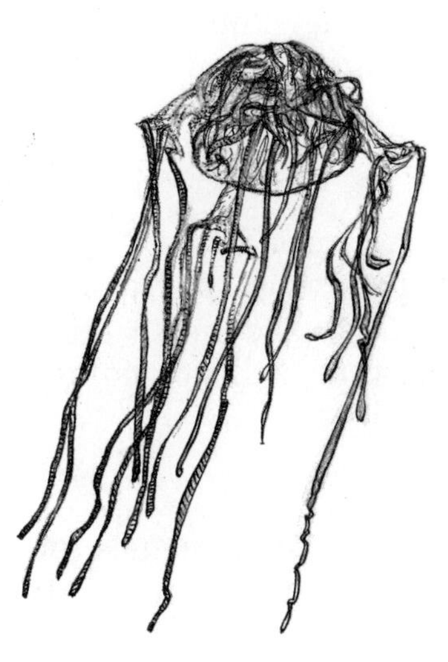

JELLYFISH

Shortly before making her unsuccessful attempt to swim from Cuba to Key West, Florida, Diana Nyad received reports that great white sharks were prowling about in the same waters she intended to pass through herself. Understandably alarmed, she arranged for a large shark cage to be built—at the approximate cost of $50,000—so that she could stay safely within its confines while stroking her way into the record books. The cage did its job. At least, it protected her from the sharks. But it couldn't keep the jellyfish away. In fact, as she swam through their midst (they're native to the region), the cage bars sliced into their soft bodies and directed their fragments into Nyad's face. Before she had completed two-thirds of the course, her eyes and mouth were so bady swollen from the stings of these creatures that she was unable to continue.

The moral? Don't neglect the jellyfish for the sharks. Their tentacles contain poisonous stingers by the hundreds, which can badly hurt—occasionally even permanently paralyze—any swimmer unlucky enough to brush against one. Happily, it's only the largest jellyfish—and some are as wide as a bedspread—that are dangerous. If you remain alert in the water, you should have ample time to detour around them.

Both jellyfish and the man-of-war are common to American waters. For most of the year, they travel alone and thus are simple enough to evade. (Keep in mind, though, that jellyfish drift rather than swim through the water. You have to dodge them; they can't dodge you.) In late summer and early fall, however, they may suddenly appear by the hundreds in the surf. The only thing a reasonable ocean swimmer can do at a time like this is gracefully retire from the scene. After a few days, they will disappear as mysteriously as they appeared, and you can return to the water undaunted and, more to the point, unstung.

SEA SNAKES

Poisonous snakes that live in the sea are only found in the southern and western Pacific. They're quickly distinguished from land snakes by their paddlelike tails. Although extremely poisonous, they will not bother swimmers as long as they're left alone.

CORAL FISH

Stonefish, scorpion fish, and toadfish—ugly names for astoundingly ugly fish—are the most poisonous of all finned creatures. Their venomous spines produce a poison that can cause humans to suffer great pain and

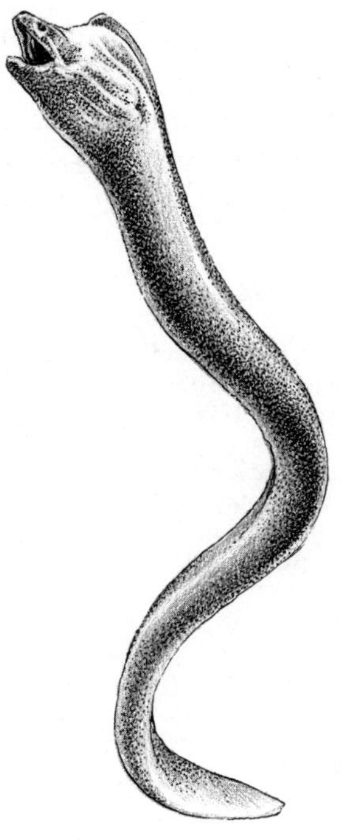

swelling. These fish live in the coral growths found off the California coast and along the shores of South America. They generally lurk beneath coral rock; the best way to keep from meeting one is to leave all stones unturned.

The moray eel is a lot less savage than it looks. Even so, its bite is so fierce that a person could drown while trying to release himself from the jaws. Moray eels live in holes beneath the coral reef, and so are more a threat to divers than swimmers. Occasionally you may see one winding its way beneath the surface. Leave it alone. It will leave you alone, too.

PLANT LIFE

Although plant life isn't going to attack you, seaweed, seagrass, and kelp can still be a menace to the inexperienced swimmer. If you accidentially swim through a patch of weed and become entangled in it, do not attempt to thrash yourself free. The panicky motions will only cause the weeds to bind more securely about your legs and arms. Just shake your limbs gently, and if there's a nearby current, enter it—the swift flow will help loosen the stuff.

Kelp, which floats in a massive tangle on the ocean surface, may present a hazard to anyone who inadvertently comes up to the surface under it. Do not try to swim through the kelp. Submerge again, and glide to a clear area.

POSTSCRIPT

A lot of this chapter has necessarily been concerned with hazards—from the ocean itself and from its occupants. But you have as much right to be there as any life form; it is your ancient birthright. Challenge the ocean's unbounded force and it will inevitably defeat you. Accept it for what it is and it will accept you—for it is as benevolent as it is fierce, and to swim in it is to be cradled by a timeless and joyous sovereign force.

BIBLIOGRAPHY

Allardice, James. *The Medical Aspects of Competitive Swimming*. London: Pelham Books, 1972.

American Red Cross. *Adapted Aquatics*. Garden City, N.Y.: Doubleday, 1977.

—*Advanced First Aid & Emergency Care*. Garden City, N.Y.: Doubleday, 1973.

—*Lifesaving: Rescue & Water Safety*. Garden City, N.Y.: Doubleday, 1974.

—*Manual for the Basic Swimming Instructor*. The American National Red Cross, 1974.

—*Standard First Aid and Personal Safety*. Garden City, N.Y.: Doubleday, 1973.

—*Swimming and Water Safety*. Garden City, N.Y.: Doubleday, 1968

—*Teaching Johnny To Swim*. Garden City, N.Y.: Doubleday, 1977.

Anderson, William. *Teaching the Physically Handicapped to Swim*. London: Faber & Faber, 1968.

Andrews, Capt. W.D. *Swimming and Lifesaving*. Toronto: W. Briggs, 1889.

Ankeney, Jeanelle. *Any Child Can Swim*. Chicago: Contemporary Books, 1979.

Arellano, Mick. *Teach Yourself to Swim...Despite Your Fear of the Water*. New York: Hawthorne Books, 1978.

Armbruster, David. *Swimming and Diving*. St. Louis: C.V.Mosby, 1968.

Atterbom, Hemming. "Swimming Physiology," *Swimming World*: January, 1978, April, 1978, June, 1978.

Bascom, Willard. *Waves and Beaches*. Garden City, N.Y.: Doubleday, 1964.

Bennet, J.A. *The Art of Swimming*. New York: Collins, Brother, 1846.

Besford, Pat. *Encyclopedia of Swimming*. New York: St. Martin's Press, 1976.

Bettsworth, Michael. *Drownproofing*. New York: Schocken Books, 1977.

Bory, Eva. *Teach Your Child to Swim*. Sydney: The Tradewinds Group, 1976.

Boy Scouts of America. *Handbook for boys*. Garden City, N.Y.: Doubleday, 1976.

—*Scout Handbook*. North Brunswick, N.J.: Boy Scouts of America, 1972.

Brewster, Edwin Tenney. *Swimming*. Boston: Houghton-Mifflin, 1910.

Bridge, Raymond. *The Complete Guide to Kayaking*. New York: Charles Scribner's Sons, 1978.

Cassill, R.V. *The Happy Marriage and Other Stories*. Purdue University Studies, 1966.

Chavoor, Sherman. *The 50-Meter Jungle*. New York: Coward, McCann & Geoghegan, 1973.

Clarys, Jan and Leon Lewville. *Swimming II*. Baltimore: University Park Press, 1975.

Colligan, Douglas. *Creative Insomnia*. New York: Franklin Watts, 1978.

Colwin, Cecil. "Butterfly for Beginners," *Swimming World*: February, 1978.

Cooper, Kenneth. *Aerobics*. New York: Bantam, 1969.

—*The Aerobics Way*. New York: M. Evans, 1977.

—*The New Aerobics*. New York: M. Evans, 1970.

Cooper, Kenneth and Mildred Cooper. *Aerobics for Women*. New York: M. Evans, 1972.

Corsan, George Herbert. *At Home in the Water*. New York: YMCA Press, 1910.

Counsilman, James. *Competitive Swimming Manual*. Bloomington, Ind.: Counsilman, 1977.

—*The Complete Book of Swimming*. New York: Atheneum, 1977.

Craven, Margaret. *I Heard the Owl Call My Name*. Garden City, N.Y.: Doubleday, 1973.

Cross, Frank. *Handbook of Swimming Pool Construction, Maintenance, and Sanitation*. Westport, Conn.: Technomic Publishing, 1974.

Cureton, Thomas Kirk. *The Physiological Effects of Exercise Programs on Adults*. Springfield, Ill.: Charles Thomas, 1969.

Davidson, James West and John Rugge. *The Complete Wilderness Paddler.* New York: Alfred A. Knopf, 1976.

Diagram Group, The. *Enjoying Swimming and Diving.* New York: Paddington Press, 1979.

—*Rules of the Game.* New York: Bantam Books, 1974.

Duxbury, Ken. *Seastate and Tides.* London: Stanford Maritime, 1977.

Engel, Leonard. *The Sea.* New York: Time Inc., 1961.

Fillingham, Paul. *The Complete Book of Canoeing & Kayaking.* New York: Drake, 1976.

Firby, Howard. *Howard Firby on Swimming.* London: Pelham Books, 1975.

Fosberg, Gerald. *Modern Long Distance Swimming.* London: Routledge & Kegan Paul, 1963.

Franklin, Benjamin. "The Art of Swimming," *Collected Works,* ed. by Jared Sparks. Vol. VI. Boston: Whittimore, Niles, and Hall, 1856.

Fraser Dutton, Geoffrey. *Swimming free on and below the surface of lake, river and sea.* London, 1972.

Furlong, William Barry. "*The Fun in Fun,*" Psychology Today: June, 1976.

Gabrielson, M. Alexander, Betty Spears, and B.W. Gabrielson. *Aquatics Handbook.* Englewood Cliffs, N.J.: Prentice-Hall, 1968.

Gallagher, Harry. *Sprint the Crawl.* London: Pelham Books, 1976.

Hemingway, Ernest. *The Short Stories of Ernest Hemingway.* New York: Charles Scribner's Sons, 1938.

Henning, Jean. *Six Days to Swim.* North Hollywood, Calif.: Swimming World, 1970.

Higgins, John. *Swimming and Diving.* New York: Arco Publishing, 1977.

Higgins, John H., Alfred R. Barr, Ben F. Grady, and Jack Martin. *Swimming & Diving.* New York: Arco, 1977.

Ingmanson, Dale and William Wallace. *Oceanography: An Introduction.* Belmont, Calif.: Wadsworth Publishing, 1973.

Jackson, Charles and Christina Jackson. "Sex Gap in Swimming Narrows," *American Corrective Therapy Journal:* Nov.-Dec., 1977, reprinted in *Swimming Technique:* Spring, 1979.

Jacobson, Cliff. *Wilderness Canoeing and Camping.* New York: Dutton, 1977.

Jacobson, Michael. *Nutrition Scoreboard: Your Guide to Better Living.* New York: Avon Books, 1975.

Kent, Allegra. *Allegra Kent's Water Beauty Book.* New York: St. Martin's Press, 1976.

Killanin, Lord and John Rodda. *The Olympic Games.* London: Barrie & Jenkins, 1976.

Krauser, June, ed. *Swim-Master.* Ft. Lauderdale, Fla.: USA National Publication, 1978-1979.

Kroeber, Frederick. *Public Swimming Pools.* S. Brunswick, N.J.: A.S. Barnes, 1976.

Law, Donald. *The Beginner's Guide to Swimming and Water Sports.* New York: Drake, 1974.

Leahy, John. *The Art of Swimming in the Eton Style.* London, 1875.

Leonard, George. *The Ultimate Athlete.* Avon Books, 1977.

Leonard, Jon. *Live Longer Now.* New York: Charter Books, 1974.

Lessing, Doris. *Stories.* New York: Alfred A. Knopf, 1978.

Lilly, John. *The Center of the Cyclone.* New York: Julian Press, 1972.

—*The Deep Self.* New York: Simon and Schuster, 1977.

Malo, John W. *Wilderness Canoeing.* New York: Collier Books, 1971.

Mirkin, Gabe and Marshall Hoffman. *The Sports Medicine Book.* Boston: Little, Brown, 1978.

Morgan, William P. *Contemporary Readings in Sports Psychology.* Springfield, Ill.: Charles C. Thomas, 1970.

—"The Mind of the Marathoner," *Psychology Today:* April, 1978.

Morisawa, Marie. *Streams: their dynamics and morphology.* New York: McGraw, Hill, 1968.

New York State Department of Health. "Swimming Pools and Bathing Beaches," Bulletin 27.

Nyad, Diana. *Other Shores.* New York: Random House, 1978.

O'Neill, Frank. *Sports Conditioning.* Garden City, N.Y.: Doubleday, 1979.

Patios, Porches, and Pools. Secaucus, N.J.: Chartwell Books, 1977.

"Peak Performances—The Factors that Produce It," *Psychology Today:* Feb., 1978.

President's Council on Physical Fitness. *Aqua Dynamics.* Washington, D.C.: U.S. Government Printing Office, 1979.

Ruck, Wolf. *Canoeing and Kayaking.* Toronto: McGraw-Hill Ryerson, 1974.

Russell, Sir Frederick S. and Sir Maurice Yonge. *The Seas.* London: Frederick Warne, 1975.

Ryan, Dr. Frank. *Swimming Skills.* New York: Penguin Books, 1978.

Schlitz, Jack, and Karen Rabe. "Personality Traits of State Level Swimmers," *Swimming Technique:* Winter, 1979.

Schollander, Don. *Inside Swimming.* Chicago: Henry Regnery, 1974.

Schumm, Stanley A. *River Morphology.* Stoudsberg, Pa.: Dowden, Hutchinson, & Ross, 1972.

Selye, Hans (interviewed by Laurence Cherry). "On the Real Benefits of Eustress," *Psychology Today:* March, 1978.

—*Stress Without Distress.* New York: Signet Books, 1974.

Shepard, Francis. *Geological Oceanography.* New York: Crane, Russak, 1977.

Sinclair, Archibald. *Swimming and Lifesaving.* London: Health and Strength, 1906.

Singer, Robert. *Coaching, Athletics, and Psychology.* New York: McGraw-Hill, 1972.

Smith, R. Philip. *The La Costa Diet and Exercise Book.* New York: Grosset and Dunlap, 1977.

Steedman, Charles. *Manual of Swimming.* Melbourne: H.T. Dwight, 1867.

Stenuitt, Robert. *Deepest Days.* New York: Coward-McCann, 1966.

Suinn, Richard M. "Body Thinking: Psychology for Olympic Champs," *Psychology Today:* July, 1976.

Strung, Norman, Sam Curtis, and Earl Perry. *Whitewater!* New York: Macmillan, 1976.

Swimming Pools. Menlo Park, Calif.: Sunset Books, 1970.

"To stay hearty, get sweaty," *Medical World News:* Jan. 9, 1965.

Twain, Mark. *The Adventures of Tom Sawyer.* New York: Harper and Row, 1965.

U.S. Department of Health, Education, and Welfare. "Medicine for the Layman," Washington, D.C.: National Institute of Health, No. 79-1808.

U.S. Navy. *How to Survive on Land and Sea.* Annapolis, Md.: U.S. Naval Institute, 1943.

Usinger, Robert L. *The Life of Rivers and Streams.* New York: McGraw-Hill, 1969.

Weihaupt, John G. *Exploration of the Oceans.* New York: Macmillan, 1979.

Wennerberg, Conrad. *Wind, Waves and Sunburn.* Cranbury, N.J.: A.S. Barnes, 1974.

INDEX

T

U

V

W